BALTIMORE

Imprint

Nedra Brown

BALTIMORE *Imprint*

Dedication

I dedicate this book to any women who are trapped in abusive situations. May this book serve as an inspiring field guide to allow you to see that you can walk away from anything or anyone that is not serving your well-being. May you utilize my transparent account to compare in contrast the pathology of abuse, lack of self-love, and awareness to find healing, value, and self-love to uplift yourself and remove yourself from any toxic environment. I would also like to dedicate this book to Keniyah Brown and Amina Robinson. May this book serve as a reminder to you both that women are to be cherished, valued, respected, and loved. If either of you ever finds yourselves in a space where you are not treated with value or care, may my story serve as a reminder to you both why you must gravitate to a space that is truly deserving of your presence.

Acknowledgment

I would like to acknowledge my mother, Diane Brown. Thank you for being my first example of what a strong woman and mother encompass. Thank you for always doing your best as a woman and showing me the benefits of hard work, faith, resilience, and determination. Thank you for leading the way for me and future generations of beautiful, dream-catching, excellent women! May your lessons, knowledge, and legacy live on long after you have departed this life! Thank you for being a great mother, grandmother, and muse, I love you!

Contents

Prologue

*W*e all enter this world as divine beings with a purpose. Living through stages of development that have been predetermined for each of us upon our arrival. Lacking the complete understanding of why we are born into our cultures and how God makes his selection process. Some of you may have never thought about the how or the why. In contrast, there are those of you who have spent every waking moment trying to understand the how and the why in-depth—wondering why you were implemented into your specific family, neighborhood, events, and overall existence—trying to keep a positive outlook. At the same time, you feel the reigns of negativity taking over your being daily. As you try to understand why God would have allowed you to be touched inappropriately, beaten, verbally abused, frightened, sad, hurt, and lost in this physical experience, we are forced to be a part of.

I know these feelings and perspectives all too well because I carried them with me the majority of my life as I questioned why God would allow my innocence to be ripped from me at such an immature age—asking why I felt alone when I had been born to two adults that were supposed to shelter me from those feelings. Walking through my childhood carrying a load of resentment based on hurt and trauma from unfortunate events that tailgated me into my adult life. I often wondered why I had never felt entirely kept, safe, or loved. I had felt the sting of trauma; in response, I had buried it so deeply within my being that, at times, I was able to convince myself that certain things did not happen. I told myself that I was ok because I was strong and could overcome anything. Although strength had always been a proper component of who I was, I would learn that strength was not always a superior quality to uphold when trying to heal. It is ok to recognize and own the fact that you are not ok, and, within doing so, you are not deemed weak due to your lack of upholding strong emotions that shield you from your truth.

Although I had spent the majority of my life trying to flee from my pain, I realized that addressing my past pain would be essential for me to show up fully equipped and able to walk in my purpose. Introducing me to a culture of cognitive dissonance that permitted me to reject new mechanisms based on my belief that the ones I knew were the only ones that existed. I had spent my entire life questioning my experiences. I was viewing them as the dreadful things that had happened to me. But I would soon find relief and prosperity when I changed my outlook. Recognizing that those events did not just happen to me, but they happened for me! Utilizing my pain to fuel and build my purpose. Working from the inside out to become the best version of who I could genuinely be.

CHAPTER 1

Where Do I Begin?

I sat at my screen, thinking, where do I start? As I watched the FaceTime screen pause and my frustration rose to its peak, I began to wonder how it was that I had reached somewhere that felt as though it was nowhere at all. You see, to tell you this story, I would have to brace myself, pause, cry, laugh, ponder, and recant the days of yesterday. The days that I had thought I had broken away from kept me very much a hostage within my right. The days I had outgrown but still held onto like a baby gripping the nipple of a bottle after being told that it was now time to transition over to a sippy cup. You see, I am now grown and fully grown in my entire person. Yes, yesterday molded me, but today had awakened me in a way I could not have imagined.

You see, I am now a woman, and I am the woman no one saw coming. As I rose to the occasion of my unanticipated glow-up, I started thinking of how I came to be this phenomenal being. Reflecting on my past days of self-doubt, fear, trauma, and inconsistently loving all of who I was. Based on the judgments of others. I was entering rooms where I was the topic of discussion before my arrival due to my childhood reputation. That was considered unfavorable based on the many street fights I had experienced. Majority of which came about due to my dire need to protect my youngest brother.

I watched as he consistently acted like an aggressive big mouth who could never walk away from an altercation. Depending on me to show up later serving as the predictable big sister who hated altercations. Yet I didn't mind getting my hands dirty with the filth that came along with physically harming someone. People often tried to make me feel less inadequate enforcing their judgments that were never accurate. I was a child who had no clue about what lay beneath the surface of my being—clinging to the statistical observations that were thrust in my direction—fearing the day when I could rise out of bed and be me. No one looks at a little girl that's hurting and asks what it is that is leading her down a path of self-destruction.

I had become accustomed to people looking at me and placing labels on me based on their poor observation skills that, at times, I encompassed those labels willingly. I told myself that there was no need to try and show up as all of me because I was never seen, respected, or understood. I had spent such a significant portion of my life feeling inadequate. Allowing others to determine who I was and who I would become that my transition was at times just as overwhelming as my trauma. I once was a fetus, and from a fetus, I grew to be a baby. From a baby, I grew to be a young girl, and from a young girl, I grew to be a statistic, and from a statistic, I grew to be a disappointment. I later grew to be an inspiration, an overachiever, and a beautiful spirit from those disappointments. You see, to have love, you have to have once had hate.

To have happiness, you must have to at once have had sadness. Few of us are born with silver spoons laid amongst silver platters with long, drawn-out written instructions of what this world is and what it will do to you upon your arrival. Some of us are born into lives filled with broken promises and countless misfortunes, but those very things that cause us to be so broken mold us to be so beautiful. So, I will tell you a story of how I came to be. I will show you how the sad become happy, how the broken become whole, and how the meek become vital, for this is the type of story the world does not tell with open arms. You see, the world is full of many poetic injustices that never get described, but this is a story you will want to hear, you will want to tell, and you will want to remember. For when it is over, you will be full, full of questions, full of sadness, full of happiness, full of hope, and most importantly, full of inspiration. Through my story, his story, and our story, one can understand this crazy boundless process called life.

We can make the spiritual, mental, and physical connections of who we are and who we are to become through our diverse experiences. You see, the little Black boy and the little Black girl have never been of the highest value to the world. It is for that reason alone that the little Black boy and the little Black girl must hold their heads high and seek the best existence for themselves that the world has to offer for, it is when we aim high that we can avoid sailing too low on the outskirts of poverty, pain, and disappointment. So, I will tell you this story and let you do as you wish with it, for it is a story of hope, growth, and manifestation that should be shared amongst all who care to hear a realistic tale of triumph.

I sat on the edge of the bed as calmly as I could, trying to fight the urge to give any response at all. It had been seven years since I had become engulfed in the same whirlwind of insanity. Trying to break away from the love, the pain, and the disappointment that was always sure to reveal itself. Once I walked down the same toxic path as I made my way through a life that brought me nothing but dissatisfaction. Due to my desire to repetitively pour love into an empty vessel. A vessel that had never drunk from a cup filled with nothing more than toxic fluids curated and concocted of the very broken ingredients of the environment from which he came. I looked at him as he ranted on and on, filling his dialect with curse words, disrespect, and half-truths. I tried to understand the darkness that had taken over his pupils as he gaslighted me, trying to create a feeling of just cause as he threw his things into trash bags screaming on and on about how no one cared about him. Observing the scars of trauma, he thought he kept tucked in. Hidden from all, including himself, but that was never the case.

I stared deep into his soul, torn from the imagery as I felt his pain. Every meal he never received. The fear he encompassed every time his foster mother allegedly forced him into the shower with her. The evil human spirits who had invaded his innocence, forcing him to commit acts of intimacy. The trauma from his childhood had stripped away what little he had left. He continued, screaming vigorously about how I did not care about him. The woman who met him as a girl and gave him all he desired, giving him all that I had to provide, sometimes leaving myself empty and depleted from the over-pouring and lack of reciprocity. I watched him narrate his feelings in the same way he had done for seven years playing the blame game, making it seem as though I was in the wrong.

I was dropping the ball on this frivolous unpredictable emotion we call love. Through this nagging parasitic emotion, I realized how conscious and abnormally unconscious I had become. From loving this scarred soul that wanted all the love and attention in the world but could never give it back in the same format, he had received it. Love isn't a complex concept when done amongst those who know what the word truly means and how it can and should be manifested and distributed. Still, he didn't have a proper understanding of the concept. He raved on and on about how he did not care about what I had recently acquired. Downing my preference to live in the big house, in the pleasant but predominately Caucasian neighborhood deeply embedded in Albemarle County. He started acting like I had sold out due to my desire to offer my children and his child an adequate lifestyle.

He threw his things into bags and disrespected me repetitively, trying to withdraw a negative response as he said something that made me aware of his true feelings of inadequacy within himself. "I'm going to take my shit and go back to the dirt where I came from," he said. Trying to make me feel a level of pity for him he did not deserve and only desired due to my inability to continue to indulge him in the way I had done effortlessly before that very moment. I recognized that my mother-like qualities had somehow transferred from my parenting duties and became an essential component in my relationship. I had always been this naive, giving spirit believing there was good in all people. I gave the benefit of the doubt even in situations where the suspicion of a person's character stripped away my ability to provide them with any benefit at all. I would soon learn the mental and spiritual cost of what happens when you deny yourself the reward of relying on your instincts and intuition.

If it quacks like a duck, walks like a duck, and looks like a duck, you best believe it's nothing more than a damn duck. I tried to look at him, extracting all my emotions and feelings of attachment for this broken person trying to figure out what kept me rooted so profoundly unable to walk away entirely. Only having moments where I'd turn my back and stay in my corner. At the same time, I watched him act as if the unbearable feeling of not engaging with me while I turned away was overwhelming. It was as if he were a small child whose mother had told him to stand in time out, secluding him from the world. Ignoring his dire need to be back in his mother's arms, laughing, talking, and playing around with the rest of his day. A man knows there is no time out in the real world.

Life goes on and on with or without our entire presence waiting at the gates of each day. Ready to go along with the motions of adulting whether we feel up to it or not. I assessed myself as I watched this man, who was still a boy, give me the highest hopes. I looked at him, feeling a surge of emotions fighting off the urge to want to take my fist, ball it up, and give him the punch in the face I thought he so rightfully deserved, but I refrained from doing so. I had been that person so many times in my life, and within this toxic relationship which kept me rooted to things, places, and feelings I had no desire to be attached to anymore. There I was, sitting at the core of my life, waiting patiently as my 31st year approached me slowly. Observing all the growth and manifestation I had walked into humbly, I was still very much in a mental place of stagnation, searching for things I did not need from people I would never be able to acquire them from.

Only to turn around momentarily, ripping the hope from my being and treating the event as though it was something I rightfully deserved when we both knew I did not. I started to think of how broken entities sometimes attach themselves based on the familiarity of another impaired essence. Recognizing in that very moment that I had formulated a trauma bond. This bond would prove daunting due to my partner's desire to intentionally become a product of his environment. Trauma that had forced him to conform to a reflection of his experiences. I had spotted early on what made him so dark, tired, and torn at the seams, and I had consciously made it my duty to repair him. While unconsciously establishing a trauma bond with him based on our shared traumatic childhood experiences.

I saw his hurt, felt his neglect, and saw his potential, but the potential was a lie. It was a lie because there is no secure way to know if it exists or if we simply want it to. A person can have all the possibilities of greatness present inside of them. Still, without the ability and desire to bring it to the surface, it becomes a resting potential that could never make it to the surface, leaving it just a figment of perception that may never come to be. I wanted him to see what I saw, what I had seen from the first day we laid eyes on each other. Still, there was no form of sorcery in the universe that could allow him to see those things without it being of his desire to do so. He took his stuff in and out, unloading the closet and strolling to the car, trying to trigger me with lies and insults that did not fit who I was, hoping to get a response. He needed a reply badly.

Through this constant unfavorable exchange, he felt my love or believed he did through toxic outpours and cries that would tug him back in my direction a few hours after our negative blowups and breakups. He needed to hear me say something, something that would give him an inclination that I wanted him to stay and that I would allow him to come back, but I gave him nothing. He tried stalling, taking out fewer items to his car at a time, trying to provide me with room to stop his charades and invite him back in as I had always done, but I could not. What was it that kept him in this dysfunctional bubble of nothingness? Why did he prefer the same things repetitively? Why did he prefer this behavior? Why was he choosing to inflict a level of self-sabotage that was unlike anything I had ever experienced before?

Why was it that a man who gave so little felt as though he deserved so much? I could not understand how someone could have someone of my caliber in their grasp and treat it as if it were of no value or use at all. Why couldn't he go away and never bother me or desire my intimacy again if he were going to treat it as if it were of such poor quality? Yet I stood, reattached to him and his demons after a divorce. How was I standing in the same puddle of mud I had just gained the courage to walk away from? How could a man love a woman or children if he could not correctly love himself? The answer was simple; he could not.

He was ready to unload his bags into his room at his mother's house as he prepared himself for a round of marijuana, social media engagements, and sidebar affairs he had just tried to make me believe he was not engaging in. He grabbed his last items and hopped into the foreign vehicle that he cherished over all things and people. I locked my door and retired to my bedroom as I thought about his specific choice of words before his departure. "You don't give a fuck about me for real," he said as his phone went off and he tried to get louder and louder. He tried to talk over the social media notifications and the messages from his secret counterparts. That was of no substantial match to the woman he was gaslighting and mentally derailing out of sport and utter frustration for her intuitive ability to read through his trail of lies and constant bullshit.

A weak woman with limited intelligence can be a man's prized asset when the goal is to utilize and abuse her in whatever nature he is allowed, Precisely. But a wise woman who believes in observing the world around her can be a thorn in a man's side. As he conned his way through life, dishing out half-truths, community penis, and a bed of lies he had played graciously in since the beginning of time. I had been this thorn of insight and intellect my entire life as I constantly relied on the belief that the watchful eye is the phenomenal mind's best friend. I had learned early on as a child that people will always give you a better understanding of who they are by half of what they say and most of what they do. Based on these observations, I began to walk through life learning to pay close attention to the things people did rather than what they said. Playing along with people's charades and pretending not to see when seeing was one of my most potent abilities.

I listened to friends tell me things instantly, reading into the situation. Seeing the truths, they presented willingly. While also being able to salvage the ones they tried to hide. I knew who was honest and who only pretended to be. Leaving me to recognize that majority of my people were not my people. They had been present actively during the struggle and stress flooded years. I felt as though they liked my broken story. Loving the rendition of me that had been judged, talked about, and hated. Fleeing from my side as soon as the dynamics of my life began to transition. They hated the new version of Nina that consisted of self-love, awareness, growth, and abundance. I remember all the flooding emotions roaring inside of me during my awakening. As I listened to a Tyler Perry interview via YouTube. I was comparing in contrast as he talked about a rocket and how the bottom portion disassociates itself from the rocket as it reaches higher altitudes. He highlighted the analogy that the people in our circles often are the same way, instantly helping me apply his theory to my current culture of life.

I Recognized that my people were fleeing because I was reaching higher altitudes internally and externally. And the reach was unexpected. Although people often saw something in me, it was overlooked. Based on their belief that I would never recognize my abilities. Therefore, I led the people around me to believe that who I was to them was all I would ever be. Familiarity makes it impossible for understanding to be reached regarding growth when people feel they know all of you. People never consider that knowing all of you isn't possible when most of them barely know themselves.

That was a trait Jeff and I shared. The only difference was that I used mine to observe and approach things and people properly, and he used his for-manipulation purposes. He spent his life learning people and responding to them based on their desires and preferences. He could talk his way into and out of any situation, for it was through his harsh upbringing in the cold streets of Baltimore, Maryland, that he had learned how to do this no matter what environment he was a part of. Jeffrey Jones was born in Baltimore, Maryland, to Clarence and Roberta Jones. Growing up in a circle of poverty, hardships, and struggles, he learned to look at the world and its people based on what he felt they could do for him. Having made it through incidences of child neglect, sexual abuse, and being born to parents who had their fair share of battles with drug addiction, Jeffrey had a different rendition of what love was and how it looked. I was born to Melvin White and Dorothy White, who, like Jefferey's parents, were together since a young age and were also married.

My parents experienced many complex issues as well. They battled their way through infidelity, financial hardship, and separation. Based on these components, I grew up with a toxic diluted version of what love was and what it looked like in my reality. The sting of childhood scars and mutilated relationships ran rapidly through my core as I thought back on my past, full of things I had no desire to be a part of. The things that used to put me asleep at night as an innocent child were no longer a part of my atmosphere. I became the little girl who longed for her father's presence as she cried herself to sleep wishing she were in a different physical space than the one the universe was currently offering and making her feel rightfully belonged to her. Like Jeffrey, I knew what mental neglect felt like, what physical neglect looked like, and how a beautiful soul could look in the mirror and feel invisible due to the scars that bound my self-esteem to a place of negativity. I Recognize that even the best moments could not strip away the mental and emotional bondage that held me close.

These components silently made me feel as though I could not see myself in its complete entirety due to the hurt and pain that stood in front of my reflection. Screaming out to me, "this is where you are, and this is who you'll be." I Overlooked all of the beauty and potential that lay still. I waited to be recognized and utilized to allow myself a chance at life. It was an opportunity that had constantly perished away from me as the world labeled me based on my pain and unfortunate experiences, trying to depreciate my inner glow that they all could see despite my ignorance and lack of awareness. The light that always made me noticeable in a room full of other energies that the naked untrained eye would feel was superior to me and my offerings. The glow that made people want to diminish my inner persons effortlessly.

I had known these experiences since my arrival into this life. People often tried to make me feel like I would not be smart enough, capable enough, or strong enough to escape the chains of adversity. Through these chains, I would find my peace and prosperity while trying to help another damaged soul find the same. I later concluded that I could not do so for anyone other than myself. Jeffrey and I had so many similarities. Like me, Jeffery was silently intelligent, although he had not made it past the ninth grade. His ability to self-educate and self-inform his brain of things he needed to know and the ability to enlighten his mind with content that made him equal to those he met was intriguing.

He measured up in quality compared to his constituents despite his education. Jeffrey had grown up in an environment unlike my southern hospitality-based upbringing in Charlottesville, Virginia. Jeffery grew up on the rough side of Baltimore, Maryland, living a life that would have put reruns of "the wire" to shame. He hadn't known the beauty of a comfortable living, consistent love, and protection of a maternal figure, or the solace of a peaceful life. Clinging to the short, structured experience he had when he lived under his grandmother's care. For it would be his grandmother who would give him his first taste of structure and true care. After departing from his grandmother's home and returning to his mother, Jeffrey lost the structured living environment and turned to the street to make money, support himself, and find solace. This made him grow to feel as though the world was full of vultures, and he had to consume the hearts of the willing and able before they had the opportunity to consume him first. He had taken his things for the millionth time, speeding off full of aggression as I lay in my bed, rewinding the scene repeatedly in my head. I felt as though I had committed some injustice towards him by deciding not to engage myself in the pool of toxicity I had been drowning in for years.

What was keeping me so unhappily rooted in this relationship that had given me no positive outcomes other than the child we shared? I tried to make sense of my emotions as I once again became plagued with feelings of guilt for choosing me, as I had failed to do consistently so many times throughout the relationship. I tried to make sense of my decision-making as I assessed the relationship's probable yet very predictable outcome. That had become the talk of my constituents as I made a fool of myself publicly walking in faith with a man who had proven himself to be unfaithful numerous times. My phone began to chime, alerting me of the multiple text messages I had received from Jeff as he gaslighted me, making it seem like I had done something wrong to him. Accusing me of being fake, saying how he felt unloved and undervalued, calling me bougie bitches, and accusing me of not knowing how to love anyone but myself. Fuck you bitch; the text read as the next would intercept before I could read the entire message.

"You think you're so much; you are not shit, he said." He continued; it doesn't matter what you do; you will never be shit. He sent one offensive text after another, trying to remove my dreams, ambitions, and achievements, all within a single text thread. Hoping he could break me down mentally. Utilizing my emotions, I shared my fears about everything I was trying to do with him. Leading me to question what it is about the growth of a Black woman that makes the people around her want to stifle her? As if it isn't hard enough for a woman, in general, to recognize her strengths and start owning them.

I often wondered why a Black woman's growth is usually unacceptable to her peers. Peers that have watched the struggles, hardships, and emotional outbursts of sadness as they watch her strive to find her place. Finally gaining traction internally, having them deem her as an offense. Not because she didn't deserve or earn her new position but felt an offense because her growth was not anticipated. Under normal circumstances, I would have ignored his harsh words, but this time, I could not. Day after day, I had been working on two new manuscripts. I had grown up obsessed with fiction novels and had taken the initiative to create my own.

I was trying to make a path to pursue a career as a writer. Feeling a burst of life flourish inside me every time I sat down to write. I could not focus my ambitions anywhere else because I felt God's hand nudging me in a new direction. I frequently reached out to Jefferey for feedback, watching over FaceTime as his face balled up with anger as I read my manuscript aloud. I was waiting for him to tell me what he thought. Jeff sat on the other end of the phone, acting as if he had no feedback to give. At the same time, his face displayed shock from listening to the story's content.

He wanted to tell me it was good. He also tried to tell me that he couldn't believe all of the progress I had made while writing the book. But he paused and could not. Instead, he focused on Ben's character, asking me what made me select the name. I was not sure what prompted his line of questioning, oblivious to where the conversation was headed." I chose Ben because all of his siblings' names start with B, so I had to keep that going, and Ben is a common name," I said. I watched as he frowned his face up with anger." Bitch quit playing with me; he said, you think I'm stupid."

"You named him Ben after my old manager, "he said, flooded with anger. I was confused about who Ben was and why he would think I would formulate one of my characters after his manager, who I did not know. He had been the king of unemployment. Jeffrey never stayed at any place of employment long enough for me to interact with his crewmates personally. "You can act dumb all you want; you probably were sleeping with him." Describing who Ben was and having me hang up after assessing that he could even accuse me of such a thing. I recognized that he did not believe my character was compiled from his manager at that moment. Nor did he think I had slept with his manager.

He was railroading me for sport, deliberately trying to drive me crazy. While also trying to discourage me. He was hoping to stifle me during my period of innovation because he did not want to see me succeed in anything. Fearing where he would end up if I moved forward and obtained a better culture of living. Many people in my life held this same dynamic with me. Nina White was full of light and possibilities, but her environment tried to wire her to believe otherwise. Imagine trying to steal someone else's value, capability, and blessings simply because you were not knowledgeable enough to explore your own. Praying a person you were drawn to because of their light would allow your ugliness to dim their light altogether.

For many reasons, the Diary of Janay Wilkerson was near and dear to my heart. I knew he would not be satisfied until I dropped the idea altogether." You aren't shit bitch, and you won't ever be shit, and this book isn't going to get anywhere," he said, hanging up the phone abruptly. There I sat, slumbering in disbelief that a man who had not done anything positive with his day could come home and try to derail his partner in such a way mentally. Due to internal issues, he was battling within himself. How could he have the audacity to say these things to me? The woman who worked twenty-four-hour shifts every other day, going to school full time, juggling a small business, and three kids.

The woman who had filled his gas tank up multiple times in one week. The woman who made sure he could get to and from work fed him and purchased the pack of cigarettes he was currently chain-smoking as he drove around in a blind rage, mad at his own mistakes and misdeeds. The woman who was giving more than she ever took. Loving more than she was loved and providing while waiting patiently for him to one day get on his feet and return the gesture of providing for his family. I had never had a man talk to me or treat me in this way before, and I could not understand what kept me rooted in such horrible treatment. I made excuses for him as I assessed and applied the mental and physical scars of his childhood, trying to rationalize his irrational behavior. Normalizing it as the psychological effects of unexamined and untreated mental illness and distress due to years of abandonment, exposure to an impoverished environment, physical abuse, sexual abuse, and psychological drawbacks from being held in solitary confinement. I did this frequently concerning his misdeeds.

I tried to make excuses for the why and the how when I knew deep down inside the reasons, I gave were not completely plausible. They were partially valid even though Jeff was making choices daily to be a bad person, and he knew right from wrong despite his trauma. I wanted him to heal so severely from these things that I had somehow convinced myself I was his savior. Convincing myself that I could heal him if I just continued to stay and not give up on him by walking away as so many others had in his life. Even going so far as convincing myself that God himself had put us together for me to lead him out of the dark space he had sat in for the majority of his existence. I told myself that I, the woman who had also experienced traumas and setbacks, could be the key. The woman who was currently an aspiring Doctor of Psychology could utilize what she had been learning those long-drawn-out nights online and apply it to the life of another.

Hoping to fix things that had gone unfixed for such a long time. I didn't know that I would impose pain and abuse upon myself. Within the process of loving this tormented soul, overriding everything I had once known to be accurate and of value, trying to help someone who had no active desire to help themselves. I was learning that I had grown from the previous relationships that had caused me issues. I had been overlooking them for so long I was not even aware of their existence. Through those relationships and failures, I had indeed discovered who I was, what I stood for, and who I wanted to become. So, I will take you on a journey that became a journey of pain, growth, self-discovery, and self-healing. I'm going to tell you about the past and the present.

Frequently jumping in and out of different periods of my life and my life while with Jeffrey. I will discuss how our parents' psychological foundations, environments, and personal experiences helped us formulate various aspects and ideologies behind what love was to us as individuals. I'm going to show you how it is effortless to become a product of your environment. While conveying how it is easy to choose to be anything but that from which you originate. I had occurred many fates of those around me many times, fitting in while also standing out. Longing to break away from the communal bondage that held me so close yet kept me so far away from who it was I truly desired to be. So, I will start at the beginning and work my way to the end, giving you my story, his story, and our story.

It's amazing how much of the past we honestly can recollect when we analyze the days that have passed. The days we thought we would never get ahead of. Due to the many adverse events that enter our lives, taking a seat at the table against our wishes. My story serves as one of the many accounts that offer a glimpse of the psychological drawbacks of the broken African American family. This story is not the type of story that begins with roses, butterflies, and honey gliding down the tip of the tongue to the back of the throat filling the air with happiness, peace, and prosperity. This type of story fills the heart with yearning while filling the eyes with tears, the brain with disbelief, and the spirit with pain. You see, I had felt all of these emotions while sitting down to tell a story that had taken place, leaving me with bruises I at one point would have preferred to feel as though it didn't exist. No one cares about the little girl who has been left to stew in a pool of tears of dissatisfaction from her environment. This story is my story, but this is his story too.

This story is the story of his pain, a cold world that did not care to leave him spiritually rooted to his mothers' breast as she searched the world for a place that could be his. Did she find this place? And if she did, could he safely and peacefully say this place was his? Or was it there's? We often hear these broken stories, but we never stop to distinguish what caused them to be tarnished internally. At the same time, we assess the fragments of their human persons being torn at the seams and left on display. Displayed amongst a cold world that was not designed to love, understand, or heal them from the broken environments from which they came. I will tell you my story while telling his story, in conjunction with our story.

I will make you laugh, make you inquire, and most importantly, understand. Understand that the world we are born into is not always the world we belong to. I will make you know-how for some of us. The calm before the storm is sometimes only a diversion, for the storm that is coming to disrupt, disembody, and dishearten the souls of the innocent. We all start with a clear vision, a fearless outlook, and hope, unattached to anything outside ourselves and the wombs from which we have risen. Still, for some of us, this existence does not last for long. Some of us know why the caged bird sings, for it is a song that carries on through the coldest of cold nights. The hottest of hot days, leaving us caged to that of our own abandoned and abused lives. As we wait for freedom to sweep us up off our feet and hold us by the hand, taking us to a better place, better places than we've ever known.

As we sing our beautiful tunes. Allowing the notes to ring through the atmosphere innocently. While our listeners are unaware of the brutal dressings of pain, each lyric and note come wrapped in. Some may argue that we have a choice from the beginning. But what if I told you a story where the alternative, we believe we have been given unconsciously was ripped to shreds long before we ever came to be. A story where the generational pain and curses of those who stood before us precedent over those who came after. I know of a story like the one I am describing because it is mine, his, and ours.

CHAPTER 2

The Beginning

When I think back on life, I recall so many events that shaped me into the woman I am today. I could write endless paragraphs about things I endured during my childhood. I could tell you a story about a bright and beautiful little girl who never really knew how smart and beautiful she was until life hit her from all directions. I could tell you a story about a little girl who never knew the tone of a kind conversation or word of encouragement because she was judged and criticized frequently by those around her. This led her to feel as though kindness was an unreal concept. So the little girl evolved to be kind, compassionate, and catering, frequently dishing out the energy she had never received but had always hoped. The ego is a tricky character who forces us to cling to false behaviors due to ignorance. It is easy to mishandle others when you have been mishandled. But it is a complicated and noble sentiment when you are willing to forgive, love, and value others despite the lack of familiarity with those concepts. For as easy as it is for us to model positive behaviors, it is just as easy to model negative behavior patterns.

It is also easy to lack a healthy approach to love when you believe you have never been adequately loved. And that was the culture of my environment. I was surrounded by beautiful women and men who never recognized their beauty due to the mutilation from childhood scars that never healed. I could tell you the story of the little boy who displayed the signs of borderline personality disorder due to growing up in dysfunction. I could tell you how that dysfunction caused the young man to inflict later the same harm he had witnessed as a child on his wife, child, and any relationship partner he encountered. The trauma from his environment would lead him to have an intense fear of abandonment, which would often lead him to display troubling behaviors that would cause his counterpart to abandon him due to his unstable behavior. I could tell you how the boy would grow to lack stability, control his anger, and have manic episodes—living a life engulfed in chaos due to his unresolved mental illness and identity-related issues. I could also tell you the story of a girl who became a teen mom, dropping out of school because she had no help, resources, or guidance during a detrimental time in her life. Finding herself turning many corners in life and getting knocked down. Always possessing a strong sense of resilience, picking herself up and moving along despite the vital force of gravity that always seemed to push against her.

You see, I could tell you so many stories. Stories engulfed with trauma, pain, self-doubt, verbal abuse, and physical abuse. The story I want to tell you the most is the story that is filled with growth, evolution, and, most importantly, overcoming odds. Even as I type these words and recall the days that have passed, tears flow from my eyes. Not because I am weak, hurt, or sad but because I am relieved. Relieved that I made it through numerous monumental hurdles that were supposed to keep me down, keep me stagnant, and keep me unaware of the true power I possessed.

I didn't write this story because I have finally found perfection; I want to humiliate my oppressors or dwell on my hurt from the past. I wrote this story because I want girls and women like me to know there is a rainbow on the other side waiting to be claimed after the storm passes. I want women to know that they can heal, grow, and evolve from harsh situations and find peace and happiness. So, I'm going to share my story in hopes that someone will read it, recognize the issues, and make a change in their situation just as I did.

I sat at the table by the window, waiting for Barbra to come downstairs to join me for breakfast. I worked as Barbra's nurse aide for over six months and had watched her rejuvenate rather quickly. Upon entry into her home, I was made aware that she was on her death bed and didn't have much time left to live due to her breast cancer that had metastasized. Barbra was accompanied by her parents, who were significantly up in age. She was a 60-year-old single woman with no kids or husband. She was also the only child, so her parents often remained at her bedside. Before my arrival, Barbra had never had an African American at her table or home. I still remember the day I arrived at her home feeling extremely out of place.

I remember being led into her living room with a dining table. This table would be my last residence inside the home until Barbra's condition worsened and her family and friends were forced to have me intervene. I sat at the table every day for 12 hours straight, only moving when I needed to relieve myself of the urge to urinate; I often let it pile up until I felt I would explode. I would sit at the table, make my to-do list, and plan out all the goals I dreamed about daily. While sitting miserably in a rock-hard chair that was not designed for my butt, which felt like it had been wiped out of existence with every passing 12-hour shift. I would watch Barbra's parents, aunt, and friends navigate rotating shifts up and down the steps to and from her bedroom, never asking or insinuating any desire for my help. This would go on for weeks until things finally somehow became worst. It was starting to appear that I was getting paid to do nothing because nothing is what I would do daily.

One day I sat at the table making my list of goals I planned on accomplishing. At the top of the list, I had three things. Get a driver's license, get a car, and go back to school to obtain a Ph.D. in psychology. Ironically enough, I would achieve two of the three within a few weeks of compiling the list. I sat making my list, frequently getting up to move around so my butt would be relieved of the pain from the hard chair, and my blood flow to my legs would be back circulating correctly. Barbara's mother, Ms. Hawkins, came running down the stairs. "She is vomiting, dear, and it's everywhere, and I could use your help," she said in her southern accent that I grew fond of after hearing her talk more and more. I rushed to Barbara's bedside, cleaning the vomit, helping her to wash up, and changing her clothes. I could tell by the expression on her face that she was highly uncomfortable. Here she was, a grown woman who had spent her life being independent, successful, and in control, and she was being washed and dressed by a little Black girl. Who, in her opinion, did not appear to be of age—asking me my age frequently as if she was going to entrap me in a lie based on her disbelief that I was, in fact, an adult.

I started talking to her, making conversation, trying to lift the uncomfortable expression off her face. I wanted to assure her that it was okay and comfortable with me. Whatever I did that day must've taken effect because, after that, it was no more sitting at the table in the hard chair feeling like my bottom was depreciating. "What's for breakfast, Nee"? Barbra asked while strolling to the table, looking as if she weighed all of one hundred pounds or less. "Rice pudding," I replied. Rice was the norm for her daily.

Although she had suddenly been coming around to regaining her strength, her appetite had still not caught up to the rest of her. Anorexia was forcing her to consume little to no food per day. She sat at the table in her nightgown that looked as if multiple people could fit inside due to her weight loss. She drank her coffee and consumed a little of her rice pudding. She took in small, elegant bites until her stomach could no longer accept the idea of food consumption. "What's new"? Barbra asked, sitting at the table waiting to hear the latest in my young and chaotic life.

It was as if she had a front-row seat to a never-ending soap opera. Barbra listened to my funny tales about my young crazy adventures with my friends and my dating struggles. Barbra knew there was always an exciting story resting on the brim of my tongue. An engaging story waiting to be shared with her. Story sharing was a routine she looked forward to." Nothing's going on," I replied, shocking myself with the statement because, for once, I could say that, and it was the absolute truth. I had taken a long-term vow to be celibate and secluded until I met someone, I felt had substance, so there were no dating stories for now.

"I've decided to get my license," I said in excitement. After all, what 25-year-old didn't have a license? I questioned myself as I let the words roam free and proudly off the tip of my tongue. "Well, Nee, I'm glad to hear that; besides, you need a license. That way, you can get me to and from my appointments,". Although I was her caregiver, she had been relying on the help of her circle of friends to get her to and from meetings. Having a license would give her friends freedom during the week and relieve them of their transportation duties.

They didn't mind taking her to and from, and this group of women would be my first introduction to what a girl tribe looked like. They would call daily, come over with food and gossip, and most importantly, they took good care of Barbra in the way I had never seen women cater to one another. I became significantly in awe of how they reciprocated love, friendship, and reliability. I told myself one day I would have my girl tribe full of love and care instead of jealousy and envy like most women I had encountered. Barbra would later welcome me into her circle of friends, having me sit in on brunches, girl talk, and learning from a group of women who were significantly older and more resourceful than any of the women in my group of friends. When the doorbell rang, I sat at the table, filling Barbra in on my plan to get my license.

The door opened, and it was Joanna Barbra's long-term friend and one of my favorites in the group. Joanna and Barbra had been friends ever since Joanna's kids were little and had attended the same church, shared the same group of friends, and had been through thick and thin. Joanna had become a widow after the death of her husband John, and it had become clear that Barbra was one of the people that helped Joanna get through that tough time. Hence, as a good friend, Joanna was present daily helping Barbra to get through the physical and mental rut cancer had implemented on her unwillingly. Joanna sat at the table, ready to hear any new news we had to share to go along with the hot coffee and beaming sun that shone brightly through the blinds. "Nee has decided to get her license" Barbra said proudly. "Well, I think that is a beautiful idea," Joanna replied with a sweet smile conveying how proud she was to hear that I was taking a step in the right direction to fully develop my independence.

We sat at the table engaging in girl talk while watching my Facebook notifications repeatedly go off. I glanced at my screen, noticing I had multiple messages from Jeffrey Jones. Jeffrey was making his daily rounds, as I liked to call it. He liked every photo and post I had posted within the week. Thirst trapping to get my attention, but I gave him nothing. I glanced at his photo, thinking how cute and well-dressed he was in all his pictures, but still, I did not engage. At the time, I was self-absorbed and based on my desire to elevate, I didn't focus much on romantic interest.

I left work that day preparing to study for my drivers' exam because it would either be a hit or miss the next day. Feeling like it was nothing more than a distraction, I knew I needed to stay on track. I tried to convince my brother to let me use his vehicle. Still, he decided to compromise his friend's vehicle instead of his own due to his fear of my driving. He convinced his friend to let me use his car for the driver's test. Aware that I had no experience with how to drive. My friend Janelle had given me two driver's lessons prior to me taking the driver's test. Referencing after each lesson that she felt it was more appropriate if we both showed up in helmets for the next lesson. Nonetheless, I was determined to obtain a driver's license. I was always this determined spirit, and sometimes that determination could be so elevated it could be deemed crazy.

Most people would have walked into the D.M.V. knowing they would pass the test because they had practiced extensively. After all, that is practical. On the other hand, I walked in the D.M.V. knowing I would pass my driver's test and had not practiced driving much. Luckily for me, I passed the test after two attempts and was able to go back to work later feeling good; I had accomplished one of the things on my list. The following week, I got paid, so I decided to get a car to further my independence. I walked into one of the most infamous dealerships in my town where your job could act as your credit. I drove away in a 2012 chevy cobalt that felt like I was driving away in a Beemer.

My brother took me to the dealership, following me in his car, laughing extremely hard as we exited the dealership in our separate vehicles. We pulled up to my apartment at the same time. My brother Melvin Jr hopped out of his car laughing at how incredibly close I was sitting to the steering wheel, comparing my driving skills to my grandmother's. My grandmother had been infamously known amongst her children and grandchildren as a horrible driver. I laughed, refusing to disagree with him because I had no real clue how to drive after I departed from the dealership, reading a book about how to do so. Teaching myself as I exited the parking lot based on things I had read and learned along the way after having the car in my possession for a few weeks. Later that week, I received a call from the dealership representative who had sold me the car.

He was checking in to see how my vehicle was operating and how things were going, so I thought. I had times when I could be completely oblivious to a man's attempt to flirt or gain traction with me. Mainly because I was always self-absorbed, focusing on real-life issues. Issues such as being a single mom to my two children. I had no help, so my only focus was my goals. Based on my desire to elevate and get myself to a more stable position in life. It was typical of me to apply something from a book to real life, for I had always had the belief that if I did enough research on something, I could do it, which was usually the case.

I answered Jamar's string of questions about my car and his service, not thinking much more about it, continuing with my day. The next day Jamar sent me a friend request on Facebook, and I accepted. I got to work the next day, and I noticed Jamar had sent me a message via inbox. I realized his after-visit survey was probably an attempt to make his move. Still, he somehow decided delivering his attempt via Facebook would be the best way. I opened his message, reluctant to find the message content was nothing like I had assumed. He was respectful and polite, sparking enjoyable conversations from the start.

You will soon come to discover that I had a pattern. A good conversationist was always my weakness. He was also cute, well-spoken, and well-versed in how to communicate respectfully and effectively using more than two-syllable words, which was a step up from most of the idiots that flooded my inbox frequently. Although I thought he was nice, I felt it was vital that I stay focused. So, I moved the conversation out of my mind to keep my focus exactly where I thought it should be. I was good at doing this, but I would soon learn the repercussions of not trusting my initial process. I had set a goal to stay focused on my kids and me, and had I done that, things most likely would have picked up for me sooner. But a hard head will make a soft ass, and I would learn that abandoning my goal to be celibate and alone until I met "the right man" would cost me some adversity.

A few days later, Jamar asked me to go out on a date, and after being influenced by Barbra, I went along. She was constantly telling me that I needed to find someone, and to this day, I'm not sure if I wanted to find someone all of a sudden because of my desires or hers. Barbra often tried to influence me to find a husband, leading me to realize later that her lack of a partner and family was one of her biggest regrets. I guess that is why I took to her suggestions despite them not being a part of my initial vision. Jamar worked at the dealership, but he was knowledgeable and could do something more had he chosen. He also worked a second job, and like me, he was a workaholic.

He often focused on his bag and goals, so we had that in common. He was also an advent reader, often going to the public library checking out books that ranged in topics from Mandela, Marcus Garvey, to the art of war. I instantly fell in love with those components because I hadn't come across many Black men who loved to read. Or self-educate, and this was something I found extremely attractive. During this period, I had been off and on in a situation with a guy named John, who I had known for a long time. John was a local celebrity in my small town. He was known for his innovation skills and local philanthropy. When we met, he had falsely informed me he was single. After forming an intimate relationship for an extended period, he came clean with me, telling me that he had not been honest.

I was distraught with him because I didn't see him as a dishonest person. After finding out the truth, I cut off our relationship. I was starting to feel like there was no point in becoming wrapped up in the dynamics of dishonesty in relationships because everyone, for the most part, had been dishonest in my experience. Even I had been dishonest regarding myself clinging to mechanisms that were very lonely and secluded for me. I told myself that alone was what I preferred. I felt it needed to be my preference due to an intense fear of becoming involved with dishonest people. I had decided to keep him as a close friend afterward because despite his dishonesty with me initially, he and I had built a bond and connection that was hard to ignore. John was respectful, thoughtful, and genuine despite his initial lie, and I found solace in having him as a long-term friend.

His Pisces spirit was indeed compatible with my Capricorn energy. Although this was true, I discovered that his emotional and spontaneous character conflicted with my realistic stiff spirit at times. He preferred to keep his head in the clouds dreaming his big dreams. In comparison, I chose to keep my feet planted firmly on the ground. I was only focusing on things that were attainable quickly. I avoided things that required more creative energy than what I was willing to give at that time in my life. He was the person that inspired me to become a nurse aide after sharing with me one day the benefits of doing so.

This led me to sign up for a C.N.A. class pursuing the career and finding that it brought my life increase in many ways right away. I secretly admired John because he was very goal oriented. Despite growing up in the hood and small town of Charlottesville, Virginia, he was able to take his dreams and build a future that was well beyond the life he came from. Being around innovative, strong, and courageous entities can be helpful to you when you are in a transformational period. Watching John move on to build a progressive life and lifestyle encouraged me. I realized I could do the same one day. John knew that I had been going on dates with Jamar, and I made Jamar aware of John because I knew we all knew some of the same people. During this period of my life, I was more of a free spirit that did not genuinely care to be tied down. I was young, focused, and dating.

Imagine admiring Lori Harvey's dating routine and reminiscing about the good ole days when your routine was similar. During those days, I tried dating with the goal of settling down, Often finding that I did not feel ready for a solid relationship. Still, I also did not respect or want what came along with casual dating. Capricorn women can be complicated because we genuinely want what we want when we want it. I had always been one to desire the whole thing and never the half. And despite that dynamic of my personality, I would soon step headfirst into a situation where the entire thing would never be available to me. Although I liked Jamar, I found out how his previous marriage had ended, and I was starting to see a side of him I did not have room for in my life. He was intelligent and romantic, but he was a man who required the attention of multiple women, and I didn't want that.

I enjoyed my time with him because he was well versed in the romance department. Always making me feel as though I was the center when he had other women in his life in reality. Looking back, I guess I was selfish about how I viewed things with Jamar. But I felt like he was also selfish for not giving me the same level of honesty I had been giving him. It was fair for him to date other people, especially since I was. Still, I didn't think it was appropriate that he was lying about it, which turned me completely off. Men often think women are better off being lied to about their significance. In reality, being honest allows us to choose what we do and don't want to be a part of. I understood why he felt he had to play it as though I was the only one.

But I also understood how and why that would not work for me. His opening with lies would only mean that would be our permanent dynamic. That was not something in which I was interested. I decided to cut things off with Jamar and kept my situation with John because John and I were always honest. And the connection was something I valued. Although I was trying to stick with John, I was still dating other men trying to find the better option. Frequently running into John while in the company of other men. Having him convey to me with his facial expressions that he did not approve.

Later receiving a call or text where he would touch base on the other male party I was accompanied by. Making slick comments while also trying to appear unscathed. I embodied an unattached demeanor on the outside in fear of catching feelings and getting hurt. To an outsider looking in, it would appear that I gave zero fucks, disregarding men, and their feelings the way they often do concerning women. The reality of it was I didn't care, but that was based on seeing what happened when I did. I started recognizing how I was placing myself in limbo, trying to date and explore what was out there. Feeling like I didn't have room for a relationship in my life while also feeling like I was the settled type.

Learning later to be okay with that component of me. I was the settled type dating amongst men who were not. Although John and I were not exclusive, he made me realize that being true to my real nature was okay. I shared aspects of who I was with him that I had never felt I could with anyone else of the male form. John was the first man who allowed me to understand that being soft and submissive was okay. Having been in many relationships with liars, cheaters, etc., shaped me into this strong anxious independent woman. I felt I did not need a man for anything.

In reality, I didn't, but it was still okay to let a man in. Making myself feel as though I had to be vigilant, stern, and insubordinate. Concerning my partners because men were not to be trusted. When had I ever been involved with a real man, I would have never developed such anxious emotions regarding cultivating relationships. Men were not my issue because all men don't come into your life to harm, hurt, and disrupt your process. And I would later realize that my ability to select the wrong partners was causing me the problem. John was the first man I had allowed into my life mentally and physically on my level.

He never took more than he gave, disrespected me, and consistently placed all of his cards on the table after being initially accompanied by his original lies. Allowing me to understand that there were still good men left in the world. As much as I was intrigued by who John was, I later realized that fear kept me in positions where I would let him in, then boom, shut him out again. I wanted someone good in my life, but the reality was I was afraid of John because he had not been the ball of deception, I was familiar with. I often had moments where I felt like things could be more due to our connection. Dropping the idea altogether every time, I considered the way he had initially approached me as a single man when he was not at that time. Although he had come clean later once the relationship with his ex-ended, I still felt as though a man that would cheat with you would cheat on you.

Especially if he doesn't give you an option to choose for yourself. And although that happened, I told myself that because I was afraid of so many things about this man. At times I asked myself which action was crazier. Falling in love with a good man who showed me things that helped me grow as a woman, keeping the truth from him due to fear of something good? Or falling in love with a man who showed me nothing but bad, stifling my growth, while making excuses for my love because I felt he needed my help to grow?

I started feeling like I valued John's friendship more than I was willing to admit out loud. I began to see how our situation was becoming compromised. We started out moving in a way that didn't require any structure due to my busy life, and then all of a sudden, things felt different. There were times when he acted as if he was feeling away about nothing. And there were times when I would do the same. I knew if I had to choose, I would much rather have him as my friend than my ex-friend, so I cut off the intimate relationship trying to hold onto the friendship. It felt right to do so at times, while other times, it did not. A month went by when I hadn't heard from John after his last text telling me that I was fake, which translated to "I don't understand why we are not being intimate anymore."

I wanted to explain why I had made my choice, but I didn't feel comfortable doing so. And I think that was partly because I was starting to make choices that were strides mentally even for me. I cut John off, only keeping him as a friend I would talk to here and there.

After all, how could he understand my desire to be celibate when we had always been intimate. I actively chose to be celibate and secluded until God sent me someone, I felt was indeed for me. I went to sit in the television room with Barbra counting down until I could leave work for the day and cruise around in my new car overlooking the fact that I wasn't the most skilled driver. I got home after work and went to pick my kids up from the after-school program.

This was pivotal because I walked my kids from after school every day before my first car. It felt good picking them up in a vehicle, and I could see the happiness and disbelief in their eyes when I pulled up to the school with a car that was our car. Later that evening, we returned home to our nightly routine. Dinner, showers, and our traditional family movie night until one of us fell asleep on the sofa. Movies were my favorite hobby to engage in with my kids. I loved watching movies trying to understand the writer's content and guessing which direction the storyline would go. I never liked doing things most people my age did. I always felt this kept me from finding a friend group and relationship I was completely comfortable in.

I had always found solace in being a homebody. Enjoying the company of my Living room, my tv, a good book, and my kids. I never wanted to go out, party, or do most of what my friends did due to becoming a mom at such a young age. Gaining the nickname granny from my college friend and old coworker Tia. Who dished out the nickname after picking up on my old-fashioned ways. I could later understand why settling down seemed like the right dynamic for me due to how I carried myself. Sure, enough, I would learn that the only people I didn't mind constantly being in my personal space were my children.

Growing tired of friends and romantic relationships once they interfered with my alone time was my norm, but I knew I needed to be myself comfortably. Often feeling like balance was not something I could have because the people who liked my presence often wanted to become engulfed in it, leaving me to feel a level of suffocation I could not become comfortable with. Later leaving relationships abruptly because I didn't know how to tell people that they were overcrowding me. As I got older, I started to see how my energy could be misleading at times. Due to my ability to become wrapped in with my partner loving the bliss of togetherness. Shortly after becoming tired of it altogether, I felt my lone wolf spirit creeping in. Murmuring to me, "bitch ditch his clingy ass, so we can have some time alone."

I loved the idea of love, family, and the act of inclusion amongst those I cared about, but I also loved my space. Feeling the peace of time alone where I could sit, think, watch a good movie, or do nothing at all without having to cater to someone's desire to gain my attention when I felt tired of engaging. I later understood how my aura could often be confusing for the people in my environment. Once I articulated that I needed my breathing space. Leaving many people to feel as though I was wishy-washy when in reality, I was just catering to a component of self-care that would always be a part of my spirit. This behaviorism would often be interpreted as me being fake. The irony is once I would decide to let go of the stronghold, I had on my dire need to be to myself, it would be with someone who encompassed wishy-washy behavior in the worst ways imaginable.

I had gotten my new car, and it had inspired this newfound ambition that had been tugging at me effortlessly. At the same time, I kept it hidden gracefully, just living life and being a mom. I often lied to myself daily, unconsciously telling myself all I could do were the things I was. I unconsciously trained myself to believe that there was no room for dreams in the land of realism because a single mom could not afford dreams. Dreams took time and money, and those were two resources on which I was always short. Many of you read that last line and felt my testimony. How many of you have told yourself this very same thing? If you have, I want you to pause, take a deep breath, and remove that thought from your mind because it costs nothing to dream.

This was something I would later down the line realize. I had been deprived of my ability to live out my dreams, not due to my lack of time or resources but simply due to my lack of faith in myself. The world shapes us to believe that there is no room for dreams when you must study, work a nine to five, and be a parent but that my friends were a load of bullshit I held onto closely. Bullshit, I fed myself so that I wouldn't have to step out on faith and do what my heart was nudging me to do. So, if you've been telling yourself these same lines, I hope that by the middle or end of my story, you realize this is a disservice to yourself, and you go after the things you want. I had been riding around for weeks enjoying the company of my kids, which was my norm. Spending my days after work getting everyone dressed up so we could cruise around, making stops to see friends, and enjoy the liberty of no longer having to walk to and from every location we went.

I had experienced my fair share of days where I got down due to the lack of progress not having a car presented for me. I did not get the jobs I wanted due to transportation issues, consistently applying to places I could walk to and from. The places within walking distance never paid enough, only allowing me to pay my bills, keep food on the table, and spend my days broke until the next pay period, where I would do it all over again. I thought about my days working at Cold Stone. Going in and opening the store solo, made all the ice cream cakes, and did the inventory while running the entire store alone until it was time for me to go home at the end of the day. I would walk to work, then walk to my kids' school to pick them up after school, and we would walk home in the rain, sleet, and snow. I did this every day, often being passed on the street by people I knew who would see us walking and never stop to give us a ride.

I had friends with cars and family, none of them gave me a hand with transportation, and I was always too independent to ask. You see, I was then and very much now a firm believer that people close to you always see your struggles even if you are too ashamed or humble to tell. I felt it was okay to ask for help, but I also realized my circle was unwilling, only able. I would also later recognize that this dynamic needed to be altered. I would learn that majority of the people around me only liked being around because they benefitted from my shortcomings and hardships. Always calling me to see how I was doing, waiting to hear the sad, stressed, struggling components of my life to enhance the quality of their own lives. This very dynamic would be the very reason all these people would soon flee from my life once I got myself together and in a better position.

When the phone rings, and you answer and the context changes from sadness, hurt, and humiliation to progress, positivity, and success, no one wants to talk. Especially not people who have benefited from those calls where you're crying about your life that at the moment feels extremely hard. You see, those people needed that from me. Not because I deserved the subliminal ugliness and bad energies hurtling around me, but because they were miserable, and it's nothing like hearing someone else's pain to help lesson yours. I would soon learn that quality will always be a better preference over quantity. It is best to have a few good friends who value you than to have an endless supply of people around who could care less. I would realize these people who were not my real friends were only able to prey on me due to my inability to accept what was right in front of me.

I would ignore red flags because I felt I needed the presence of others around to be okay, not realizing I was clinging to a toxic pool of haters who saw my abilities long before I ever would. Secretly laughing at my stagnation, glaring at me closely, praying I would never realize my full potential because Nina, who had struggles, self-esteem issues, and stress, was far more interesting than a woman with self-knowledge. Barbra was getting stronger every day, and my days at work started to feel a lot less like going to work and more like leaving one home and going to a second home. Barbra had been urging me to go out and date, often referring to my need for a husband. I desired this for myself, but there wasn't exactly a tree sitting outside filled with eligible men waiting to be picked from. So, I did what felt easiest, and I stayed put. I always told myself that God would send me the perfect husband who would be a great match for the person I was when the time was right.

Notice I said when the time was right...... had I waited for the right time as I should have, things would have most likely gone different for me...but I will get into that soon. Barbra and I spent the day doing what we did best: store hop! We had spent the day coming and going stopping at our favorite antique stores, talbots, and whatever else we could think of. I loved those days with her because the day would fly by, and I could get back home to my kids. I often reflected on how far I had come since my cold stone days of working around the clock and barely bringing in enough income to make ends meet. Always reminding myself that no matter how far I climbed as far as progress was concerned, I would never forget the days of not having and not doing because those days had molded me significantly as a woman and a mother. This was a regular exercise for me!

Gratitude was vital energy to have, and I never wanted to forget where and what I came from and made it through. My new job provided me with peace of mind, financial elevation, and most importantly, I was valued by my client. It felt good being appreciated and respected for my hard work because this was a component that was always missing, especially in my new line of work as a nurse aide. Often, I would be treated like the help, feeling like my presence was as significant to my employers as an enslaved person's presence who had graduated from being a field slave to a house slave. Feeling as if I knew exactly what it felt like to be an indentured servant. I know some of you read that last line and felt it was a little dramatic but growing up in Charlottesville, Virginia, I had experienced my fair share of experiences feeling the sting of racial inequality. Especially in my line of work.

Having friends in the same line of work and similar fields like nannying, we often sat on the phone sharing our stories, all feeling the same way. It was conversations with my friends and coworkers that confirmed my feelings and their level of realism. It is easy to deduce that you're being treated unfairly or ungracefully when you're in a room with others, and there is no internal or external component linking you to these people. A woman of color will often walk into a room and feel differences that may or may not exist based on race, gender, socioeconomic status, and educational background. This is why I preferred hearing my friend's stories. They served as reminders that those feelings were not in my head and that they existed whether the people amongst me wanted to acknowledge their behaviors. Therefore, I felt incredibly grateful for the individuals who hired me and treated me like I deserved to be treated.

The people that treated me like a human being and not some inferior little Black girl hired to help. After Barbra, I would find the clients' dynamic that hired me would change. I would be blessed to come into contact with people who valued my help and my intellect, treating me the way I desired to be treated. I enjoyed the pleasures of not having to walk everywhere, and my new car was now my most prized possession and resource. I would go to work every day feeling proud that I had gotten my license, my car, and like so many other achievements, I had done so independently. Being a single mom of two children and not having any help or resources doing things on your own, especially things that require time and money, can feel monumental. Especially when you've reached out to people asking for help and being disregarded. I remember wondering why I could never rely on anyone outside of myself during those days.

I remembered the days when I cried because I didn't know how to keep my bills paid or provide for my kids. I remember how I used to cry and question my life because I would work so hard and never feel like I had what I needed to provide for my kids adequately. People would often say things to me, complimenting me on how well dressed my kids were or how nice my home was, never having a clue that I was struggling in the ways that I was. Not knowing that I was often living paycheck to paycheck, relying on the lump sum of a refund check from school or my tax refund to do certain things for my kids and my home. I remember those days so clearly. Getting those lump sums that during that time felt like so much. I ran to home goods and the world market to get the décor I wanted and couldn't afford regularly due to my bills. Or showering my kids with clothes or little gift baskets to put a smile on their faces after feeling guilty for struggling and not being able to do the things for them I wanted to because the bills and food came first.

I remember going to food banks to get groceries when food got low, and money was not an option because all I had was what I needed for my bills. I remember my kid's fathers getting their new cars nice clothes and walking around with every new pair of Jordans that came out, not even offering so much as a pair of socks to me for my kids. You see, I was a special kind of unlucky because I had acquired not one but two nonexistent fathers who didn't give a damn whether or not my kids had or didn't have. Both were consumed by their selfishness, only offering a hand here and there when they thought it could get them into my bed. Realizing that it wouldn't and seizing all false attempts to be in their kids' lives. This was something I blamed myself for over the years. Blaming myself for the lies I had been told.

Two long-term relationships left me with nothing more than disappointment, hardships, and children I would have to provide for on my own. Often being lied about and painted as a mad baby momma who stifled the father's ability to see their children. For years, these false narratives enraged me because I knew the truth. Never being fully redeemed from these narratives until these men had other children they neglected in the same way. Leaving the past in the past, allowing them full access to their children with no boundaries in place only to learn that with or without boundaries, these men were not and would never be interested in my children in the way I would have preferred them to be. I had learned that I was more than what had been done to me. Sure, these people may have caused me some pain, disappointment, and suffering at times, but it was through these unfortunate events that I finally saw me and all of me.

Rising above adversity and using my experiences to be a better version of myself. For years I would stare at my children, assessing the pain they felt from their fathers' absences and blaming myself. Blaming myself for every time I spoke up. I was blaming myself for standing up against every mal behavior against my children and using my voice. Every time I advocated for myself in the relationship, I spoke out against cheating, lies, and carelessness. Wishing I could've been or would've been a different type of woman. This very dynamic kept me embedded in my marriage for so long.

Telling myself that I needed to stay with my abusive husband so my youngest child would never have to know the pain of neglect from her father like my two oldest children had. Telling myself that if I left and he stopped being a father due to my absence from him, it would be my fault. Consistently fighting my urge to be vocal, smart, and intuitive. Because I secretly felt those qualities were the main ingredients to being a single mother. The women I knew who had their relationships intact were silent. I started questioning if advocacy was my mistake. Did I need to transition to a quieter, stifled version of myself to have a happy ending? Hell no! I did not, but it would take time before I understood that.

I recalled the memory of being five months pregnant and extremely ill with hyperemesis gravid arum, which would become a lifelong nemesis in all of my pregnancies. Each time it presented itself in a heightened, miserable form, making it hard to consume anything. I Recall me putting out my sons' father mid-pregnancy and making a conscious choice that I could do it alone. You see, I knew in that very moment when I told him to leave that he would not be a resource for my unborn son. I had grown up in a culture where it was pertinent that a woman like me realize she was lucky in unfortunate situations. The societal environment I came from told me that a woman with kids should take the man with the money and the minute version of care. To most, you see a man with money, and some respect was far better than no man and no money.

Sometimes we get ourselves into these relationships that devour us whole. We cry and complain about the person and the outcome overlooking the fact that we saw it coming all along. This was something I had seen many times. Even my mother had adopted and settled for this horrible rendition of love at times. Still, I was determined that would not be me. I had never been blind, nor was I one to pretend or place blame solely on one person. He had been wrong for the things he was doing behind my back, and I had been wrong for allowing it for so long because I felt I didn't have solid, tangible proof. How many of you have ever been in this position? You know something is going on, but you have no evidence or way of proving that your hunch is simply more than just a hunch.

Having people tell you, girl, it's your hormones. Or girl, that man takes good care of you, and your daughter you are tripping. But I knew I was not wrong. Dating in specific environments can be tricky. My friends thought I was crazy to complain because my son's father gave me any and everything I asked for. He introduced me to a level of life I had never seen before, showering me with money, gifts, and respect. These components made me feel as though he was the most genuine man in the world.

But I was no fool, and I always thought if it felt too good to be true, it most likely was, and, in his case, I was not wrong. The disrespect behind closed doors made him not suitable for me. Although it would take time, I would find the strength to walk away from him based on my hunches that would not be proven until later. I lay in bed vomiting in a trash bag feeling as if I had been hit by a bus. My days were starting to run together, and each day felt more miserable than the day before. It had been a few weeks since I retired from my apartment in Prospect and moved into my first townhome around the corner in Orangedale Ave. Omar had been the answer to my prayers in the beginning.

Showering me with nothing but love, respect, and care. But my feelings for him were starting to change, and my intuition was poking at me daily, telling me he was not the person I thought he was. Before moving, I found some disturbing things, making me feel as though our relationship had been built on lies. Omar had met me one night when I was walking home from work. Like usual, Prospect was flooded with its usual entourage of the hood's finest, all swooning around a new face as if they had never come into contact with a woman before. Omar stood out to me because he wasn't like the rest of them. They all yelled inappropriate things, following me to my building constantly, telling the same genre of lies, trying to get me interested, and feeling annoyed when they realized I was not who they would have hoped I would be.

Spewing out lies and bragging about the street money they had in their pockets, not realizing that I had never been involved with a street guy, nor did I desire to be at that time. I took pride in going to work and making my own money, and I had never felt there was anything I wanted that I couldn't get for myself. "She's stuck up, they'd reply after being denied any interaction with me. I was 18 and excited I was on my own with my daughter, never really feeling concerned about a man. Omar would watch me from the street, smiling and speaking occasionally. He seemed polite, but he also gave me slow vibes that made me feel like he was a little off, judging from his body language. In other words, I felt like his elevator didn't go all the way to the top. So, I would give a half-smile in return and keep it moving, holding on to my judgments of him for quite some time. I remember one night, in particular, walking home and taking out my trash.

I exited my building, making my way towards the dumpster when Omar popped out of nowhere. I remember thinking to myself how creepy he was. I thought to myself, why was he always out in the hallways late at night? Dumb and naive as they could come. Later I would learn that the hallway was occupied during the night for where and how he made his money. Omar popped out of the hallway, offering to take the trash out for me. Usually, Id decline, but I was tired, and my shift had run a little later than I expected, so I handed him the trash and hurried back into my building before he could catch up with me.

I was quite the anomaly to most and still am on most days. People looked at me and saw this young girl who was always well dressed, hair done and assumed attention was what I would want or like, but that wasn't who I was. I was shy and abnormally introverted amongst people I had no familiarity with and preferred to be ignored. But walking around well-dressed with a nice form was not exactly the recipe for being ignored, which often irritated me. Weeks passed since I had seen Omar, and my homegirl and occasional roommate came by. Erica Harris had been a close friend, and I relied on her company during the week. Although I was happy to have my place, I hated it being just my daughter and me. I would often have friends stay over regularly so I wouldn't be plagued with anxiety.

Erica was pretty, fly, and outgoing in ways I could have never been, and that was what I admired about her. She was always herself, and she had no cut cards about any of her engagements, no matter how outlandish they could be. She did what she wanted to do, and she didn't give a flying you know what about who agreed or disagreed with her methods. Erica walked into my apartment well dressed, with her hair crimped and styled, ready for the night. "You look cute, Erica I said, trying to figure out if she was coming from or getting prepared to go to. I hated when she came over at night ready for a date because I knew that meant I would be staying in my creepy apartment with my daughter on my own. My apartment was no creepier than anywhere else I had stayed.

But it felt creepy to me because I was there alone. It felt good being independent, but it also sparked some anxiety because there was no one I could fall back on if things did not go as planned. Girl, I got a date tonight, Erica said as if I hadn't already assumed that much. With whom I asked, secretly annoyed that she would not be staying. I'm going out with Angel tonight, she said with a wide smile. But don't worry, I'm coming back, she said, lying through her teeth. I knew, and she knew she was not coming back, but I played along. What about Hank, I asked?

Have you all broken up again? Knowing they were because they broke up every couple of weeks. Girl, I'm not thinking about his crazy ass, she said, lying again. I sat and listened to Erica tell me how she wasn't thinking about Hank taking in one lie after the other because I knew within a matter of days, they would be back boo'd up again. She'd be acting as if she had not said any of the things she currently was. The next day Erica came over later during the day. I heard a knock at my door, and sure enough, it was her and Hank standing in the doorway together. It hadn't even been 24 hours since she was last in my face talking big talk referencing how she didn't care about her Ex yet; here they were standing in the doorway, both of them looking simple as hell.

We all have that homegirl that talks so big like she won't do this or that regarding her ex, then five seconds later...boom.... she's back with him. I never judged her because I knew she was bluffing each time she opened her mouth to pretend not to care about him. They walked into my apartment glued to each other's hip, Hank with a smile on his face. He loved him some Erica, and despite how she tried to act, she loved him too. Erica sat down with an odd look on her face. This was one of her looks I did not favor. It was what I liked to refer to as her "sneaky look."

I could always be sure that when she came through the door with this look on her face, she was cooking up some scheme I would not be in alignment with. I sat on the sofa, ignoring her, purposely waiting for her to let it out. "You know Hank got a brother, Omar," she said, still holding the same sneaky little grin on her face. I rolled my eyes, thinking how predictable she was with her cat eyes glaring at me, waiting for a response she knew she wasn't going to get. I tried over-talking her because I knew where she was headed. "You know Omar thinks you are so cute," she said, shriveling her face up again with the sneaky look I hated. I pretended not to hear her.

Having someone think I was physically appealing was not a big deal. I had always been more interested in conversation and mental attraction. But both of those things tended to be hard to come by with men in my age range. Their approaches were the same, long-drawn-out rants about how sexy or fashion-forward they found me to be. Leading me to believe that the dating pool was full of mindless idiots fueled by their raging hormones. Call me judgmental, but I had not been proven wrong. That is until Omar came along, or so I thought.

Me, Omar, Erica, and Hank would spend the night playing cards and laughing. I was always generally shy, and it confused many people because no one understood why someone whose outer appearance consisted of flamboyance daily could be so silent and constricted. I had spent my entire life being this way, usually only coming out of my shell showing my fun and comical side to the people I knew long-term and trusted. To make a long story short, Omar started coming around more after that night. We would talk, hang out, and spend a lot of time enjoying each other's company. In the beginning, I didn't find Omar physically attractive. He wasn't unattractive, but he was not the kind of guy I would usually be attracted to, and he was about ten years older than me.

At the time, I was eighteen, and he was twenty-eight. I wasn't looking for anything at this time in my life, and You all will soon realize I had developed a pattern. For it was when I wasn't looking for these things that they tended to pop up wrapped nicely, appearing to be everything I wanted, only for me to realize through heartbreak that it was not. You see, even now, as I sit here typing these words, I question myself. Not the current me, but the former me. Wondering what it was that made her so gullible and giving. I wonder why she felt she needed anything from anyone when everything she needed was already resting solemnly inside, waiting to be noticed, appreciated, and activated.

Still, I guess that is how it goes for many of us. I would spend the next year of my life wrapped in this relationship with this man that appeared to be everything I needed and wanted. Only to find out he was none of those things. He had made himself be someone he wasn't to get me, have me, and keep me. Later I realized keeping me would never be a plausible option because I would never settle or succumb to the mindless "pick me "version of a woman Omar preferred. Omar was quiet, comforting, and giving. Leading me to feel as if he was the male version of myself.

He always made sure my daughter and I had everything we wanted and needed, and no was a word he never said in response to any of my requests. Spoiling me from the first week, he made his presence permanent. I would go to work every day at the hospital, and when I would return home, things were not as they once were. The bills I was used to paying solely on my own became the bills I no longer contributed to. He would buy all my groceries, pay my bills, and provide me with every handbag or shoe I desired. Shopping was always something I enjoyed, but my lifestyle had changed. The shopping I was used to doing here and there or maybe once in a blue moon became a weekly regimen in my schedule.

Me and my daughter would walk into a store and touch any and everything we wanted, and he would get it. No questions asked, and no talking about what he did for us later. Luxury was always something I desired. After tasting the good life regarding financial stability with Omar, I realized he helped mold some of my newfound desires. He always admired my stylish aura because he was a style lover himself. Often encouraging me to do things during that time that was bold and striking. I remember one day having him convince me to do a half and half look with my hair.

Having the left side one color and the right another. Shooting down the idea and recalling his suggestion after seeing Nicki Minaj body the look years later. Omar was secure in who he was at that time, and he never tried to stifle who I was. Always encouraging me to show up and show out, teaching me how to overlook hate and judgments. Our time together would not end on a positive note, but I would later realize that God had put him in my life to teach me many things. Later feeling thankful that we had crossed paths due to the blessing of my son, my first encounter with ambition, and my first introduction to living a bossed-up lifestyle. Omar showed me that I could level up and better my life through consistency.

Despite his flaws and lax parenting, he was a good teacher and muse. I would work every day and leave the house with my friends with an allowance. He would send me out of the house with money on my way to make money. This allowance allowed me time to go shopping on my breaks at work. This shopping usually consisted of home décor and clothes for my baby girl, who never wore the same outfit twice. I was young, frivolous, and dumb as hell. Eighteen without a clue or a sense of direction.

Omar had created a monster. Just cute and spoiled. Spending every waking moment focusing on my child, my man, and my newly developed shopping addiction. This dynamic was significant because I saw what it was like to be with someone who made me feel like they didn't care as much as I preferred. And after meeting Omar, I saw what it was like to be with someone who appeared to care about me in ways I had never experienced. My previous relationship was a long-term relationship with my high school sweetheart. Who happened to be the father of my first child.

After ending that relationship, we would go back and forth for years doing an on-again, off-again routine. That always felt like it was too much to keep up with. We were at one-point young, in love, and dumb. Becoming young parents. Later, we watched as our relationship and friendship became compromised due to the dynamic of us being babies having babies. Kyle and I had our ups and downs, but they were minor because we were kids. After our daughter was born, we tried to get it right and never could.

Based on the fact I was always so serious, and he was young and ready to be young. And although leaving that relationship was hard for me based on all the things we went through together as kids, I never held it against him. Later I recognized that the sacrifices I wanted him to make as a young man and father were unrealistic based on who he was. And where he was at that time in his life. So naturally, I fell for Omar because he made me feel like I was getting everything from him that I didn't get from Kyle. Omar had never had someone like me, and the same went for me. I could see the admiration for who I was in his eyes every time he looked at me, making me uncomfortable.

This was based on the fact that I had made a living out of ignoring my true nature. Unconsciously I overlooked my spirit because I was never comfortable being all of me. Simply out of fear that there was no place in the culture of life I was in for someone like me. So, I went with the flow, pretending to be the person everyone thought I was. Often feeling internally miserable. Covering up my true essence daily, playing into stereotypes and the people's expectations around me.

Never allowing myself to be anything more than the around-the-way girl who had a baby young, dressed nice, had a nice body, and a nice place in the hood.

You see, for most, that was all it took at eighteen. Most girls from where I'm from aspired to look good and be popular while laid up with a man with a bag. Although to most, it would appear that's who I was or wanted to be, I had a different idea of what I wanted out of life. Omar had always talked about marrying me and a future, and although those were things that most girls would want, I felt he wasn't living right, so I didn't see it for us. When I met Omar, he told me he was a construction worker, and I believed him because I was the clueless young fool I was. Later I found out he was a drug dealer, and by that time, I was able to look past my standard moral reservations for his profession based on my feelings for him, so I thought. When in fact, I now feel it was not the feelings but the freedom of not having to worry about finances.

A part of me always knew what Omar did, but I played oblivious because no one had come right out and stated it. So, it was easy to ignore what was not known to be a fact. Again, this was me ignoring the hunch that tugged at me, telling me what I needed to be told. To make a long story short, I knew a lot more during those days than for what I gave myself credit. I spent the next year of my life feeling happy in my relationship while feeling something wasn't right. Every day I would walk out of my building and go down the street to my mom's house. My neighbor who lived directly across the hall would give me dirty looks on my way out of the building.

One day I went outside to meet up with Erica. Never speaking, never sparking a conversation, only extending countless dirty looks I didn't understand. Some would have assumed it was the loud music or a large number of visitors that angered her, but I did nothing of the sort. I remember my intuition tugging at me during this current moment, telling me there was more to Nia's stares, but I brushed it off. After all, I didn't know her, so there was no real reason she could have disdain for me. I was significantly younger than her, and I had not seen or heard of her prior to us becoming neighbors in Prospect. Erica had phoned letting me know she was almost at my building, and she wanted to know if my daughter and I wanted to go for a walk.

Walking was always a part of my daily routine, which was easy because I didn't own a car or drive. I got my daughter dressed, did her hair, and went out to meet Erica to take our daily stroll down Prospect, trying to pass the time. Although I was in a relationship with Omar, I spent a lot of time alone. He was always in the streets making his money while I was on my own. In the beginning, this was the hardest component of my relationship. I walked outside to meet Erica, but there was no sign of her anywhere. Erica was always late.

I stood outside dressed in my dark denim jeans, a bright yellow tank, a see-through mesh shirt, a colorful xoxo bag, colorful Jordan sneakers, and long braids down to my hips. Holding my beautiful baby girl dressed in her Ralph Lauren dress and matching sandals. I stood in front of my building, feeling annoyed. Once again, I had been waiting and waiting on Erica, and she was on a different schedule than the one she had conveyed to me. If she told you she was five minutes away, it was in your best interest to add fifteen minutes to the duration for your solace. A burgundy S.U.V. pulled up to the front of the building, and out came Nia, the unfriendly neighbor. She extended her infamous regularly anticipated grill rolling her eyes at me as she exited the vehicle. Nia was extremely tall compared to me, who stood five feet since the sixth grade.

Nia walked past me, and my daughter giving me the stink face as usual. She was dark-skinned, heavyset, with an enormous butt that you could typically spot from the front view at first glance. She had a pretty face that was hard to notice because she preferred to frown more than smile, but I was about to understand why soon enough. She was rude and highly bothered whenever she saw my face, which plucked my last nerve. I usually would chalk an event like this up to her being a hater. Still, we were not in the same age group or social class, and as far as I could see, she was an attractive woman and had no reason to feel anything towards me. She walked into the building, and I wanted to stop her in her tracks and ask her woman-to-woman what her issue was. Had I done something to annoy her and not know?

Erica called my cell to let me know she had something come up and would no longer meet me. This pissed me off instantly. Not because she wasn't coming, but because I knew she was lying and was laying up with Hank despite the false reasoning she had given me. I put my daughter in her stroller and went on a walk to Orangedale to visit my friend Lanaye. Lanaye was about ten years older than me, and we had become friends shortly after I moved to Orangedale Ave at the age of 17. She worked as a social worker during the day and the hood source by night. If anything was going on in the hood or the city, you better believe she knew of it.

I often walked over to visit her during the day when Omar was out making his money, and I was home alone. She always welcomed me and my daughter's visits with no invitation required. I knocked on her door, still feeling annoyed. Lanaye came to the door quickly, assessing that something was wrong with me from the troubled look on my face. All I could think about was the burgundy S.U.V. and its unfriendly owner. That nudge started to creep in instantly. It was as if my intuition were playing a game of tug of war and winning over my cognitive process. I pictured the vehicle trying to make the urge go away, but it would not.

"Girllll, what is going on?" She asked in her usual worried tone. Ready to Soak up the tea and spill some in return. I quickly went into detail, letting her know about stank face Nia and how I was starting to feel like she had an issue with me. Lanaye froze up instantly after hearing Nia's name. "What, what's that look for? I asked, secretly feeling that I knew where the conversation was headed after becoming so consumed with the hunch that came to me shortly after seeing the vehicle Nia was driving. "Well, girl, don't say I told you, but it was said that Omar was fooling with Nia when he first started seeing you."

My bottom lip hit the floor as Lanaye continued giving me the rundown on Omar's treachery. According to her, Omar lived with Nia and drove her vehicle while she went to work. The burgundy SUV I had watched her pull up in invaded my thoughts because I recognized it right away. He drove me to and from work, the store, and doctors' appointments in her vehicle. All I could wonder at that moment was, who does that? What type of man drives a woman's car around picking up other women? What kind of man has the guts to do so with two women living in the same apartment building and not fear getting caught?

This was the first red flag of many more to come. Lanaye summed up all that she knew about Nia and Omar, reminding me on my way out the door to keep her name out of it. "Girl, just don't say I said anything," Lanaye repeated, assessing the anger in my eyes as she watched me walk down the street fuming on the inside. This was always the part I hated about trusting people, specifically men. But what I would later learn is that I was not in trusting my heart and my time to a man. Instead, I was trying to build with a boy who had no desire to live a better life. Omar had spent most of his younger years behind bars for drug trafficking.

So, although he stood before me as a man in the flesh physically, internally, he was the little boy he had walked into prison as. The culture of life I came from, I saw this every day. Men would go to jail young and come out like grown men who were still in the same boyish state that they entered jail in. Lacking the knowledge, morals, or desire to be anything different other than the lost, misguided souls they had always known themselves to be. Omar was kind to me, respectful, loving, and catering. And most of my friends thought I was crazy to complain about cheating suspicions, him selling drugs, and staying out late. Still, I did not come from the type of life he did, and I had no desire to be a part of it. This created a divide amongst us in our relationship because I was never happy no matter what he did.

I wanted to live comfortably and carefree, but I didn't want the drug money to be my source of a happy life. I wanted a solid happy relationship, but I didn't want an "in the streets man." You see, that's what I feel many people get confused about. There is an in-the-street man and a street man, and the difference between the two is highly significant in the culture of a relationship. A street man is someone whose original habitat is the street. They grew up in the hood adopted the hoods mentality and culture but may or may not still reside there. Growing and evolving, adapting new mature concepts that allow the opportunity for evolution to occur.

A in the streets man is someone who is out and about roaming the hood fucking around and fucking up. Lacking any drive or desire to do anything outside of running and roaming around carelessly in the streets consumed by living a street life. Omar fell under the category of being an "in the street man" who was incompatible with who I was and who I wanted to be. I was from the street, but I wasn't in the street, which separated me from Omar. I arrived home fumigating with anger and disappointment. I waited for him all day, but he didn't come home until late that night. I put my baby to bed, and I waited and waited, but it was late, and I had to work the next day, so I went to bed.

I heard the key placed in the door late that night, and Omar entered the house. I hopped out of bed, ready to pounce and give him a piece of my mind. I entered the living room abruptly to find him staggering around, intoxicated. "So, you had the fucking nerve to pick me up in another woman's car, I asked him." He looked at me confused as he made his way to the sofa, preparing to sit and accept a side of me he had never seen before. All I could think about was punching him in the face as he sat listening to my rant unattached to the conversation due to the elevated levels of boat, also known as embalming fluid roaming around in his body. "I'm walking around here trying to understand why this girl is looking at me fucking crazy, and your raggedy ass failed to tell me it's because you were living with her five seconds before you started dating me." The more I described and expressed my anger and dissatisfaction with him, the louder I became.

Omar kneeled forward, and before I could say another word, my floor was covered in vomit. I realized I would not get anywhere trying to have this conversation with him. I rushed to get some cleaning products and towels and began cleaning up the rug while he lay in a pool of his vomit talking out of his head. Comparing him and me to Bey and Jay, diluting that our home was a penthouse. The delusions were monumental because we lived in a low-income apartment in the hood. He had compared me to Keisha from Belly and ranting about how he loved me etc. At this point, I became even more furious.

I remember cleaning him up and helping him get in the bed that night and analyzing everything he said to me in his high state. I repeatedly replayed the line; where he compared me to Keisha because

I knew what he meant. Men like Omar felt like having a woman like me was like hitting the lottery. Attractive, young, clueless, and in the damn house. Just cute, silent, and unproblematic. Never questioning his coming and going. But he was about to be in for a big surprise.

It's funny how you have no proof of anything, and then one day, the universe shows you something, and that's when the red flags start to pop up all over the place. You see, I was silent and unproblematic, but that was only because I had nothing to be vocal about until this event. Weeks had gone by, and although I was still upset that Omar had lied to me and hid his previous relationship with my neighbor, I had managed to move past it, telling myself one lie after another, trying to be complacent. He started showering me with more gifts and money, trying to make me okay with things he knew I was not okay with. Coming home daily with loads of expensive cosmetics, handbags, and clothes he had purchased from everyone's favorite neighborhood booster, Lee Lee. Lee Lee started making multiple trips a week to my house at his request. Bringing me loads of items she had boosted from my favorite department stores. I loved Lee Lee because she would keep me updated on things; I needed to know about Omar.

Dealing with someone in the streets can be challenging if you don't live that lifestyle. So, it felt good to have someone keeping me informed about what was going on when he left the house. I would confront him about things, and he would always assume it was Lanaye who told me when it was usually a compilation of people. Still, I would never admit to either party being the informant. He would insult Lanaye, telling me how she wasn't my friend, and she was miserable. Spewing out insults about her weight and her single status. Telling me she was jealous of my relationship with him. I always found that part of the conversation to be laughable given that I didn't feel there was much to be jealous of based on his duplicitous behavior. This was typical, I thought to myself.

Men always want to speak badly about your friends when they know those friends are telling you about their dishonesty. Jealous, I thought to myself. "Of a man who spends more time in the street than he does with his family, a man who sneaks around behind my back talking to other women." In my opinion, there wasn't much to be jealous of. He made his insults about my friend, and in return, I responded, talking my usual talk that to him seemed unrealistic. He hated how vocal I was about his backhanded lifestyle. He hated how aggressive I could be when I spoke up about things I disagreed with. This was a characteristic he was starting to get tired of.

He wasn't used to dealing with someone who couldn't be bought. Sure, I would take the money and the gifts, but I would never just shut up, and I would never stop asking questions, and that was something he, like most unfaithful men, hated. He wanted me to be someone I was not, and I expected the same from him. We would constantly argue about what I was hearing. He would permanently deny my inquiries, telling me I needed to stop listening to rumors from jealous females. Finally reaching his breaking point after hearing allegations piled on allegations and telling me that I needed to go find a white man or a Christian. After hearing him say that I realized he was telling me in that very moment that he was who he was, and maybe who he was didn't fit with the person I was. I would get upset, break up with him, and put him out.

Watching him walk out of the door with his things bagged up. I never uttered one word or appeared to care. I was a different person during those days. I often reflect on how I learned so much about relationships from this relationship. I also learned that it was okay to show emotion and be gentle with people because the only human being I showed genuine love and care to was my daughter during this time in my life. Omar left that day and spent the next few days blowing up my phone, begging me to let him come back. A few days passed, and I spent the day vomiting up everything I tried to put in my body.

Although I had experienced hyperemesis when I was pregnant with my daughter, I was no longer familiar with the symptoms because that had happened over two years before this event. I ignored the vomiting telling myself it was probably something I ate. The next day Omar continued to call my phone back-to-back, and I didn't answer. During those days, I was the queen of unbothered. Showing emotion was something I was able to avoid at all times. No matter how deep something hurt or cut me to my core. I Never allowed myself to invest my feelings into anything or anyone truly.

I told myself it was the best thing to do to avoid the hurt and sting of disappointment and heartbreak that came with emotional investment. My youngest brother Gavin decided to check on me that day. Gavin and I spent the day hanging out, and it took my mind off of my Omar troubles. I left Gavin in the living room to go to the bathroom. I Sat on the toilet feeling the urge to urinate but what was expelling from my body was not urine. I started passing clots the size of a fist and bleeding heavily. My stomach began to cramp, and suddenly I felt as if I was going to pass out.

I yelled for my brother, and he rushed into the bathroom immediately. Calling my mother on her phone, I instantly explained what was happening. My mother explained to us over speakerphone that I was having a miscarriage. We needed to call the ambulance right away. Calling the ambulance when you live in the hood is like alerting the media. Everyone rushed outside to stop and stare as they watched me being carried away on the stretcher. The bleeding continued and had not slowed down upon my arrival at the hospital. Shortly after arriving at the hospital, Omar walked into my room, greeting my brother and me.

He had found out where I was from, one of my neighbors, and came rushing to my aide despite us not being together. The doctor informed us all that I was pregnant and had suffered a miscarriage and would need to undergo a surgical procedure for them to scrape out any excess tissue left over from the discarded fetus. I would later go through a series of miscarriages throughout my young, stressed existence. Often taking in the many complex emotions that come along with the event. Brushing them off as if I were okay. Later, I learned that each miscarriage had taken a part of me during each event. Except in the case of the child, I miscarried with Omar because I could sense that having a child with him was a bad idea.

Based on all the things, he could not contribute to the wellbeing of another at that time in his life. That day before I went into surgery, Omar questioned the doctor repeatedly. Wondering if there was a chance the child could have survived. The doctor explained there was no chance and carried me to surgery immediately. I saw tears forming in Omar's eyes concerning the child we didn't even know was forming in my body. As he tried to hold back his tears for the loss of his first child, my brother sat in the corner trying to hold back laughter. To him, it did not make sense that Omar was upset about a baby he didn't even know existed.

Later I would think back on this event, trying to understand how a man could shed tears over a fetus yet later choose to abandon an actual living child. I didn't cry or share Omar's feelings of disappointment. As horrible as it may sound, I felt absolutely nothing. I didn't want any more children at that time, and after breaking up with Omar, I felt God had done at that moment what was best for everyone. After my surgery, Omar escorted me home, making the miscarriage the highlight of our conversation. He disclosed to me that he had always assumed he couldn't have children based on the fact that he had never had any. I didn't want any more children because my first experience as a young mom showed me how inconsistent some fathers could be.

Having another child from another relationship didn't feel like a smart choice, so I made it clear to Omar that I was uninterested in having another child. You see, the smart thing to do to prevent another situation like this from happening would have been to seek preventative measures like birth control, but I did not. Again, this was another stupid act that I could have handled differently. Still, I was young and dumb, walking around thinking I had things figured out when in reality, I didn't have a damn clue. A few months had passed, and things were going a lot better with Omar and me. I had convinced him to get a job and slow down on the street life, and we spent our days doing things in a way that I felt was more comfortable for me. Omar would go out here and there to make his money or attend outings he knew I was not interested in being a part of. He would return home at a reasonable hour. No more boat use and gossip about him doing the wrong things.

Finally, I started to feel like things had started to normalize. One day I went outside of my building to find a note plastered to the front of every door in my building. The note stated that there had been complaints that people had been selling drugs in the buildings after hours. The note urged all to report any activity witnessed. This plagued me with anxiety because I knew that put Omar on the radar to be reported. Omar had stopped going out to make his rounds, and his clientele started to come to him. Knocking on the door at all hours of the night, grabbing their fix, paying, and returning once they were out. It had reached a point where I started to feel extremely anxious.

I would go to bed at night and have bad dreams, picturing the feds bursting in my house and dragging him and me away. All my daughter had was me, and I knew I could not let that happen. A few days later, a note was placed on my door and my surrounding neighbors stating that Omar was officially barred away from Prospect due to complaints of his drug-selling activities. What I was not seeing at that time was that God was consistently trying to remove Omar from my life. We were not compatible, and we did things that were different, too different. I had made a habit of keeping people around that didn't make sense for the person I was and the person I wanted to become. I would realize that my struggles in life were often self-inflicted due to my keen ability to overlook the things God was trying to show me.

I decided to let Omar know that he had to shut everything down. I knew he would not stop selling drugs, but I couldn't have him doing it from my home because it was too risky, and I knew it was only a matter of time before he would end up in jail. During those days, I should have realized the lack of respect for me and my child. A man who loves something will protect it at all costs, and he was not protecting my child or me in the way he should have because he did not truly care. He constantly put my home and livelihood at risk to elevate the drug money in his pockets. Compromising the little, I had to get more for himself. You don't know what you don't know, and unfortunately for me, there was a lot that I did not know at that time in my life. I would later understand that I went through all I did to learn and gain wisdom. Still, unfortunately, my learning process would be intense due to the many wrong turns I would take by choice.

CHAPTER 3

When A Woman's Fed Up

I had a talk with Omar, and he agreed to shut everything down the next day right away, and he did. It took a few weeks before the feen traffic stopped, and occasionally in the middle of the night, I would hear him turning away people expressing to them how we had a child, and they could no longer knock on the door. A few weeks passed, and the traffic had ceased. But the warning letters were still being plastered on all the doors in Prospect. People were coming to me telling me that Omar's ex-girlfriend, Nina, and many others were upset about him getting the bulk of the Prospect customers as his clientele. People felt Omar was Taking money out of other people's hands by taking over all of the drug traffic in the neighborhood. I didn't know what to believe, and as far as I was concerned, there were plenty of suspects who had the motive to turn Omar into the Prospect office. I didn't care who the culprit was because I had grown tired of Omar, his lifestyle, and his illegal profession. I wanted stability but I didn't want Omar in the streets selling drugs. Every time I closed my eyes to sleep all my dreams were consumed with nightmares and anxiety. Each dream was the same, the Feds would bust in, take Omar and I would wake up, sick, and full of fear. Afraid of when the hour would come that the ball would drop and Omar would be held accountable for the only lifestyle he had ever known. I loved how he spoiled me but I would have rather had him, a regular life, and less stress than continue to live the lifestyle we were. I never helped him with any of his dealings but I couldn't help but feel guilty for my allowing Omar to live the way he was. I didn't want my child living in a family-like the one I currently was indulging in. A man should provide but how could Omar provide if he were locked up, or dead and those were the only two fates I could see awaiting him based on the lifestyle he was living.

In my opinion, we had reached a dead-end. There was no point in finding the culprit because there were so many to choose from. The more this went on the more I started losing sleep and suffering from anxiety during the night. I had started vomiting, and I could not keep anything down for three weeks. I was so consumed with stress I didn't realize I had missed my menstrual. I decided to make a doctor's appointment right away.

Omar and I arrived at my appointment, and the vomiting had not suppressed. The nurse handed me a bag, and I started vomiting nonstop. They ran labs and asked me to urinate in a cup. The doctor and the nurse re-entered the room shortly after I handed over the cup of urine that was equivalent in color to a glass of Arizona tea due to the vomiting and dehydration. "Congratulations, you are pregnant," the nurse said as if I looked like I wanted to be congratulated. I was sitting in a doctor's office, vomiting up my entire existence. So, to me, the moment was anything but celebratory.

Omar's face lit up like a Christmas tree. He was happy he was getting a second chance at fatherhood after the miscarriage, and I was miserable. We left the doctor's office that day, full of emotions. He was happy because he was getting the child he wanted, and I was bland on the inside. I didn't feel happy, and I didn't feel sad; I just felt miserable and weak from the morning sickness that would quickly evolve into all-day sickness. A few weeks had passed, and the illness was getting worse and worse. Every week I was at the hospital getting fluids and given prescriptions for Zofran that did not affect my pregnancy nemesis, hyperemesis gravid arum.

Omar continued to spend his days out in the street making his money reverting to his regular schedule of being gone all day while I stayed at home pregnant and miserable with my daughter, who was two at the time. This was clearly no way for an eighteen-year-old girl to be living but during these days I was clueless about life and my future. Every day I would wake up crying and feeling terrible. Things suddenly felt as if they were moving backward, and the only thing that had changed was that I was now Omar's pregnant, miserable rendition of Keisha lying in bed with a toddler throwing up every five seconds. The notes were still being plastered on everyone's doors daily, and my anxiety kept me up at night, along with heartburn and morning sickness. I kept telling Omar I wanted to leave Prospect, but I never felt like he listened. My cries and complaints often felt like he was summing them up to be merely nothing more than pregnancy emotion fluctuations. One day Omar came home and told me to start packing up my things.

I lay in bed looking at him with zero interest waiting for the next round of vomiting to start. "I got us a townhouse in Orangedale," he said. "Three bedrooms, a room for Kylie, a room for us, and a room for my son," he said, glowing like he always did anytime he referred to the unborn golden child! That day I packed all I could with what little energy I had in my body, and the rest Omar took care of. He had paid some local friends to pack up and help us move everything into our new home. That day I was so happy to get away from Prospect that I didn't have a care in the world. I was happy to be living across the street from my mom again and a few houses away from my friend Lanaye.

Omar hated Lanaye, but I knew it was because she knew things about him that he didn't want me to know. My youngest brother had graduated from high school, and he had decided to move to Atlanta. My best friend was back from college, and after experiencing some issues, she could no longer attend the HBCU she had been attending. Although I felt terrible things didn't work out the way she wanted them to, I was happy she was returning to Charlottesville to have someone around to help keep my mind off things that were troubling me. A few weeks passed, and my best friend Raye, also known as Rayneesha, and I had been spending a lot of time together. Later, she had decided she would move to Atlanta with her high school sweetheart, her little sister, and my little brother. My brother needed help getting settled, so like usual, I went to Omar, let him know what my brother needed, and he provided it without any questions asked.

We got a rental, and my daughter, Omar, my cousin Tika, brother Gavin, my best friend, and her high school sweetheart all went on a road trip to Atlanta to help them move and settle in their new apartment in the A. When we arrived in Atlanta, Omar helped purchase my brother a bed and other miscellaneous items he needed before we headed back to Virginia. During the trip, I noticed things that made me feel a certain way but I kept my thoughts to myself. Like me, my best friend was short, blunt, and vocal about any and everything she felt. This was a quality we shared, and we were very similar in the way we handled expressing ourselves to our partners. The first night before arriving at their apartment, we all stayed in a motel. We watched several prostitutes make their rounds outside as we entered the motel.

I remember joking with my best friend about how Omar and Rayshawn appeared intrigued. The next day when we got to their apartment, Rayshawn and Omar seemed eager to go for a stroll around the A without us. I remember Ray and me speaking up while clarifying that they would not be going anywhere without us. Later that day, my cousin Tika disclosed to Ray and me how she didn't like how we spoke to Omar and Shawn. Telling us, we were mean and didn't treat our partners right, always bossing them around, etc. Me and Ray both looked at each other, both ready to give Tika a piece of our minds. You see, usually, I would take someone else's advice about my actions and my words, but Tika was like cousin faith from soul food, and with that being said, her opinion was never required or respected.

Ray spoke up quickly with an irritated look on her face." I don't mean any harm, Tika, but I will speak to my man however I like, and his ass is fine, ain't nobody being rude to him," Raye concluded as she rolled her eyes at Tika, making it clear she was uninterested in her opinions. We went back to Virginia, and I said goodbye to my little brother and my best friend, who were always my go-to people daily. I had no clue that I would walk into some of the most challenging days of my life after this trip. Shortly after we returned from Atlanta, Omar made me aware that he would have to start staying out more to make the money back he had just spent on the trip. The days passed slowly, and I was still battling with hyperemesis daily. A few days passed and it was now time for my prenatal appointment.

That day, I went to my appointment feeling the same normal amount of physical misery I had felt every day due to the excessive vomiting and dehydration. After having an ultrasound, the doctors came in as a group of three, alerting me that there was an issue. It appeared to them that my son was not swallowing the amniotic fluid and absorbing it in normal amounts. The doctors alerted Omar and me that after delivery, our son would have to go into surgery right away and need multiple surgeries because it appeared his internal structure was not developed properly. That day my heart broke into a million pieces. This was when I adopted a new mechanism for my life and his. I realized I had been overwhelmed with stress from Omar's lifestyle and many other things, and I said a prayer that day, praying God would bless my son with a healthy body so he would not have to endure any form of surgery.

Omar tried staying home to offer me emotional support for about two weeks, but it was killing him. I noticed the more I needed him, the more it appeared the call of the streets could drown out my cries and desires, pulling him back as if he had a lifetime magnet glued to his body that no one could see. So, I stayed home being a mother to my daughter, battling my pregnancy sickness, and feeling scared for my delivery because I didn't know what would happen with my son. Even as I write these words and describe these events, I cry. Not because I'm sad or broken by my past, but I cry because I'm proud of myself for not letting things break me. I never really realized how much I endured back-to-back as a young woman until I decided to write it all down on paper. Omar had gone back into the street to get his money, so he claimed, and I was left alone to endure things no woman should have to on her own.

Eventually, Omar started staying out later and later, and I would address it the next day, but I couldn't do so in my normal aggressive, and I mean business tone because I knew I couldn't risk getting worked up for my unborn child's sake. So, I said it calmly and waited for different results, but they never came. Omar started sleeping with his phone under his pillow and turning his phone off completely at night. Once I noticed that, I knew there was more to his late-night engagements than making money. But I had no proof, so I waited until I felt like the pain of being constantly left on my own was more than I could bear. To this day I often spend significant periods alone in real-time. I contribute my ability to do so based on what I learned from the numerous periods I spent amongst the wrong people—learning that it is better to sit alone than to sit amongst many people who don't value you as a person, friend, partner, or family member.

So, I made a choice, and within making that choice, I knew things would change for my children and me instantly. I was at this point 19 years old with one child who was about to turn three and a child who was due to be born in a few months. I knew I didn't have any help or support, so staying in my misery felt like the best thing to do for the longest time. It kept my bills paid, food on the table, and stability for my children. Although I no longer had my own because I was no longer working, I felt like Omar would do the right thing for his child. But I was wrong, and I was about to be in for a big surprise. One day Omar came home late, and I decided I had taken all I could take.

His money was significantly low for someone who claimed to be out in the streets making money all day and all night, and he was starting to show signs of inconsistencies with the way he was moving. I knew there was more to his late-night engagements than he told me. While he was running the streets doing him, I was at home all day with my daughter, weak and ill from my pregnancy feeling morbidly depressed, worrying about my unborn child and the direction of my life. I never wanted to be the kind of woman who stayed with a man for stability. I realized I had evolved from an independent woman to a dependent woman who was now stuck in a relationship she knew was not suitable for her with no resources to leave. I was fed up with Omar and his behavior, and I had taken all that I could take. That day I chose a path that was considered by many to be a dumb path, but in my heart, I knew it was right despite the trials that would come with my choice.

I waited for Omar to get home, telling myself that I needed to advocate for myself differently. When he arrived home that day, he was shocked at me laying on the sofa, ready to speak to the things I thought I knew at that time. I made it clear to him that I no longer wanted to be with him anymore because I was tired of asking for things, I knew I would never get. I was also tired of him trying to buy my silence, spoiling me with gifts, money, and material things. I enjoyed them initially, but he didn't realize that what I desired could not be purchased. He took his things that night after hearing me make my last and final plea, and unlike all the previous times, he didn't beg to stay or ask to come back. Leaving me alone, pregnant, and depressed at the age of 19 with no one to turn to. My siblings and best friend were all away at college, and there I sat in a deep lonely hole, afraid of what was next for my life and the life of my unborn child.

Omar stopped going with me to my appointments, and shortly after, I didn't hear from him at all. I went through the last four months of my pregnancy alone, never getting a checkup text or visit from Omar, leading me to deduce that it would be me on my own once our son was born. I didn't want to prepare for that dynamic, but deep down, I knew it would be the only one available to my son and me. I would spend my days dwindling deeper and deeper into a level of sadness and despair I had never known before. Battling with depression unaware that depression would be a mood I would sit with for an elongated period. As I asked myself what I did to deserve such a lonely and hurtful fate. As I watched the man who had promised me so much regarding myself and my child act as if we no longer existed. I will forever remember this time because it was one of the coldest experiences I ever had to face.

I often assessed the situation, thinking of things I could have done differently while I sat in a pool of self-doubt, blaming myself for the fucked-up behavior of a grown-ass man who was still sitting in the behavior patterns of a lost little boy. Unwilling to take accountabilities for all of the poor choices he would make regarding my unborn child in the days that lay ahead. The first month came around for the rent to be paid, and I expected Omar to show up with the money, but he did not. I called and got no answer, and I realized I was on my own, sick, pregnant, and broke. I started selling my designer handbags for money, Omar's jewelry, his rims, and anything of value I could to get the money to pay the rent. I decided to speak with my landlord and was honest about my situation, and he and his wife agreed to work with me on getting my rent up to date. Had I known Omar would stop providing, I would've waited and planned my exit from the relationship out a little more meticulously, but I felt I was doing what was best for my unborn child and me. The time came for me to have a baby shower and my cousin Jayla, who was also my son's godmother, planned the event.

I wasn't in the mood, and all of the people I wanted to be there, such as my best friend and brothers, couldn't be. So, I felt like having a baby shower was pointless. I knew my cousin was only trying to brighten my spirits, but the thought of a baby shower with just me, her, my daughter, and my aunt Sheryl seemed depressing. Nonetheless, I made it through the baby shower, prepared for another night of lying on the sofa sick and pregnant with my three-year-old when I heard a knock at the door. I went to the door to find Omar standing in the doorway with a dumbfounded look on his face as I let him in, thinking he had come to make things right or apologize for all the doctor's appointments he had missed, but that was not the case. He came in and sat on the opposing sofa, asking me how I had been. I looked at him, feeling like we were off to a horrible start with the idiotic opening question he had chosen of all questions.

"How does it look like I'm doing, "I asked? He said nothing in response to my sarcastic comment, so I led the conversation to where I felt it needed to go. "Let's see; I've been here for weeks with no help, no money for bills, and no transportation to my appointments," I said, "walking to the hospital for every appointment while sick and dehydrated. So how should I be doing?" I asked sarcastically, waiting for some form of apology I would never get. Omar wouldn't even look at me; he refrained from making eye contact with me during the entire conversation.

Conveying to me just how much of a coward he truly was. I didn't know much about why he was handling me the way he was, but even back then, I could smell the stench of a new woman all over his presence. Sure, I had heard stories of men handling themselves the way Omar was, which was a familiar dynamic amongst the young men in my environment. Although that was true, I could tell that Omar was not just mishandling me for sport. It was as if I had become his enemy, and he was trying to hurt me in the worst ways possible. Making himself believe that if he treated me like I deserved it when I did not, he would somehow come to believe the lie himself. He then proceeded to say that he didn't want to leave and never would have left my side, but I put him out. Typical, I thought to myself.

"You left me," he said, gaslighting me, pretending that I was the cause of things when I had made him leave due to the things he was doing wrong. It was at that moment that I recognized that I had given him the exit privilege he had been waiting on for weeks, or possibly even months. When he met me, he had multiple situations going on in the background that I knew nothing about. Walking away from all of those situations convinced I was the good thing he had been waiting for. Only to grasp a stronghold of me and my heart and dispose of both once the next thing came along that looked like a better opportunity. This led me to the understanding that men are creatures of habit. Most of the time, the behavior carries on, and the only thing that becomes new or indifferent is the parties involved.

Omar was now ready for a new party to enter his life. Uninterested in what that would mean for my child or me because, in his mind, nothing mattered but his desires. He would be the first man to teach me the importance of observation. For it was through these unfortunate circumstances that I would enter into that I would learn that all humans have patterns. Patterns become easily identifiable when you learn to pay close attention. He then concluded his phony attempts to show care and retrieved the rest of the things he had left behind. I lay on the sofa with my daughter watching tv, trying to avoid saying or doing anything to interrupt him from tying the last knot to the closure of our relationship.

He approached the living room with his things, asking me where his jewelry and rims were amongst a few other things. I explained to him that I had sold everything valuable to get the money to pay my bills for a few months until I could return to work. He was upset but knew there was nothing he could say in response to my reasoning for selling his things. He took the remainder of his belongings that night, and I didn't hear from him anymore. It had suddenly been as if he never existed to me, and I never existed to him, and honestly, it tore me up inside because I never would admit it outwardly, but I was afraid. So afraid that night after he left, I experienced my first panic attack and was rushed to the hospital. I thought I was going into labor, and it terrified me. I tried to calm down, but I could not.

My mother came across the street and retrieved my daughter, and I went in the ambulance on my way to the hospital to give birth, so I had assumed. Shortly after monitoring me, the doctor explained that I had experienced a panic attack and was extremely dehydrated. So, they pumped me with fluids and kept me overnight, and the next day I went home. I was breaking down from fear; I would spend my days sitting at my friend Lanaye's house getting things off my chest I didn't feel comfortable talking with anyone else about. She had been a social worker for years, so she had a natural way of making me feel comfortable disclosing the things I was going through. I told her I had an upcoming appointment, and she agreed she would be my ride to and from. That day I was scared to go in because I knew they had planned to give me a date I would be induced to go into labor with my son, and I was terrified.

I had no family or friends that could be present, and all I could think about was all of the issues my son was supposed to be born with. So that night, I prayed, cried, and promised myself that no matter what happened, I would pick myself up and be the best mom to both my children I could be, and that was a promise I would keep. That day I went into the hospital as a terrified nineteen-year-old girl with no support. My mother kept my daughter for me to give birth, and both brothers were away at college. My pride wouldn't allow me to call my dad to be there with me out of pure embarrassment because I felt I had let him down. The bright little girl he had seen so much it had done nothing more with her life other than becoming a teen mom and a statistic, and I couldn't face him. Knowing this was a path I had created for myself after laying in a bed of countless mistakes, telling myself this was now who I was, and all I could be was a mom. My mom contacted Omar, and he came to the hospital a few hours after talking to her. He arrived with a look on his face that showed he was not interested in being there.

One thing led to another, and before you knew it, we were in a full-blown argument, and my blood pressure had skyrocketed. After seeing my blood pressure, the nurse told Omar he had to go. He left the hospital that day and never came back. Later I was informed that the nurse had taken action to have him barred away from the hospital after the incident. Fearing that I had been in a violent situation with him. A small part of me felt relieved I didn't have to look at him during the process because it was too emotionally triggering for me. A few hours passed since I had been induced, and the labor pains started to kick in. I started having another panic attack once I realized things were in motion. In a few hours, I would be welcoming another child into the world on my own with no true indication of what physical state he would be born into the world in.

CHAPTER 4

Abandonment

I took in a deep breath as I felt my chest flustered with all of the stress and strife of the previous days I had lived. I was feeling the stress of every nap I had missed. Every meal I had struggled to put on the table, and every man I had been in a serious relationship with and bared a child who was now the product of a single mother. Exposing my heart to the countless disappointment that love had always seemed to give me in return for my loyalty. The child support checks that never came due to never being paid. Or the ones that made it to my bank account in the form of 83 dollars a week. For my oldest child, who required more than that just for nourishment.

The stories I am willing to share with you all are no different from the ones many of you already know. Due to these unfortunate dynamics, I spent many of my days weary because I was miserable from the plague of hyperemesis gravid arum and the sting of being cheated on by my drug dealer boyfriend. He was ecstatic in the beginning that we were having our first child together. Only to find out later during the process that he had been cheating on me with a girl who was pregnant by someone else.

I have to admit it was a big, massive bite in the butt to give birth to my son and realize that as a result of me breaking up with his duplicitous father and putting him out a few months later that I would be raising a son on my own. During those days, I got my first glance at how cultural concepts are unconsciously established. Some of those cultural concepts are why many young men and women in the Black community grow to love and be loved improperly. Growing up in urban communities, you hear similar stories people experience, never questioning why that may be so. It wasn't until I started approaching my thirties and looking at life with a different paradigm that I realized my role in some of the harsh experiences I had been through as a young woman. Realizing that I had always been this ball of light people notice, sometimes for the right reasons and other times for the wrong ones.

Nevertheless, I realized that although I had always had a shine to me, I had allowed my luster to be diminished by people, places, and experiences. All because I didn't see myself in its entirety. Allowing people to make me feel less than or like showing all of who I was could not be permitted. The gag is God said fuck um! Do you, and I finally decided to listen. When overlooking the past, the present, and the future, like most, I often saw my future just as clear as I saw my past. Telling myself that all my experiences would never go in vain because somewhere there is a little girl who is just like me going through the same things I did.

Trying to make it out of the emotional rut she never asked to be in. I know that girl exists because I have had the privilege of seeing her in my mother, my mother's mother, my friends, and family members.

Looking at mirror images of myself, wondering how different some of those cloudy mirror images could be if they had just had someone come along to offer them some Windex and a paper towel. So, I stand before you figuratively today trying to be the Windex and paper towel to another woman or young girl walking around with that cloudy dust hanging over her image of who she is and who she could become. Growing up, I witnessed many things that tarnished my idea of self-care. Most of the Black women I knew were always in roles of giving. They were giving to their husbands, giving to their jobs, and most importantly, giving to their children.

So naturally, I grew up believing that a good woman is a giving woman. Always making sure her house was clean and comfortable. She went to work. Her bills were paid, and her kids were well taken care of. I know to most of you, this seems like a pretty open and shut concept. Many of you may even feel like this is an adequate depiction of what a "good Black woman "is. But I was going to learn how wrong I was.

There is absolutely nothing wrong with being a giver, but in reality, the giver needs to receive as well, and I was going to learn how depleting life can be when you put everyone before yourself. That day I gave birth to my son alone, and God gave me the miracle I had been praying for. When my son exited the wound, they took him right away because they had already made me aware that he would need surgery and I would not be able to take him home. About an hour later, the doctors entered the room, informing me that the issue they thought he would have with his stomach not being appropriately developed was not the case, and he was healthy and didn't need any surgeries. All I could do was feel gods' presence with me at that moment. Despite the fear and pain that I had built up inside, God had yet again showed me his power and will to provide for me, and I found reassurance in that miracle and continued to keep moving despite my circumstances. Two days later, my son and I left the hospital, and I started doing what I did best.

Which was making a way for my children and me despite the lack of support and resources I did not have. As I type these words, tears fall as they frequently have throughout the cultivation of this story. I don't cry because I'm sad or it's too hard looking at my past, but I cry because I admire that young girl who was often alone, scared, trying to push past fear. Despite the constant adversity, that girl was always able to rise above her circumstances, which is the biggest blessing. Days turned into weeks, and weeks turned into months, and before you knew it, I had established a new routine. My cousin sweetie pie had given me a job at a hotel where she was a manager, and I was back working instantly. I would go to work and leave my kids with a neighbor.

My neighbor Edina was a white woman from Bosnia. I had become close friends with her children. Although she was from Bosnia, she had more swag and gangster energy than any white woman I had ever come across. She and her daughter were my muses for the character max in the diary of Janay Wilkerson. She took care of my kids for free, ensuring she fed them and kept them safe while I was at work. Her daughter Dee Dee and I had just become close friends, and she stepped in to help me after seeing that I was young and trying. Identifying with my struggle as a mom of two on my own because it was a struggle, she had known after her children's father was murdered in front of her.

I would spend my days cleaning the hotel rooms and crying in them, frequently feeling overwhelmed and worried about where my future was going. I wanted a change badly and didn't know what that change would look like for me, but I knew my kids deserved more than what I had or could currently give them at that time. I was sad about how Omar had been handling me. I couldn't sleep or eat, losing weight frequently to the point where I was no longer the Nina everyone knew—identifying how the Nina with the nice curves, butt, and hips had gone from cornbread fed and thick to anorexic looking and thinning out by the day. My weight had gotten so low from depression and lack of appetite that people were spreading rumors that I was potentially doing drugs. It bothered me that someone would make up a rumor about me, but it made sense after staring at myself in the mirror due to how crazy I looked. My son was a calm baby and never cried much or required to be held all day like my first child.

Although he was calm sometimes at night, I would pick him up and hold him all night, watching him sleep due to my inability to sleep after developing insomnia that would be a nemesis that would come in and out of my life frequently during my times of distress. One night I went to retrieve my son from his crib when I noticed he was extremely pale, and his lips were blue, and it looked as if he was not breathing. I called my mom right away, waking her up out of her sleep. She came to get my three-year-old daughter while me and my newborn left in the ambulance, rushing to the hospital. This would frequently happen until my son was finally placed on a breathing treatment and diagnosed early with asthma. This heightened my insomnia due to the fear that I would wake up one night, and my son would not be breathing, so for a long time, I would make myself stay up at night even when I felt tired. I had let all thoughts of his father go out of my mind because I was not one to dwell on things that I knew I couldn't change.

I had tried to find answers to what was going on with Omar but never had any luck. Little did I know that the answers would find their way to me once I stopped searching. One day I was walking across the street to get my kids from my mother's house when a car passed by me, stopping at a halt in the middle of the street. "Nina? Is that you," the person asked from the driver's side. I approached the car to find that it was Omar's mom. Me and her had always had a good relationship, but after I broke up with Omar, I had not heard from her.

She emphasized how she didn't know who I was walking down the street due to my weight loss. I invited her to my house to see my son for the first time, and she gave me a box of pampers, wipes, and milk. She was easing her way into a conversation about her son. Asking me if I had heard from him when she knew I had not. She then assured me that Omar would be helping me raise and provide for our son despite us no longer being in a relationship selling me dreams I knew I could not afford to buy. So, I did what I had always been known to do in life: speak my mind. I listened to her spoon feed me bullshit, and when she was finished, I gave it to her raw.

Informing her that I knew he would not help me pay bills because since I had left the relationship, he had not. Letting her know how he never called, never came by to see my son since he was born, and never paid one bill or inquired if I had food or needed anything. She left my house that day, and I never heard from her again. She was coming by to try and clean up his mess, but I made it clear to her that selling me dreams was not a requirement for me to be ok. Sure, I wasn't ok. I felt like a hot mess, but I had a million and one things to worry about, and her son not being present was not on that list for me. It's funny how we live in a world where telling the truth and speaking your mind will make people dislike you. I could've gone along with what she was saying to me, been quiet and complicit, but that wouldn't have gotten me much, and the little help she would have been willing to give me in exchange for my silence and lack of acknowledgment was not worth it in my opinion.

A few weeks later, Omar showed up at my door to lay eyes on his son for the first time. At that time, our son was three months old. He took me to get him a single can of milk, and he had forgotten that he had evidence inside his car that would clue me in on what was going on. Giving me incite as to why he had been handling me the way he was and why he was not trying to be present for my son as he had intended to be initially. I hopped back in the car after buying the milk when I looked at the dashboard of his car. Feeling sick instantly as my stomach hit the floor.

I looked at the family photo and tried to figure out if my eyes were playing tricks on me. "What the fuck is this?" I asked as I pointed to the picture of the newborn baby, the girl, and him in a family photo looking like a low-budget version of the Huxtables. "So, you had a whole family hidden away," I asked, recognizing that the baby boy in the picture was about the same size and age as my newborn son. He snatched the photograph from me, giving no answers. He yelled at the top of his lungs, making claims in response to what I was saying, telling me that the baby was not his. I couldn't believe what I was seeing or hearing. "You think I'm some dumb bitch you can tell anything to."

"What type of clown shit is this? Who takes a picture with a newborn baby that's not theirs," I asked? He said nothing back in response. "Precisely no one, you fucking liar," I said as I took the milk and slammed the door entering my house broken into fragments that even I couldn't recognize. Calling my mom crying, telling her that I had found out Omar had another son, deducing that as his reasoning for not being present or supportive of our son. Wondering why he was mishandling things in the way he was. Wondering how a man could choose between two children and not feel guilty.

Questioning why he was handling me like I was a side chick, he had accidentally gotten pregnant when we were together, and it was something he had wanted initially, and I did not. That entire day I stayed glued to my bed, leaving my kids with my mom while I lay consumed with thoughts, questions, anger, and sadness. A week later, I visited Lanaye. She told me that someone had informed her that a month before I had given birth, Omar was spotted at the hospital with another girl bringing her balloons and flowers to labor and delivery. I instantly knew he had lied to me and the baby he was not claiming as his son was his. A few days would pass after I received that information from Lanaye, and I would find out the truth. Later that week, my cousin called me, giving me all the details after talking to Omar's brother.

She informed me that allegedly Omar had been cheating on me while I was in a relationship with him and pregnant with a young girl who was also pregnant. Allegedly The girl had been pregnant by another man but met Omar and started dating him while she was pregnant, and the baby in the picture was her son; she had given birth to a month before I had my son. Hearing that Omar was telling the truth about that component didn't offer me relief. Hearing that he was allegedly sleeping with a pregnant woman who was pregnant with someone else's child disgusted me. After hearing the full details, I decided I needed to let it all go and move on with my life.

My friend Raye had been living in Atlanta for some time, and after hearing what I was going through, she offered my kids and me to come live with her in Atlanta to have a fresh start and get on my feet. Agreeing to help me find a job offering her help after all of her failed roommate situations. It appeared we both were in a bind after being let down by people we depended on, so becoming roommates seemed like a great idea. My brother Melvin Jr agreed to pay for all my moving expenses to move to Atlanta, so I began packing and selling as much as I could out of my home so I could leave and start over. Omar had not contacted me to see my son after the one time he had shown his face, and due to his actions, I was convinced he did not care. So, I started getting myself together to leave. Like usual, news in the hood travels fast, and within a few days of me packing, breaking my leasing agreement, and selling and giving away furniture and décor, the word had gotten back to Omar that I was leaving. Within a week, he found out and had me summoned to court for a custody hearing. I received a court notice in the mail and was advised by my family to stay and go to court despite my plan to leave and take my kids and go to Atlanta voiding the court request altogether.

I was furious and confused about why Omar was taking me to court after showing no interest in our child. After several weeks of home evaluations and court proceedings, the judge ruled that we would have joint custody. Giving me and Omar set days and times where we would have our son. The judge then informed me that I could not go to Atlanta and take my son. He made it clear that if I were to move, I would have to leave my son behind unless I could plan for him to return to Charlottesville every week for Omar's visits. Omar was so happy to hear the judge make that ruling because that was his initial reason for taking me to court. He wanted to keep me from moving, knowing I would not leave my child behind. Omar would pick up our four-month-old child for two weeks, taking him back for the weekends to stay with him, his new girlfriend Ashley, and her four-month-old son.

The thought of them playing house with my son bothered me a lot, but I knew there was nothing I could do but let him go despite my personal feelings towards the situation. After being consistent with his visits for two weeks, Omar dropped my son off, and we didn't hear from him again for months. I would spend months leaving messages for the guardian ad litem and the court complaining that the visits were not taking place, trying to get full custody of my son, and having no progress. Being told there was nothing I could do if I didn't have an address for my son's father. I didn't understand what Omar's issue was. He was not present consistently for our child, nor did he ever pay his child support, which was less than two hundred dollars a month. It didn't make sense to me why he was being so spiteful. Not wanting to help me out as a parent while also not wanting to see me go and get somewhere in my life.

I had been the one let down, lied to, and humiliated, yet he was being spiteful and vengeful for a wrong he created. He wanted to keep me from moving on despite his lack of desire to be present for my son. My son would be nine months old before I would see Omar again. After having the courts deny me of moving, I had to move in with my mom due to breaking my lease, preparing to move to Atlanta, and being dismissed by the judge. I was living in a small bedroom with two small kids. One day when I was walking home from work, I noticed Omar's car in Orangedale at the bottom of the hill. I knew he was there for one reason and one reason only.

To replenish his drugs to sell. I was furious with him for how he had handled things with me. Most importantly, I was angry that he had taken me to court, discontinued his custody requirements after two weeks, and kept me from going to Atlanta. I knew I would probably never have an opportunity to confront him again, so I decided to approach the car to say what I felt I needed to say. Soon as he saw me, his eyes got big as he looked over to the passenger side, realizing the energy I was bringing to the car in front of his girlfriend. I started giving my spill about how horrible he had become—yelling outside about how he was an absent father and a clown for choosing to care for someone else's child over his first-born child.

" Hold up, don't bring my son into this," his girlfriend said from inside the car as if she had not been warned of my reputation. So, I approached the car, ready to give her the ass-whipping I felt she rightfully deserved. I pulled on the door handle, ready to drag her from the vehicle as she locked herself inside the car. I was more than willing to take my frustrations out on her, Omar approached me screaming for me to go home, yelling, trying to discourage me from laying a finger on her as she sat in the front seat, silent. At that moment, I wanted nothing more than to drag her from the car in front of him, feeling like she was at fault for how he had treated my son. Later I recognized she wasn't to blame. Sure, she knew about me and knew he was in a relationship and had a child on the way, but she didn't owe me anything.

Him neglecting his responsibilities and doing my son wrong was his fault. Even though later I received confirmation from him that she did not like my son being around because she felt like she should have come first, his actions were still at fault. He went on to have multiple children with his girlfriend. Helping her raise her son and their children never establishing a relationship with our son. Stepping in and out of our son's life, only trying to see him when he would leave his girlfriend, be with other women, and establish new relationships— ending all communication with my son once he was back in the relationship with the mother of his younger children. He was taking his girlfriend through similar trials like those I had faced with him.

Omar cheating on her repetitively with other women allowed me to see that although it was hard to leave that relationship with nothing and start from scratch, I had made the right choice. After losing everything and having to start over, I would rebuild my life from the ground up, which would be something I would have to do often in my life. Becoming no stranger to trials and triumph. I constantly reminded myself during hard times that drowning was not an option for me. I looked to my kids to grasp the strength to keep going despite my desire to give up.

CHAPTER 5

When Trauma Comes To Dinner

started this journey debating what I wanted to tell and what I wanted to leave out. Being an African American around the way girl, we often grow up looking at hardship, struggle, adversity, and mistreatment in the face daily. Asking ourselves what form will I receive today? Will it be judgment? Adversity? Disappointment? Often living our lives with minimal expectations. Because our environments have taught us that we don't deserve to expect anything.

Accepting people's judgments as our truths even when we know deep down inside that those rulings are not truly applicable. Sometimes I reminisced around yesterday. Taking a long hard look at the old me. The adolescent version wondering where it was, I got all of my strength—wondering how a little girl could muster up so much faith in faithless situations. Clinging to hope when hope was often denied of her. Thinking to myself, what is different now?

Where had that undeniable strength gone? Overlooking the past while walking towards the future. Feeling grateful that despite all of the harrowing experiences I had faced as a child, a young adult, and a grown woman, I had been fortunate enough to find my purpose and walk in my faith even when faith was a dismantled concept in my life. We often hear about women drafting their stories of hardship and struggle. Waking up one day, saying to themselves how their stories hold significance and should be shared. Because somewhere, there's a little girl or an adult woman going through the same things and seeking guidance. I've been the product of divorce, sexual abuse, verbal abuse, hatred, physical abuse, street fights, dating drug dealers, a teen mom, and the unfortunate list goes on and on.

I faced many events where I felt plagued, helpless, hopeless, insignificant, and distressed within those situations. I Often questioned God even as a small child, trying to understand how he could love me and torment me with so many burdens back-to-back. Never offering me a moment to be able to take a deep breath and pause and allow the rest of me to catch up with all that had occurred and all that was occurring. Looking at myself and feeling weak while being strong as I wiped away my tears, chucked up the deuces, and carried on with my day as if nothing had occurred. Asking God why and never got a response. You see, I would ask him that repetitively over the years.

Why me? Why this? Why now? And I would never hear a reply. I asked God why from the age of eight when my parents first separated. And I started witnessing my mother getting beat by a man that wasn't my father and appeared to have no regard for a woman or her body. Seeing him beat her repetitively to the point she would curl up on the floor in a fetal position like a wounded animal. Face tarnished, lip busted, and blood leaking. I wondered how God could allow my innocent eyes and heart to undergo such experiences.

Asking for his presence to be permanent, begging for him to show up in those moments where I felt alone to the point where I felt there was nothing more for me to do but to allow this man to continue to hurt my mother, or I hurt him. When I was eight years old, I would experience the first of many traumatic events that would lead to one of the most traumatic events of my life. At age eleven, I would have a breakdown from the unaddressed Trauma taking matters into my own hands, almost killing a man in hopes of freeing my mother from the bondage of abuse that my brothers and I had witnessed for four years without having someone step in to intervene. You see, even as I type these sentences, I realize there has always been a certain casual demeanor I held when discussing the incident. Because for such a long time, I had put it out of my mind. Telling myself that although it happened, and I got through it, I was alright. I know many of you are wondering how a person can genuinely be okay after experiencing something so traumatic at such a young age. And the truth is they can't, and I would soon learn from Trauma in my future that the Trauma of the past can be laid to rest, ignored, and overlooked, but it will always have a way of showing up to dinner uninvited until it is adequately addressed.

I remember the event like it was yesterday. My brothers had gotten dressed and left the house excited to go to the local carnival with some friends, and I stayed home. Although the carnival was an annual event, we all attended. I had lost interest due to an experience from the previous year. I had gone to the carnival with one of my little brothers, my best friend Raye, and her siblings and gotten on a ride, and after having a bad experience where I thought I would leave injured, I decided the local carnival was not for me. So, I stayed home with my mom because I preferred to be around her as much as I lacked showing it. I often felt neglected due to the duties of single motherhood that kept her away from home more than I preferred her to be.

I remember running my bathwater, planning to take a bubble bath, binge eat snacks, and watch lifetime. I was addicted to watching lifetime movies, never considering that my life would soon become the plot for one. Soaking in the warm water playing in the bubbles as I had done since the age of five. I was enjoying the quiet from my brothers not being home. I laid back on the flimsy bath pillow I had gotten from the Dollar Store that was now depleting due to the lack of air. Making myself comfortable when I heard a loud noise penetrating my bubble of serenity. Then I heard another loud thump followed by the word bitch!

Then another and another until the screaming and crying took over the entire apartment. I knew instantly what was going on without having to have a visual depiction at that moment. I hopped out of the tub, wrapped my towel around me, and ran into my bedroom, slipping on some clothing. Rushing out to my mother's aide, I witnessed him pounding her repetitively as if she were a man and he was in a prison brawl. I Screamed for him to stop as I watched him punch her in the lip, splitting the dermis instantly as the blood began to flow from her mouth.

There was nothing but fear and anger roaming through my body at that moment. I wanted him to stop because it appeared to me that if he didn't, he would kill her or harm her worse than he ever had before. I was angry with God, never understanding how he had not answered one single prayer. For years every night, I would talk to him, begging him to remove this man from our lives. Taking away his disrespectful language and his harmful hands. Praying that God would strip us from the trauma and allow us to have a sense of normalcy again. Yet here I was again, standing over him as he beat my mother as if she were some worthless illegitimate figure in the universe that didn't deserve to be loved and cared for properly. As children, we wake up greeting each day, feeling the comfort of our parent's love and protection hovering over us as we navigate our way through an unpredictable world. Never imagining or anticipating a time where we would have to serve as the comfort and protection for our parents.

Unfortunately for my brothers and me, our parents' separation left us wounded in ways we never spoke of. The knowledge of those wounds had been embedded in all of who we were and who we each would become. Forced to grow up fast, living our childhood lives as miniature adults. Taking in the unpleasant aroma of the trauma, our environment served us casually. With no adults rushing to our aid. No aunts, uncles, parents, teachers, or authentic good Samaritans coming to rid us of the agony. My parents had separated and started new lives, none of which included the well-being of their children.

My dad was navigating his way through single life, starting over, and looking for love in all the wrong women. Trying to find my mom's replacement. In comparison, my mom was looking for stability, companionship, and someone who could help her financially. It never dawned on them how their selfish desires could affect their children. Robbing us of a stable life filled with love and comfort like the life we had known when they were together. I watched as my mom picked herself up off the ground running to the kitchen, crying, closing the door behind her. She hoped to get a few moments of peace away from the evil man who seemed to find pleasure in beating her down consistently in front of her children. He followed her into the kitchen again, trying to go at it for a second round. Hitting her repeatedly as she tried to get away and run into her room as he followed closely behind

I could have walked away and called the police or another grown-up, but I had done that many times and no resolution had been found. I drifted off into thought, thinking about the last fight event where my mom would be getting the crap beat out of her while me and my brothers were forced to watch. In the past me, and my brothers had jumped him beating him with baseball bats at my request after he had hurt our mom, but it wasn't enough for him to stop harming her. He ran towards the house hallway, making his way towards my mom, ready to attack her again. Shortly after, he'd do his usual exit. Where he would hurt her and leave her in tears to fend for herself as she assessed her bruises that were always both internal and external. He didn't know that this time, that exit would not be an option for him.

I had watched him do this routine repeatedly, and after seeing this last incident and seeing my mother's face, I was determined this would be the last time he would harm her. Usually, he would leave the house for a few hours only to return later, living, breathing, eating, and acting like nothing had ever happened. I walked into the kitchen, picking up one of the knives from the knife set on the kitchen counter. Before I could fully understand what would or wouldn't happen due to my thought process, the knife that was once embedded in my hand pierced through his chest. Bringing him to his knees in an instant. I stood in front of him as he gasped for air, falling to his knees looking at me as if he were shocked. He was surprised that a knife had been placed in between his cold heart by me, a little girl who had watched him beat her mother aggressively for four years.

I stood over him, watching as he faded, falling to the ground. I offered him no assistance as I stood over his body, waiting to see him take his final breath. I needed to see him depart, telling myself that doing so would save my mother because it had become apparent that she had no intention of fighting back or removing him from our lives. So, at that moment, I thought I was doing the only thing that could be done: to kill him before he had another opportunity to beat and potentially kill her. My mother heard his body drop to the floor, rushing out of her room as she stood in shock, screaming while taking notice of her kitchen knife that was now piercing through his chest. She screamed, asking me questions that I don't recall hearing until this day. I stood in the center of the hallway, frozen and numb.

I did not feel sad, hurt, or scared of the ramifications of my actions. I never once worried or wondered what was going to become of me. This was my first experience with shock. I didn't feel anything. It was as if my entire being had become numb and still waiting for the final result to kick in and my family no longer had to be traumatized in the way we had been from the actions of this dark spirit who had made it his duty to harm. Shortly after, my little brother Melvin entered the house. He was shocked to see what had occurred during his absence.

Within seconds my mom had called my cousins who lived in the same apartment complex. Having them rush to our aide immediately after she had made them aware of what I had done. I didn't move or say a word. The adults roamed around the apartment, taking the knife out of his body, and hiding it under my mother's mattress. Trying to develop a story while the ambulance and police were on their way. They asked me to go to the back of the apartment and wait until they informed me to come out, so I did as I was told and went into my room. My cousins Julia and her daughter Toccara came into my bedroom, telling me to shut my mouth.

They had constructed a story for the police and informed me that I was inside and had not seen anything. The police arrived, and my cousins and mom gave them a false story, telling them that her boyfriend had been stabbed by someone outside and no one had gotten a good look at the person due to them fleeing the scene right away. The police officers heard the story and made it clear that they knew the stabbing had taken place inside the home. After finding the knife under the mattress, the leading officer approached my mom, telling her that she needed to start telling the truth about what occurred, or he would have to place her under arrest. The fear of the word arrest made her come clean. The officers realized the trauma I had just experienced was life changing. Having me transported in a police vehicle would have added much unnecessary fuel to an already explosive fire. She made the officers aware of what happened, and the officers agreed to allow me to come to the station with my mom in my cousin's car.

When I arrived at the police station, I was taken into a room and questioned. I told the officers and the woman who had been sent in by the social services what had taken place. They then separated me from my mom and questioned me again. Later, I would find out from one of the counselors that the questioning segment for my mom and me had been filmed. That day I left the police station with my mom, and I was informed that I would undergo counseling. I was also told that my brother would have to do the same because he walked in on the tail end of the incident. After the stabbing, my mom's boyfriend was taken into intensive care, where he would remain for a while.

Being informed by the doctors that had the stabbing been a few inches deeper, it would have killed him. After the event, I underwent counseling, and my social worker Iesha Ogbomo had been seeing me regularly. She would pick me up, take me to lunch, and do activities where she would gradually slide in conversation about the event. Asking me what I was feeling and frequently checking in on how things were going after the event. My mother was made aware that her boyfriend would be getting out of the hospital soon, and he was not allowed to be around us. She was informed that if she had him around us again, placing us in danger, we would be removed from the home and taken into foster care. After hearing this, I felt a huge burden lifted off my chest.

After finding out he had not died, my biggest fear was having to be around him again. I thought to myself finally were free, but I would soon learn that was not the case. Sure, enough, after being released from intensive care, the devil had returned to our lives. My brother and I were still going through counseling and being questioned frequently. My brother would show up to each counseling session as if he were mute. He never responded to questions, comments, or anything from his counselor as he kept his nose embedded in his book reading until the session was over. After months of being coached and prepped, I met with my counselor and told her exactly what my mother had told me to.

Iesha decided to go another route, trying to get the truth out of me. Iesha knew I was an intelligent kid, and she knew if I were willing to kill to protect my mother, lying would be possible. Especially since I knew my brothers and I could be taken away. Every time I sat down for a session, I kept spewing out the same lies repeatedly, telling myself it was the right thing to do. My brothers depended on me, and I couldn't allow us to be taken away from our mom and risk being separated and placed in a foster home. One day I left home and went out with Iesha to smoothie king to get smoothies. I remember that day being important because I had never had a smoothie before that, and the introduction to the Angel food smoothie was something I enjoyed.

We grabbed our smoothies and walked around old navy looking at clothes, which Iesha and I appreciated. She loved to shop and look nice, and so did I, so she often used fashion to bond with me and make me feel comfortable. After walking around old navy and window shopping, we headed for her car, where we sat and drank our smoothies and talked like we usually did. She went on to ask me if I had seen my mom's boyfriend since the incident waiting for me to tell her the same lie, I had been for weeks. She allowed me to lie, and right after she told me, she knew I was not being honest with her. She then told me that she knew my mom's boyfriend was still living there, and I was lying to protect her. I refuted her accusations, convinced I would continue to lie so that I wouldn't be separated from my brothers.

I knew how things went with kids who had gotten placed in the system, and I told myself trauma while being together was better than us facing trauma and being ripped away from one another. Iesha then went on to say to me that on our initial police visit, when we were questioned, they had to videotape our interviews—telling me how she and her colleagues watched the video multiple times, recognizing right away that my mother seemed more worried about her boyfriend than her child. That day, I told myself that my mom was probably more worried about him because she was fearful, he would die. She was concerned about what fate I would have to face as a minor if that were the case. I had no reply for Iesha's comment because I knew even then as a kid why she told me that and what she was hoping to get in return, but I was not going to tell the truth, and get my mom in trouble and have me and my brothers be taken away from our mom and our home. So, I lied with a straight face and went on as if that were the truth and I was sticking to it.

A few weeks later, I went to court for the incident where he was charged and put on probation based on my testimony. I was not charged with anything, and the judge ruled it as self-defense, stating that it was clear that I was trying to protect my mother. As a kid going through this experience, I remember feeling so many different things. Often, I resented my mother because I didn't understand how a woman could allow certain things to occur, especially in front of her children. I Often blamed her for all of my trauma because I didn't understand how she could allow herself to be a victim of abuse after knowing her mother had gone through those things. But I would soon learn how generational curses can be handed down effortlessly to the point people apply unhealthy cultures of living to their lifestyles because they lack the knowledge and courage to break the cycle. Learning through my own experience how hard it can be to break away from relationships that aren't healthy due to fear.

I was normalizing unhealthy behaviors because of being in environments where those behaviors occur frequently and are normalized by the people experiencing them. I would gain a newfound sense of respect for my mother after going through my relationship issues, where I would learn through experience that abuse can be hard to escape—normalizing the trauma in my marriage, telling myself that my husband did not want to harm me intentionally. But it was his unaddressed trauma that made him do so. Frequently hurting, embarrassing, and manipulating me for sport. Helping me understand how accurate the phrase "hurt people hurt people "was in my specific situation. I stood in the middle of my room, assessing the shattered glass that had overwhelmed my new area rug.

I was taking in what had occurred, wondering how it was that I had always managed to be intuitive and stupid within the same instance. I was ignoring what I already knew, hoping for different results—often finding a way to believe in the unbelievable—in contrast, infringing my faithful hope upon the hopeless. The last seven years of my life had been filled with so many ups and downs I still don't know how I could have made it this far. Yet here I sit, Growing, healing, and learning from my experiences, trying to understand what I should take away from each event. Hoping that a woman somewhere on this planet will read these words and find the strength to walk away from anything that is not serving her well-being.

Whether it be a toxic relationship, a toxic friendship, or a stressful work environment, sometimes change can scare us more than the hardships we face. I glanced at my arm as I watched the blood fall to the carpet. Looking at the deep lacerations on my left arm, trying to understand how it was that I had not felt any of the cuts take place. For seven years, I had endured event after event in my toxic relationship. I always looked past my partner's many flaws, telling myself that he was scorned and needed my help. I made myself his savior when there was no morsel of his being who wanted to be saved. Realizing after the last physical altercation, we would have that he preferred staying in his toxic space mentally and physically, for it was the only home he had ever known. I watched as my phone went off, and he sent me text message after text message playing his usual role of the narcissist from hell.

I ignored each text telling myself I had come to the end of the road in the relationship, and after what had occurred, I was not going to look back. I realized how I had let myself down, my kids down, and altered my blessings repetitively by keeping myself in a space with a man who had done nothing but dragged me to the point all I had were the internal skid marks of treachery invading my being. I looked at my oldest daughter as she stood in the hallway with tears filling her eyes. She was tired of seeing me go through the things I had, and I finally looked at her, seeing what the Trauma I was allowing was doing to her and her siblings. At that moment, I understood how my mother had fallen into the situations she had and been blinded by what it was doing to us. Realizing I was not that woman, nor did I have any desire to be. I had spent my entire childhood judging my mother for her mistakes in her relationship choices and experiences.

Yet I was immolating them unconsciously, causing my kids the same fear and hurt I had always vowed not to as a mother. Looking at my daughters and seeing them cry and hurt was all I needed to know that it was time to walk away. I had fought for my marriage way longer than God had intended, and he was now showing me that there would never be any form of resolve with a person whose only desire was to break me down. It was the only dynamic he had ever desired because it was who he was. I had witnessed how he had emotionally tormented his ex. Breaking her spirit and dragging her through the mud. After she had been nothing but a resource of love and help to him.

I listened to his stories about her as he painted her to be the obsessed drug addict he had to walk away from because of her unhealthy habits. Only to find out from others that the account he gave me was inaccurate. He had lied, cheated, and taken all that he could from her. Leaving her with nothing in the end but lies, heartbreak, and diplomatic interaction. As he dangled me in her face. Gloating about marrying me and having his first child wanting to crush her from the inside out. Hoping to create feelings of inferiority in her as she watched him dangle me playing it out to her and everyone else that things in his corner were perfect.

Constantly using the imagery of who Nina was to attract another woman's eyes. Depending on my popularity and haters, to give him a constant space to do his dirt in. Counting on the dislike and envy that other women in my community had for me as a tool to create a safe space and community amongst which he could cheat. Never understanding the aspect that was taking place. Being ok with recruiting women whose only interest in him was based on their dislike for me. Gripping onto other woman's ill intent to steal my happiness as they had their fun with him behind my back and smiled in my face. Feeling good about the things they knew about him that I did not.

He had left Baltimore, planting himself in a small new community of women who were not real women. Diving headfirst into a population of local hoes whose only goal in life was to connect themselves to whatever man they could. Often equating their worth with their ability to snatch up a man who belonged to someone else in most cases. Jeff saw the envy other women held for me utilizing it as a tool. Listening as women talked about me sharing their feelings of hatred towards me with him. At times, I remember thinking, why do women feel comfortable telling my husband how they felt about me? Pondering over why so many women hated me when I had done nothing to them.

I later realized that they shared those feelings of envy with my partner because they could see that same energy in him. Although he had initially been drawn to me for my qualities, he also hated me for them. Often resenting me for my inability to conform to the person, he thought I should be. He was drawn in by my sense of style, ambition, and independence. While silently resenting me for my ability to be vocal, intuitive, and aware of things in most cases, I had no tangible map guiding me to the conclusions I always developed based on his behavior. I now look back on these days and realize that as much as the people around me were afraid of my being, I was just as scared of myself. Often clinging to spaces, I knew I didn't belong out of fear.

Fearing what people's response would be if I allowed them to see all of me. Can you imagine stifling your true nature to make other people more comfortable? This was something I had done the majority of my life. I was constantly battling with my feelings of displacement. Feeling as though I didn't belong with any of the people or places, I had come to know for most of my life. I was feeling a desire to break out of this shell of fraudulence. Abandoning the imagery of the fly, popular, around the way girl who everyone knew was with the shit.

Allowing the intelligent, ambitious dreamer to show up and take her place at the table. Telling myself that the other pieces of who I was could not be presented because they did not fit. Constantly shrinking myself to fit in spaces I didn't even want to be in. I often feared who would switch up on me if I showed myself in a complete form. The problem with pretending is. Eventually, you get worn out. And that's what finally happened. I became tired of hiding and holding onto people I knew didn't fit.

Later welcoming all of myself and watching as friends became enemies, strangers became investors, invested in my life based on all of the community gossip that never seemed to stop circulating, and people I knew my entire life started treating me like a stranger. Because to them, I was. The craziest thing about all of that is when I finally walked away from the abuse, fake friendships, unsupportive family members, and I started loving all of me, shit got real. I started seeing that the more I decided to make positive, progressive changes, the more people's energy became negative concerning me. People always say it's lonely at the top, and I wasn't even close to being at the top, and I saw how real things get when you decide you want better for your life. Suddenly, everyone's energy went from you heard what happened to her? To who does she thinks she is?

In the minds of my peers, I was not supposed to be able to rise above the hurdles I had. Nor was I supposed to have an awakening and start cultivating a better life for myself. The talk shifted from Nina's humiliating marital issues to Nina's glow-up. And let me just say that was a shift no one wanted to see, acknowledge, or speak on. I started to witness firsthand how God was building me up right before the people who had harmed me, conspired against me, and gossiped about my shortcomings. Reminding me that no weapon formed against me would ever prosper because God had made all of it a part of who I was supposed to be. During this process, my enemies were sick because every time they looked up, I was blessed in front of their miserable faces. So many times in my life, I had heard the phrase small towns breed small minds. I was never giving it much thought. But I would soon find out that small towns not only produce small minds, but they also generate small, minded intentions. Learning that although I had endured so many challenging experiences, there would be a lot more waiting for me around the corner. And God was preparing me for a future that would be bigger than any malicious attempts against my spirit ever were.

CHAPTER 6

The Pregnancy

My relationship had been moving fast, much faster than what I was used to, and although I liked Jefferey, there were many times when I felt overwhelmed with anxiety. I had not shared my life and space with anyone other than my kids for such a long time, and it made me feel uneasy. Jeff had been trying to get me to go out on a date with him for a while. Barbra was the person she was prying, as usual, convincing me that I should give Jeff a chance due to his consistent effort. The night I agreed to go out on a date with Jefferey, the beginning of the date was horrible. We started at the movie theater, and we went to see one of the worst movies I had ever encountered. I had sat for as long as I could, watching as Jeff squirmed around in his seat as if he belonged in a Preparation H commercial.

It was making me convinced that he was on drugs. As I judged and labeled him silently. Telling myself I was going to leave this date and never talk to his weird ass again. I sat still, feeling uncomfortable as Jeff continued to move around in his seat awkwardly. "I think I'm ready to go," I said. Shocking him as he tried to figure out how I had let him pay for tickets, refreshments, and gas only to decide I would be leaving the movie after twenty minutes of the showing. But my mind was made up.

So, he agreed that we could leave. He grabbed my hand while walking towards the car, asking me to drink and sit and talk. I started telling him that I was tired and had to get up early for work the following day. But he would not take no for an answer. I agreed to have one drink, clarifying that I would be going home after that. We arrived at the UVA corner, sitting down at one of the local spots to have a drink as I had agreed. At first, things were a little quiet and awkward.

Leave it to me to break the ice with a joke. Allowing Jeff to loosen up, I didn't understand why he was so shy when it was his idea to drink and talk initially. A group of college students came in, and I noticed a beautiful Asian girl who had more butt and hips than me, which was quite a ratio for a woman that was not of African American descent. "Good lord, where in the world did, she get all that?" I inquired, sparking a laugh from Jeff because he had noticed long before I did. At that moment, I thought back on how Omar and I shared times like this. I had always been the kind of woman to admire the beauty of other women because it was something a lot of women fail to do, especially when out with their partners.

But I always felt there was no harm in a man taking notice of another woman's beauty in my presence or my absence. After all, aren't we all visually motivated creatures? What is the point in having eyes if we can only utilize them to admire the beauty in the world during certain times? After getting Jeff to loosen up, we started having the most intoxicating conversation. He was drinking drink number two, and I was still drinking number one, babysitting my long island due to me not being much of a drinker. "You're not going to drink?" he asked as if it wasn't obvious based on the small sips, I had been taking in.

"Your welcome to finish it," I said, not wanting to waste my money. He grabbed my glass, gulping it down in a short period, making it clear to me that he was no rookie in the drinking department, unlike myself. We sat in the bar talking for hours and hours until it was finally 2 am. I glanced at my phone, realizing I would pay for my night out when I got to work the next day. As much as I knew I needed to leave and get myself ready for work, I did not want to. On our way to my car, Jeff started holding my hand, walking me to the car, and I felt extremely uncomfortable. PDA was not my lane, and it made me feel uncomfortable that someone I had just met was so direct in a way that I was not.

The next day I went to work and shared the tea with Barbra about how my date had gone with Jeff, and she was excited to hear a good report. The next day Jeff and I got together again. Then, the day after, and before you knew it, we were inseparable. He met my mom, and I met his mom right away. I got the vibe from his mother instantly that she did not like me despite her trying to pretend as if she did. But I ignored my instinct about her feelings about me because I did not care about that dynamic. Although I liked being around Jeff and spending time with him, I felt confused.

A part of me loved his time and attention, but there was another part of me that felt indifferent. I liked having time to myself, always had, and it was always a conflict of interest when I would tell Jefferey that I wanted time to be alone. In his eyes, people in a relationship spent all their time together, but I did not have the same outlook. I would go along with Jeffrey's desire to be around one another constantly, but I was never content with that dynamic in the back of my mind. That was my first mistake, and I would learn the importance of starting how you want to finish. A few months went past, and Barbara's chemotherapy began to turn. The treatment that had been proven to be a success was now failing.

Shortly after she became ill again, I started to get sick. I was constantly vomiting up the same yellow fluid, convinced that I had maybe become contaminated with her fluids. Barbra was becoming worse by the day, and we were all starting to prepare for her decline. She could no longer go out, becoming confined to the bed while receiving hospice care. Although I knew how things went, I tried to convince myself that she would pull through. I worked twelve-hour shifts at Barbra's, managing to get my schoolwork done during her rested periods.

One day I arrived at work sick and unable to keep anything down. I was still trying to show up for her because she had made it clear that she preferred me to be the caregiver there for most of the day. Me and my coworker Allison gave Barbra a bed bath while taking notice of how depleted she was. After helping Barbra, my nausea became worst, so I left work to go to the emergency room. Jeff and his mother met me at the hospital, looking at me as if I were crazy when I told the doctor I wanted to be checked for cancer. As my anxiety took over, I assisted Barbra with gloves as I recalled a handful of times. The doctors took a urine sample noticing how dark my sample was due to the vomiting and dehydration.

The doctor arrived back moments later, informing me that I was pregnant and was experiencing hyperemesis gravid arum once again. Jefferey appeared ecstatic about the news while his mother sat in her chair, looking depressed. That same day I found out Barbra had passed away while I was at the ER, and it tore me apart. I felt horrible that I had not been there when she died. Not realizing that God had done me a favor because had I been there, it would have been too much for me to handle, given my attachment to her. I got home that night crying my eyes out with Jeff there by my side the entire time. Although he had proven himself to be a horrible person regarding me numerous times, the early days were not as terrible as they later transitioned to be.

Shortly after, I became too depressed to work. Often excepting cases and not showing up, feeling as though I did not want to be in my line of work anymore. I was still paying my bills, but my car note was due, and I could not pay it. So Jefferey paid it for me for a few months. He was constantly trying to lift me out of my depressed state, finding that he was not having much luck. Shortly after, I went back to work, accepting two private cases telling myself I had to work harder because I would have another kid in a few months. For months Jefferey was helping with my kids, bills and being emotionally and physically accessible to me when I needed him to be.

.

One day he approached me, insisting we get married. Initially, I thought he was just talking. I know what you're thinking...married? To him? Clearly, I was not thinking straight. The term young and dumb was definitely sufficient, to say the least. Once he made it clear that he was serious, it made me speechless." Let's do it;" he said, leaving me in a confused state. "Do it when?" I asked, trying to understand where he was headed. "Let's do it now," he said. And that's what we did! We arrived at the courthouse nervous and ready to change our lives tremendously. I remember us standing in front of the room holding hands, shaking. With our eyes watery as it appeared, we both wanted to cry. I had never been so anxious, happy, and terrified simultaneously. As I realized what it was, we were about to do. That day I walked away one year older at 26, pregnant, sick, and married. I felt like I had finally found my person—the person I was destined to spend my life with. For the first few weeks of married life, I was in an ultimate state of pure bliss.

We shared the news with our families that day and got mixed reactions. After hearing the news, Roberta sat on the phone with Jeff trying to hide her disdain. She was seething on the inside as she asked to speak to me. Ready to put on her poker face despite the internal hatred she felt for me. "Congratulations," she said, shocking Jeff and me after not receiving the negative commentary she was usually known to give. "Well, I guess I can't say shit to you now because that's your husband." Sparking a laugh from the both of us as I said to myself, "you sure cant!" Little did I know my fairy tale would be ending long before it ever really began. After my weeks of bliss and happiness, things started to change, and Jeff did a complete 360. I remembered hearing stories where women would share that they had no clue that they had married someone who was the complete opposite of who they presented themselves to be. Always thinking silently that there was no way a woman could marry someone and have them change overnight. I soon learned from experience how true that dynamic can be. He had moved in, got comfortable, and was no longer doing the things he did initially. Since my first pregnancy, I had always had to battle with the stress I endured from having hyperemesis.

Making my pregnancy experience a miserable event day in and day out. I would awake during the day to vomit nonstop. I frequently skipped meals and lost weight because I could not keep anything down. My pregnancy had been going terrible, and it had gotten to a point where although I was still working two jobs, I could barely get out of bed in the mornings. I would work one case during the day and another at night. I had been at both jobs long enough that my clients respected my hard work and reliability, so my clients didn't mind my frequent trips to the bathroom to vomit. Under normal circumstances, my body could have handled working the two cases at once because hard work was something I had become accustomed to.

But my pregnant body did not agree with it, and I would come home daily with swollen feet and an upset stomach due to overexertion. Jeffery had not been much help when it came to responsibilities. Yet I didn't mind in the beginning telling myself that it was okay. I had gone through a relationship with my son's father having him pay all the bills and handle my financial needs. After he had abandoned those duties abruptly, leaving me with nothing and no resources, I vowed to never put myself in a position to have to depend on anyone ever again. I told myself that it was better to be independent than dependent on someone who could potentially let me down. So, I continued to work, take care of my kids, and pay all of my bills on my own, telling myself that I didn't need a man to take care of me.

I convinced myself that all I wanted was someone who would love me adequately. I know, right, stupid as fuck! But you live, and you learn. I did not realize that I had a lovely apartment, kept a kitchen full of food, paid all my bills, had my car, and had my own money. Although these were things, I had been doing before Jefferey, moving in should have meant that he was contributing consistently, and he was not. My rent was seven hundred and fifty dollars a month, and I always paid it alone. I'd go to work feeling miserable, come home and clean my house on my own, and take care of my kids on my own.

Still, I never complained, nor did I see how convenient my lifestyle was for Jefferey and how inconvenient he was for me. Jefferey would get his paycheck and blow it within a week. Sometimes, this can be common when you're paying bills and taking care of financial obligations with your income, but that was not the case for him. He would go to the mall and buy new clothes, two-hundred-dollar sneakers, and use the rest to go out with. Spending the leftover majority on cigarettes, drinking, and the club. A week later, he'd be in my face asking for gas and cigarette money. As if he thought of me as his human ATM.

Each time I offered him the stability he lacked, never considering how daunting that routine would become for me. In the beginning, I didn't mind due to me trying to redeem myself after my relationship with Omar. I always felt like I had become dependent in an unhealthy way. Recognizing that Omar did not always have it like he tried to convey to me. He was simply trying to keep up with our initial introduction of big stacks, designer ensemble, and the spoiled girl vibe he had introduced me to in the beginning. He later came across Ashley, who often walked around dressed like she had been displaced, liked money, and wanted to be taken care of but in a different way. At that time, Ashley didn't keep jobs and was no fan of working.

Meeting Omar and having him provide for her and her son, who was not his child, was like winning the lottery to her. She didn't require high-end anything and simply wanted nothing more than to have all her bills paid and some money placed in her hand. Omar didn't realize that I never required those things; he just took one look at me and assumed that I did. He was offering me a new lifestyle that was never expected until after introducing it and carrying on with it for so long. After assessing how I had contributed to the discord between Omar and me, I tried being a better partner to Jefferey. Offering help in areas where I usually would not in a relationship. I taught myself that a relationship is a partnership where the woman should contribute.

I was ditching my city girl's attitude where I required the man with the bag and adopted the perspective of a woman who was ready to build and go after her own bag. Instead of being the Nina, I was with

Omar, who only received never considering the option of giving in return. I had always been the type of person to share what I had, especially when there was someone with a need that I knew had less than me. Exempting myself from being the giver in a relationship because I was taught that a man should be the giver, especially after watching my parents set that example for me. My parents married young and often faced struggles financially as young adults. Although they had numerous hardships, my father went to work and allowed my mother to stay at home with us. This led me to think that a man was supposed to be the sole provider.

So naturally, I never felt that I should provide anything to a man financially, allowing myself to let Omar play the role of the provider. Later I recognized that he couldn't keep up with it as he originally had because it was not who he was. Omar was practicing the art of being a trick, splurging the bag on whatever attractive young woman he could find—using his bag as bait. Willing to give, do, and be something, he wasn't until the next woman came along with her hand out, ready to receive her prize. I fumbled the bag by confusing the tricking dynamic and providing the same thing.

I think I began to cultivate a giving spirit with Jeff after looking at all the times in my life I needed assistance and never had any. I was explicitly looking at all the times in my life when I needed resources that people around me had in abundance and were unwilling to share. Telling myself that I would always try to be a blessing to others because I knew what it felt like to need and not have. Although it was a noble sentiment, I would learn that it was one I needed to reshape. Helping people in need was not a bad idea, and it was also one God would never frown upon. But helping people who had ill intent towards me, disrespected me, or simply would not appreciate it was a concept that needed recultivating. For months I watched Jeffery do what he wanted with his money, never offering me anything outside of an outfit when he tried to drag me to the club or a pair of overpriced sneakers.

I always turned down the offers, trying to get him to understand that I was a grown woman. Who desired more than clothes and shoes? Equating it to a lack of understanding because he had only been in relationships with the same class of women. Women who felt like a man offering them clothes and shoes were a come up. He would not understand why I did not want what he was showing me. Before my pregnancy, I would allow Jeffrey to drag me out to the club with him against my desires. I had been to the club many times, constantly feeling out of place because it was never an environment that I felt comfortable in—later learning myself and taking notice of my preferences to be in a lounge or hookah spot over the club environment.

Still, I would get dressed and go with Jeffrey feeling more uncomfortable at all the glaring eyes and shade I would encounter from his secret counterparts. Never understanding how I had suddenly become the object of concern for so many women I had never had any interaction with. One day Jefferey came home from work with a bag with new clothes, shoes, and eagerness in his spirit. He was ready to blow his check on the weekend like he preferred to do. Begging me to go to the club with him knowing I was in no state to go anywhere. Like always, I let him talk me into it. That night we got dressed, and we went out like we did all the time.

I endured ill grills from sideline hoes who somehow managed to be upset with me for their actions. Feeling upset that Jefferey would have the gall to flaunt me in the club while he walked around a room full of women he had slept with before me and a few he had been messing around with behind my back. I was tired of being uncomfortable and trying to interpret weird energy directed towards me, so I decided after that night I would not be going out with Jefferey to the club anymore. I had a talk with him about it, and he understood my viewpoint. He was leaving my final decision on the table with no intervention. There was no intervention simply because he knew my absence would allow him room to do what he had been known to do, which was cheating! A few weeks later, Jefferey came home from work to find me lying on the sofa vomiting up in a trash bag.

I had been ill the entire day, and it had gotten to the point where I had no energy left in my body to go to and from the toilet. He came through the door pretending to be concerned after seeing me vomit back-to-back in the bag. I watched as he checked his phone repeatedly. A few minutes later, he approached me, giving me a story about an emergency taking place with his mom. Telling me, he had to rush to her aide and give her a ride to her house, which was about an hour away. I didn't question it, and I was far too dehydrated to even speculate for a second that he was not being honest. So, I watched him leave, and I laid on the sofa praying I would fall asleep and I would feel better.

I fell asleep and woke up about two hours later, noticing Jefferey had not returned home. I called his phone repetitively and got no answer. Still, I didn't think anything more of him not being home. God has a way of bringing you light when you are in the dark, and I had been sitting in the dark clueless about who it was I had married. So, God showed up that night, offering me some light. As I scrolled down my Instagram timeline, bored with nothing better to do. I came across a picture of Jeffery and his homeboys dressed in black in red like they were a part of a high school gang.

I couldn't believe what I was seeing. There he was posted up with his homeboys in the club, having a good time ignoring my calls while I lay on the sofa feeling miserable. I was furious and shocked that he would tell me a lie just to go to the club and leave me alone while I was sick. I had always thought things were going on I didn't know about simply because my inherited lack of trust made me believe all men lied and cheated, yet there, I was feeling surprised. I was tired of dealing with dishonest people, and my feelings for Jeffrey were transitioning the more I viewed the back-to-back uploads on his friends IG. As if my night had not gone bad enough, my friend called me to give me more disappointing news and evidence that Jefferey was not moving respectfully. I answered the phone to speak with my homegirl Janelle.

Janelle had never liked Jefferey from the start of our relationship after having prior knowledge of how he had mistreated his previous girlfriend, whom she had a relationship with. Telling me from the beginning, I should not entertain him because he was a fraud. Had I listened to her advice, I would have been better off. But a hard head will make a soft ass, and after all that would occur, I would realize that her interpretation of who Jeffrey was in a relationship was spot on. "How are you feeling, girl?" Janelle asked. Hoping I would give a different physical report than usual.

"I feel like a hot ass mess. This baby is draining me, taking everything from my edges to my oxygen, and I don't know how much longer I can make it without keeping food down. "Don't do the seed of Chucky like that! Besides, look at who the father is; you should have known better! Just hang in there, and before you know it, you will have a beautiful baby girl, and it will all be worth it." I wanted to agree with her, but I didn't have the energy as I felt the vomiting sensation take over. I picked up the trash bag and let it all out, forgetting that Janelle was on the phone.

I let what little that was left pour out before I picked the phone back up. Apologizing while she sat quietly on the other end, not responding. She finally spoke up, telling me that I was a strong woman and I needed to remember that God never puts more on me than what I could handle—going on for minutes in cryptic mode, spewing out one cliché religious quote after another. I knew she had something more she wanted to say, but I didn't understand why she was stalling.

Figuring it was most likely regarding Jeffery's night out at the club. I told her how he had lied, and I had come across the pictures on I G informing me of where he really was.

She took another silent pause debating if she would come out and tell me or hold it in. I waited for her to speak up when she finally started to progress with what it was; she had initially called me to tell me. "I hate telling you stuff, especially when I know you're sick and pregnant, but I got a call tonight from someone who was out at the club. Apparently, Jeffery was in there acting like he was not married and had a pregnant wife at home. My homegirl told me she watched him on the dance floor grinding with some hoe, and he was cutting all the way up. She told me she hated seeing that because she knew how it felt, and she wished someone would have told her what was going on when she was going through it. So, she recorded it and sent it to me, hoping I'd show you and you'd leave his dusty black ass," Janelle concluded.

I waited for the video to finish loading when it finally popped up on my screen, making me feel even more nauseated. There he was in the center of the club, grinding with a girl who looked like she didn't own a hot comb or hair oil as her matted install took over my focus. I watched as he picked her up, grinding in the center of the room in a way that only a man to whom was single would be able. The humiliation was one thing, but the thoughtless disrespect made me feel confident he was not what I needed in my life. Janelle sat on the phone talking about Jefferey as if he had disrespected her while disrespecting me. Telling me how she hated seeing me go through that during my pregnancy. I knew she could relate, and I knew she didn't want to tell me, but she knew she had to.

That night when Jefferey arrived at my house, I put him out, making him take all his things, informing him that I did not want to be in the relationship anymore. For weeks he tried getting me to change my mind, and I wouldn't. He would contact me every day, checking to see how I was doing, offering to come over and assist me with things he had never helped with since the start of our relationship. I'd decline and keep it moving, telling myself that I was better alone than to be with someone who was dishonest and disloyal. I kept working both jobs and going through the motions daily, although it was rough. I'd go to work, come home, spend time with my kids and do it all over the next day. I never allowed myself to give in to my feelings of missing Jefferey.

My kids and I started going over to Janelle's house a lot like we had done previously before me and Jefferey had gotten married. We'd enjoy each other's company while our kids played. Swapping out details about our work-related stress, single motherhood, and local tea we had heard about during the week, Eventually, I started feeling sicker and sicker. I would spend most of my days in and out of the er getting fluids and nausea medicine through an I V. Jeffrey would always show up to the hospital assisting me home. Eventually, I let down my guard and let him come back feeling like maybe my absence had taught him a lesson. We wouldn't even make it through half the month before more information about who Jefferey really was would be brought to my attention. I woke up feeling sick as usual.

I rushed to the kitchen to find some saltines and a cold ginger ale I could utilize to try and suppress the sickness. I felt horrible mentally and physically. Realizing that although I had allowed Jeffrey to come back, I still didn't trust him or feel comfortable around him. Every time I looked at him, I wondered what more there was to his being that I didn't know about. Yet I tried to block it out and keep going because I knew I had more important things to worry about. I nibbled on the cracker while I sat on the sofa, trying to wait for my nausea to calm itself. I felt the sting of dehydration and weakness plaguing my morning routine as I sipped on the ginger ale, hoping it settled, but it did not.

Before you knew it, I was up moments after rushing my dehydrated body to the bathroom. Projectile vomiting uncontrollably. That day I wanted so badly to call into work and stay home, but I knew I could not afford the luxury of having a self-care day because I had bills to pay, groceries to buy, and kids to take care of, and if I didn't go and get it then I would not have it. When I think back on these days, I shake my head at the many levels of stupidity I dabbled in unconsciously. Sure, I had been the girl that was spoiled with her hand out and that had failed. I had also been the girl to spoil and take care of herself, but I should have never been the girl taking care of a grown-ass man. Nor should I have been the girl to allow a man not to contribute.

Although these days were hard for me, they taught me that I am the prize! And no man that seeks interest in this prize should ever be able to roam freely, not contribute, or not understand the assignment of what it is a man should deliver in a relationship or a marriage. During those days, I told myself that money was not significant. As long as the love and communication were there, the money would one day come through teamwork. Although this was a noble sentiment, I should have never adopted it willingly. What is it about options that make some young women feel as though they need to compromise in areas where they shouldn't? It's as if we tell ourselves that we are not worthy of all the things we watch others have.

This had been something I did often. I was telling myself that my options were limited because I had not reached a successful space in my young life. Making myself feel as though I had to be better to have the better options I silently desired. But this was only partially true. A man that is truly a man and indeed the man for you will come along, assess that you are not whole in the ways you desire, and help you get there. When my mother met my father, she was young, broke, and didn't have anything. He didn't look at her and say, "I like this woman, but she isn't enough or doesn't have enough."

Instead, he made her his wife and the mother of his children. This was a lesson I had been missing as I continued to feel that my poor relationship outcomes were due to shortcomings. When essentially, the poor results were due to my flawed selection process. I continued to hold everything down, telling myself that one day Jefferey would be on his feet, and he would contribute in the way he should. But that was a lie, and that day would never come because it wasn't who he was. Nor did he have the strength to be that person. He had been neglected, uneducated about what a man was and should be, and coddled.

He was surrounded by people who always made him feel like his wrongs were never wrong or on him. So, accountability was a concept he knew nothing about. It was ironic because, despite his late father's battle with drugs, he had been known to be a good man and father. I listened to Jeff and his sibling's accounts about their father. I often recognized how they all had love and respect for him. Sharing how he was a great father who did his best to ensure his children were loved and protected. You see, a man that loves something will treat it in the way he should.

But a boy lacks the capacity and knowledge to do so adequately, and I would soon realize that I was blind to the fact that I had been dealing with a boy and not a man. Jefferey left for work, and I lay on the sofa for a few minutes, trying to get myself together. Feeling the exhaustion roaming through my loins as I tried to pick myself up and get dressed so I could get to work on time. I put on a long white maxi dress with floral trimmings running across the top, some flats, accessories, and did my hair and makeup before exiting to work two jobs while feeling like I had been hit by a bus. I didn't feel the best, but it didn't hurt to try to look better than how I felt. Fashion had always been a massive component of who I was. I could be going through the worst shit in the world, but you better believe when I stepped out of the house, I was going to bring the slay, smile, and keep my head up because that's how I had always handled things.

I recalled an event from my past. After having my oldest daughter Kylie, I was experiencing frequent periods of being burnt out. I had gone back to school and was working a new job as a manager at the local Claire's. Juggling being a mom, student, and working woman were difficult for me during those days. One day Kylie's grandmother Janet came to pick me up to pick up milk for Kylie. I walked outside in silk pajamas, fuzzy slippers, and a headscarf. Too tired to put on clothes after being up all night with a baby. Janet stared at me as I walked from the car to the store entrance.

She was looking as if she had something she wanted to say. When I got back to the car, it appeared that she could no longer hold her tongue. Expressing to me how vital appearance was. Telling me that it was essential that I presented myself in the way I wanted to be received and walking around in pajamas and a headscarf would not give the best impression of me. Although walking around like that was not a norm for me, I understood why it was bothersome to Janet. That day I took her advice. I started presenting myself with an organized aesthetic whenever I left the house.

Adopting this mechanism even when I was tired reminding myself that I didn't have to look how I felt. Looking good always made me feel good, and fashion was always how I expressed myself. Most of my looks were often based on my emotions, and I used style to express myself since childhood. People would often look at me and assume I was not going through anything based on my outer appearance. But I was always a firm believer that you didn't have to look like what you were going through, and I always tried to uphold that concept for many reasons. I arrived at the Williams home to work my day shift as their caregiver. The Williams were a husband and wife who lived in a retirement community who both had been experiencing dementia.

I had been working as their caregiver for a while, and the wife had fallen in love with me, and I had grown to love them both. They were significantly older and had traveled the world experiencing many different cultures. The husband had made a living working as a geologist, and they would often share their stories with me, often leaving me intrigued. They had lived in Borneo for quite some time. Living amongst the Iban villagers and daily, Ms. Williams would share stories with me about their experiences. Showing me pictures and things they had brought back with them. I would sit, listen, and become enthralled for as long as I could before hyperemesis would take over, and it would be back to the bathroom for me hovering over the toilet.

That day I made it through my shift feeling completely drained. I left work and went home for a few hours to spend time with my kids and feed them dinner before taking them across the street to my mom so that I could work the night shift. Jefferey stayed at my house while I was at work, and I would usually return home around 6 or 7 am. That night I arrived at my night job where I worked with a client who also was living in a retirement community. He had been having some issues after being found in the hallway one night roaming around naked due to his Alzheimer's. So, the family hired me to watch over him during the night to make sure he would not roam the hallways or injure himself. Although he had Alzheimer's, he was still pretty sharp and knowledgeable.

He had been a former professor of Russian studies at The University of Virginia and spent his days roaming around suffering from cognitive depletion. He was a very nice man and never gave me any problems. My nights working there were often pretty peaceful despite my nausea. That night I sat in his living room reading to try and keep myself alert and awake during my shift. Reading made me feel as if dozing off was right around the corner for me, so I decided to stroll through Instagram to see what exciting posts I could find. About twenty minutes after, I received an inbox from a young girl I did not know. I opened the message, and she was in my inbox asking me for advice.

Telling me how she had often looked at my social media and admired me. I looked at her page and saw she was a local, so I let her vent through my Dm, giving her what advice I could. At the time, I thought it was an innocent attempt to get advice from an older person. She told me how this guy had approached her via social media who had been in boxing her and requested to hook up. Telling me, she knew he only wanted to sleep with her. She then told me that after he had been very progressive with his attempts, she started sleeping with him, allowing him to take her virginity, and he and she were dating and in a relationship. Shortly after, she found out that he had lied to her about being single, and she decided to keep messing around with him. I explained that she had to start how she wanted to finish.

I told her that any man that begins with a lie in his approach would end with one. Informing her that she had now made a conscious choice to be a side chick, which would be the level of respect she would receive from this man. She then went on to tell me that he had been hurting her and doing her wrong, and she was tired of being a secret. She wanted him to prioritize her, and he would not, so she wanted to know if she should tell his partner. I didn't know what to say to this stranger in my inbox, making it clear that she was ready to ruin someone's relationship out of spite and hurt. I told her that her informing the girlfriend should be contingent on her level of morals and reasoning. I explained that she should take a step back and think before acting.

It was just like me to go into Iyanla fix my life mode overlooking my life components that needed addressing. Giving advice was okay, but I needed to be taking some of my advice, and at that time, I clearly was not. "You didn't tell her when you were sleeping with him, correct? Right, she replied. So don't get yourself in some drama trying to hurt another woman because your hurt when you already knew what you were getting yourself into. She waited for about fifteen minutes to reply when she had previously answered promptly to the entire conversation. She responded, thanking me for my advice, and I went on with my night.

Two a.m. rolled around, and I received a message from the strange girl again. Are you awake? Yes, why what's wrong? I just wanted to let you know that my boyfriend is your husband. She messaged back. This little raggedy …you know what I thought to myself as anger rolled around in my pregnant belly—forging a partnership with heartburn that transitioned my night into a miserable one.

I was shocked that she had taken me through all that, only to find out she was referring to Jeff. I went to look at her page again to find out after strolling through her content that she was only seventeen years old. I was furious and annoyed that she had sent me all of those messages playing me when her initial intent was to let me know she had been sleeping with my husband. But I controlled my anger because she was someone's child, and I knew how things went with girls from where she came from. It was normalized in the hood to be sixteen and seventeen dealing with older guys. Sleeping with men for shoes, clothes, and whatever minimalistic item you could conjure up from letting a grown-ass man take advantage of you. I had been friends with girls back in the day who were fourteen messing with men twice their age.

Thinking then, it was gross and wondering what things they had experienced that made them feel comfortable enough to lay down with a grown-ass man when they weren't even old enough to buy liquor. I had also been 19, dating Omar, who was twenty-eight at the time of our relationship. And I saw firsthand how older guys manipulated younger women. Omar had been good to me until he realized I would not be willing to be the young dumb entity he thought I was. Thinking my position as the mother of his child would allow him to hold a space with me that he could not. It bothered me that this young girl had allowed Jeffery to take something so valuable from her. But I couldn't judge her because I had been her with Omar.

The only difference is Omar had not taken my virginity, nor was he married. I allowed her to say whatever else she felt was needed. It was two a.m., and I figured she had to have more to tell if she was up at that time in boxing me. I remembered what it was like to be young and dumb, but I also knew what it was like to be immature and petty, and she was definitely in her petty bag. She went on to tell me that she had been sleeping with him for a duration of time that dated back to the beginning of my relationship with him. Giving me complete details, I took them all in. Once she finished, I called my coworker and had her come to relieve me to leave my job right away. I was ready to leave work and let Jeff have a piece of my mind. I was also prepared to beat his ass!

I called my mom crying, upset, telling her what the girl had just informed me of. "I told you that you don't need to deal with him" He isn't anything but trash, and your too good to be wasting your time on a bum like him. She kept going in about who he was and wasn't trying to make me understand that we were not a good fit for one another. While I sat on the phone crying, my eyes out shocked that he had been playing me the entire time. Accusing me of guys at the beginning of our relationship when the only time I left out of the house was to go to work and come home. Yet he had been having a sexual relationship with a girl that was seventeen years old and in high school. I never looked at him as being that kind of guy. But I knew he grew up in Baltimore experiencing a culture of life that was different from my Charlottesville, Virginia upbringing. Yet, the thought of him sleeping with someone underage made me sick to my stomach.

After speaking to my mother, I calmed down and pulled up to my apartment, prepared to kick him out and keep it short and straightforward. Something about the entire thing made me furious, and as much as I had changed and been working on myself, I realized that the girl from Orangedale avenue was still very much a part of my being. With that being so, I opened the door and charged him like he was a person in the street. Punching him in his face and blacking out as I kept swinging. I was yelling to the top of my lungs about how he was disgusting and a fraud—screaming as I kept swinging when my mother ran through my door that was still wide open. Grabbing me, pulling me off of him as I continued to try to break free and beat his ass like he was a stranger to me.

My hormones were raging, and, at that moment, I had forgotten about the well-being of the child I was carrying. In other words, I had blacked out, and the only thing I kept hearing in my head was "beat his ass"! The violence in our relationship would prove to be a never-ending saga. Although he initiated most of the physical altercations, there were times like this when I would break from my emotional distress from his behavior and act out in a violent physical manner as well. Feeling as though he deserved it for all the times, he had harmed me both physically and mentally. When the truth was what I did was not permissible. Because violence, and toxicity is never ok and you can't feel justified when inflicting harm upon someone no matter what poor behaviors they may have contributed to your reaction. That night he left my house empty-handed after I had told him to take all of his things. I knew he would try and do what he frequently did, which was wait for me to calm down, and he would come back, but I had made up my mind there was no coming back, or so I thought. The next day I took his things to his mother's house and dropped them off to him and went about my life telling myself that although this was my third relationship and third child, I was not a failure. I had always had insecurities about having two previous failed relationships with two men I had conceived children with. I told myself that those relationships did not define me at that moment, and I needed to keep going.

I reminded myself that I had been a single mom to two kids previously, and I would be able to do so alone with a third. Weeks went by, and I continued to stand my ground and keep my distance from Jefferey. I had been so blind to who he was, and a lot had been revealed to me at once, but I knew it was the clarity I needed. Jefferey would call me back-to-back every day, and I wouldn't answer. He would text, and I'd ignore him. I was feeling frustrated frequently after I'd received one too many texts. I finally felt forced to respond. About three weeks later, he showed up at my job while I was working the night shift.

He begged me to come outside to talk to him. Despite not wanting to, I knew if I didn't, he would sit outside, and I didn't want to risk losing my job, so I went out to talk to him. Telling him, he needed to leave. He begged me to forgive him and give him another chance. Telling me how marriage was a battle when I interjected, explaining to him that although that's true, God never intended for my struggle to be with infidelity or constant humiliation. Turning him away as I went back to my shift, trying not to feel bad for standing my ground. My grandmother had always told me never to let a man make a fool out of me.

And as a child, I never understood what that meant. However, she would share the stories with me about how my grandfather allegedly had cheated on her while they were married and eventually left her on her own with all of their kids to be with a sixteen-year-old girl. At that moment, I thought about how my grandmother's story was now congruent with my own. I told myself that I was strong and could be strong enough to walk away from a no-good man and be a good woman despite my experiences. Reminding myself of all the stories my grandmother had shared with me, telling myself that I would have the strength to do the things she didn't think to do. Hoping my story would have a better ending than hers. Telling myself that I could learn from her mistakes, but it would be a long time, approximately seven years, before I would have the strength to do so.

About an hour after I returned to my shift, I received a call from my husband's best friend, Jarell. Jarell informed me that Jeff had been rushed to UVA hospital after attempting suicide in the ambulance. Right away, I felt a knife pierce through my impregnated gut. Feeling instantly that I was to blame for not taking him back. I left work right away and headed to the hospital to rush to his aide. They weren't allowing anyone to come in except me when I arrived because we were married. When I arrived at the hospital, I found him lying in bed, experiencing significant stomach pain due to a large number of pills he had taken.

He seemed high and talked in a weird voice that I did not recognize. I hated the things he had done to me, but the thought of him feeling so low that he would attempt to take his own life was difficult for me to process. I had never known anyone suicidal, and it was hard to try and make sense of it all. He laid in the hospital bed drinking a tar-like pasty concoction the doctors had given him to try and rid his system of the substances he had taken. He laid there telling the doctor how he had done so because he didn't want to lose me, and I felt sick to my stomach hearing the weird things coming out of his mouth. Trying to understand how a person could think that they loved someone to the point that they would rather die than be without them. Yet, on the other hand, they could lie, cheat, and manipulate that person out of the love they rightfully deserved.

One plus one will always equal two, but at the moment, I was starting to question what was right because things were not adding up correctly. Jeff could see how uncomfortable I was with him as I listened to what he said. Are you scared of me? Observing my anxious manner. Yes, I said in response to his question trying to be honest. I would never hurt you; he said as he held onto my hand. I didn't know what to make of him or any of it. How could he be sitting there trying to assure me that he would never do anything to harm me when he had just tried to harm himself.

The next day he was admitted to the fifth floor of the hospital, which was the floor where they kept all the people on suicide watch, people with mental disturbances, and people who were overall experiencing issues related to psychosis. It's so funny how God works on people. Because as a child, the two places that scared me the most were mental facilities and nursing homes. Yet through a series of events that would take place, I would make it my mission to help people living in those environments. I guess it is true that you never have a real solid idea of where you might end up and what your calling might be. The next day I went to the hospital to visit him, and I felt highly overwhelmed, fearing that I would come into contact with one of the "mentally ill" people on the fifth floor and be terrified.

As I approached my husband, I remember seeing a man I had come across many times as a child. He was a local homeless African American man I had encountered many times in passing. I watched as he paced back and forth, talking to himself, and appearing to be making very little sense. That day I arrived, and I was greeted by an African American social worker who had been in charge of assessing to see if Jeffrey could be allowed to go home or if he would have to be admitted to the facility for a more extended stay. That day I would make one of the many mistakes that would enable him to continue his negative behavior patterns and neglect his mental health, which was a lot more problematic than what he or I knew at that time. The social worker did her evaluation and exited the room quickly. During her absenteeism, Jeff begged me to talk to her to agree to let him leave and come home.

Let's just say I had been plagued with guilt blaming myself, so I went along with his request despite my fears of what he was capable of, and I was able to get the social worker to release him under my care. That day I went home and throughout every bottle of Tylenol, cough medication, and allergy aid I had in my home. During this point in my pregnancy, my health started to worsen from all the stress I had been under from watching over Jefferey like he was a ticking time bomb waiting to erupt. I was also drained from working two jobs, and I could no longer keep much of anything down. I went to the hospital one to two times a week for dehydration. One day I had been vomiting nonstop for two days, unable to leave the bed, throwing up in a trash bag all day and night. I felt so weak I could barely hold myself up to walk to the bathroom.

My mom kept my kids for two days while I toughed it out and had come over to check on me. After finding me completely depleted, weak, and pale, she called the rescue squad and had me rushed to the hospital. Upon my arrival, the doctors intervened immediately, informing me that I could have died had I not come in when I did. They admitted me to the hospital, where I stayed for a few days. They had me set up with a pump equivalent to a chemotherapy pump upon discharge. The pump would be a resource for me to have nausea medication enter my system daily from sticking myself with a needle and having the pump disperse nausea medication so I could keep it down. The pump offered me some resolve, and I soon kept down small meals here and there.

I spent a lot of time checking in on Jeff, and now and then, we would have issues that would lead to arguments where he would threaten me that he would try to" kill himself again." In the beginning, when he did this, my fear of him going through with it would cause me to stifle any opposing arguments; I had started making myself submissive in a way that was not in my nature. This went on for a lengthy time. I was beginning to feel as though the walls were caving in on me. Often, I felt like I wanted to leave Jeff but couldn't because I knew if I did, and he harmed himself, I would feel as though it was my fault. So, I allowed myself to stay and be miserable. One day I took my son out for a mom and son day, which we did more frequently before the suicide attempt trying to get my mind off of all of the things that were plaguing me.

When I ran into John, although John and I would talk here and there, I tried to keep my contact with him minimal because I knew my feelings were dangerous, and I never wanted to confuse myself with those feelings. They were difficult because it is easy for a woman to become engulfed with feelings for an old flame when her current flame turns out to be an absolute nightmare. I also learned how vulnerable I was during this time in my life, and I didn't want to open old doors I had closed for my own good. I knew he had heard about what I had been going through because he always did. Making me aware of what he had been told every time we spoke. Always asking me why I was allowing myself to go through things that I was, and never having an honest answer or understanding to give him in return.

John noticed my son and me as soon as we entered the mall. I tried to put my head down, praying that if I didn't look up, maybe he wouldn't engage as he sat at the food court table with all of his friends. But him being the gentleman he was and the Charlottesville native he was, he would never have allowed me to walk past him without him addressing me. He walked up to me, hugging me right away while talking to my son. Asking him how he was doing and being polite, although he barely knew my son because that was the kind of guy he was. John and I had been good friends in and out of dealing with one another for a long time before I started dating Jeff. I ended the relationship with him shortly before meeting Jeff, and few people knew that we had been involved except for our close friends.

John moved away, and briefly after I stopped communicating with him after Jefferey saw messages between us and told me he did not feel comfortable with John and me being friends. You look good; John said, making me feel incredibly awkward. As I stood there in complete shame, wishing I would have had the sense to pick the right guy. I had given up my friendship with him for a man who was more disrespectful than anyone I had ever met in my life. A man who was currently using his suicide attempt to extort me into staying and being in a situation I knew was no good. I could not continue to make eye contact with John because I knew he could see how unhappy I was, and I didn't want him to make any inquiries. So, I said goodbye and went on about my day taking my son out and trying not to think about it too much.

Although that was damn near impossible for me because John had a soft spot in my heart, and I knew he could tell how I felt even when I didn't say it. He knew all the things Jeff was doing behind my back, and he knew I didn't deserve them. Me and my coworker Beck had been getting closer after both being employed at the Williams home. Beck was an older woman about the same age as my mom. She was fun, comical, authentic, and I liked being in her company. One day when I got to work, she informed me that we would be taking the Williams on a field trip to the Virginia Safari Park. Since I was seventeen, I had not been there and was looking forward to a getaway after all the stress I had endured at home.

That morning I got to work; I had Beck stick me with my needle, hoping the medication would do me some justice and I would be able to enjoy my day at the safari park. I even managed to consume a hamburger and fries at the diner we stopped at on the way back home. That evening we dropped off the Williams at the retirement home and rode around enjoying the rest of the day. We later headed to pick up her youngest son, who was about seventeen at the time; they drove me home to drop me off. Beck and her son rushed to my aide, helping me in my apartment and sitting with me for a while, trying to make sure I was okay. Before I could get inside my building, I began projectile vomiting like the exorcist. I soaked in a hot bubble bath while they sat in the living room waiting for me.

When I was finished soaking in the tub, I put on a mud masked, pinned my hair up in a bun, and put on my nightgown and fuzzy socks, prepared to take a nap. Beck didn't want to leave me, so she waited for Jeff to come home, telling me she didn't feel right leaving me after seeing me vomit uncontrollably. I accepted her offer and sat on the sofa, laughing, and talking with her and her son while waiting for Jeff to come home. When the door opened and I saw Jeff walk through the door, I was happy. I couldn't wait to tell him how much fun I had at the Safari Park. His facial expression changed as he entered the room to find Beck and her son sitting in the living room with me. "How are you doing?" Beck asked as she took notice of his demeanor. "Jeff, this is my friend Beck and her son," and before I could finish the sentence, he said, "come here I need to talk to you" in a distressed tone.

I hopped up from the sofa, following him to the backroom, not thinking much of it. When I entered the room, I was talking randomly when I felt his hands wrapped around my neck as he choked me to the point I couldn't breathe. Shouting "bitch didn't I tell you to stop fucking playing with me repeatedly." I tried to get him off me, but I was too pregnant and weak to succeed. Beck and her son ran into the room, trying to get him to stop, and he would not. Suddenly, his hands were no longer wrapped around my neck, and Beck was in the hallway scuffling with him like she was a man. Her son pushed her out of the way, charging Jeff and taking the lead in the fight until he drew blood.

Jeff made his way out the door and sped off aggressively. My floor was covered in broken glass from the scattering of my favorite world market décor. Once again, he had shown me a side of him I did not know existed. I didn't understand how he could be upset about Beck and her son being in my house. He had seen Beck's son, who was significantly handsome for a teenager, and gotten consumed with jealousy. It didn't make sense to me why he would think anything of it, especially when I was pregnant, my face was covered in a mud mask, and I was married to him. When being around a man, they are interested in; a woman doesn't walk around in face masks and grandma nightgowns.

But he could not put it past me because he knew what he was doing and had been doing from the very start of our relationship. Why wouldn't he look at the handsome teenager and think intrusively when he had dabbled in a sexual relationship with a seventeen-year-old. My grandmother always said, "They can't put it past you when they know they can't put it past themselves." I could never wrap my head around Jeff's many insecurities relating to other men and me. This was a consistent problem in our relationship. He constantly accused me of men I knew and men I did not know. He felt as though I had to have a secret counterpart somewhere.

Laying safely tucked away, awaiting my call when he was not present. I lay on the sofa while Beck and her son got my house back in order for me. They both urged me to come home with them for the night, but I wouldn't agree to it. I heard a knock at the door, and it was Beck's oldest son coming to check on his mom and brother. After seeing that I was pregnant, he sat down, telling me that I needed to get away from Jeff for my sake and the sake of my unborn child. Urging me to come home with them just for the night, but I didn't. I would have many encounters where others would encourage me to walk away from Jeff.

I did not grasp a proper hold that I was walking blindly through an abusive situation. A situation that had become flooded with mental, physical, and emotional abuse. Telling myself that things weren't as bad as they were. Beck left urging me to call her if Jeff returned, promising me she would send her sons back to get me and handle him if I needed her to. I lay on the sofa crying, trying to understand what had happened and why. Replaying the random attack repeatedly, trying to determine what warranted him to feel the need to act as he did. That day he called my phone over and over, crying and begging for my forgiveness.

I declined, only to have him call me and threaten to kill himself. Under normal circumstances, I would give in after hearing that, but it had now become clear to me that he had been dangling his suicide attempt over my head to keep me trapped. So, this time I responded by telling him to go right ahead! I hung up and didn't speak with him again. I kept the event to myself, only confiding in my mom and expressing to her what had occurred. Hearing her go off on the phone in a rage, telling me that she would make my brother "beat his ass." It would be best if you stayed away from him, she raged on.

A man who will choke and charge you while pregnant is not a man you need around. I needed to listen to her; she knew from experience after all. So why didn't I? There I sat, listening to what I already knew—disregarding facts, science, and statistics based on my emotions consumed with love and care for the very person who was giving me nothing but pain. Why did I feel he needed to be saved so severely? And why did I think I was the one to do it?

These were questions I asked myself repetitively while walking in faith with an unfaithful partner and silently assessing the boundaries that no longer existed regarding this hurtful person. Succumbing to the realization that I had begun to lose who I was trying to recultivate, a relationship that was fading before my eyes. I wanted him to see what he was doing to himself and the people around him—wanting him to understand how his actions were infringing upon my health and happiness. But he would never be able to grasp that reality because I was indulging him in a way that made his actions and disrespects okay. The next day I got a call from several of his family members that lived in Baltimore.

Jeff had wrongfully informed them that me and my brothers had attacked him. His mother also called me, cursing me out and being disrespectful. Insinuating that me and my siblings had "banked him," as she said verbatim. I hung up the phone realizing nothing I could say would be heard because Jeff was a liar, and he had already changed the narrative to one that he felt would suit him. The story he told was ironic because he had never met either of my brothers at that time, and my brothers did not live nearby to assist me in that kind of way even if I wanted them to. I knew he was embarrassed and couldn't express to his mother when she asked why he showed up to her house bleeding that he had been beaten by an older woman and her teenage son for attacking me for no reason. So, he did what he did best and lied, painting himself as the victim and my circle of people as the victimizers.

That event would lead me to spend the remainder of my pregnancy independently. I finally felt as though I had been through way more than what I preferred at the hands of Jeff and his bullshit. For weeks, my routine was the same. I'd go to both jobs, come home to my kids, and try to be as present as I could under the ill circumstances of hyperemesis and keep my distance from Jeff. The pump was no longer working for me that well, and I became tired of the misery I felt. My coworker had informed me that a special cupcake she could get me from a local bakery would help send me into labor. I thought it was a myth, and after trying castor oil and getting no results, my desperation was at its peak.

That day my coworker dropped me off two lemon drop cupcakes, and I ate them within thirty minutes of one another. I was still skeptical about the possible results, so I took two teaspoons of castor oil and tried to wait it out. My bags were packed and ready to go, and my mom waited with me at my house to see what would or wouldn't happen. I waited and waited, and nothing happened for hours, so I sent my mom home telling her I would lay down and update her if anything happened. A few hours later, she knocked on my door, checking on me. We sat in my living room talking for a few minutes before I got up to go to the bedroom, and I dropped to my knees from the impact of the contraction. I don't know if the castor oil or the cupcakes helped speed along the process or the conjunction of the two, but it appeared to be a success.

My mom called the ambulance, and Jeff, as I stood in the middle of the floor feeling the worst pain I had ever felt in my life. The fire department arrived before the ambulance, and after seeing how close together, my contractions were, they started laying out tools that looked like something you would use to dissect an alien. The fireman informed my mom that they would have to deliver my baby on the floor of my room using the tools they had with them. My anxiety peaked as I watched the man sit out the devices when I exploded out of fear. Have you lost your fucking mind I yelled out as the contractions continued coming more potent and more vital; I am not giving birth on this hard ass floor, and none of you will be fucking touching me, I screamed. My mom told me to calm down while I continued to curse like a sailor from the panic that was taking over me. I felt like I had been trapped inside a bad scene from a movie.

The firefighters hovered around me, expressing that I had no other choice because my baby was coming now, whether I was prepared or not. "Back the fuck up," I yelled like a crazy woman to the top of my lungs. Jeff rushed to the back of the room, looking like he was more anxious and scared than I was. There he stood, a mere baby himself mentally preparing himself for a baby of his own. Looking like he, too, was trapped in a bad scene, he was not prepared for. I had never been so happy to see him in my entire life. There's something about the brutal pain of contractions that can make even a demon look like a savior for you as you lay enduring that kind of pain.

After cursing out the entire fire rescue team and having the head firefighter leave the room frustrated that I kept declining their help, the ambulance showed up, escorting Jeff and I to the hospital. It felt like my daughter was trying to force her way out of the wound with a two-by-four, and the pain was unimaginable. I remember thinking when I watched movies, especially old slave movies, where they show the scene of childbirth how dramatic they always were. Telling myself that it couldn't have been that bad. But let's just say that day, I paid silent homage to my female ancestors, finally experiencing what they had for generations with each life they brought into the world. When we arrived at the hospital, I was scared and crying nonstop. "Hello, miss White," the doctor said as she entered the room briskly.

With an entire team of people with her moving just as fast as she was. "So, I'm going to tell you what will happen," she said quickly. "We're going to transport you onto this hospital table, and when I ask you to push, you're going to push. You are about to have a baby." Okay, I said, sniffling up my tears. "Can I please have some medicine? Can I please have an epidural?"

"I'm afraid it's a little too late for that," she said. "So, we're going to do this the old-school way, and I would be grateful if you could stay calm, you can do it. And I want you to give her your hand," she said to Jeff. They got me onto the hospital table, positioned my legs, and before you knew it, the pain got worse. The doctor told me to push when she instructed, never preparing me adequately because I would have to push my way through horrible pain from the contractions.

Several times during the excruciating process, I felt myself fading, praying I would not die on the delivery table. Passing out frequently during the process and having the nurse nudge her fist in the center of my chest bringing me back to the event. I gave birth within forty-five minutes, and it was the longest forty-five minutes of my life. That day I gave birth to my daughter, and I realized I had an internal strength, of which I was unaware. I had never imagined in a million years I could give birth without the assistance of the epidural, and it was an experience I would never forget

CHAPTER 7

You Can't Teach An Old Dog New Tricks

*E*very day Jeff would come to the hospital and spend the night with our daughter and me. She took him in a way I had never seen a man be with a child before, and it gave me hope that he would potentially become a better person for our child. After we were discharged from the hospital, he would come over daily to babysit our newborn while I went to work. My mom would watch my oldest two children, but I didn't want to overwhelm her with watching a newborn because I knew she needed rest for work, and my oldest children were no problem for her. My best friend Raye was a manager at the local Steve madden store in the mall, and she had informed me they needed some extra help. I got a third job working there to make extra money because I knew I would need it now that I had an extra mouth to feed.

I was juggling working three jobs and taking care of a newborn and two other children.

And although it was not easy, I did a great job. I started getting back to my old routine and making more free time with my kids because I knew they needed me, and I would often see them less when I was working more. I was telling myself that I was doing what had to be done because I was still operating as a single mom even in my marriage, simply because I was still a single mom. Jeff started pitching in paying the entire light bill, and I was still responsible for the rent, groceries, gas, and children all on my own. It was hard having him back under my roof, but I didn't want to be the mom of three with three absent fathers, so I put up with it telling myself that my daughter needed her father. I knew that if I were not with Jeff, he would not be a part of her life, and I knew that because I had been through it before. So, it was easy for me to see it in him, although I didn't see it in the others.

I needed to keep my kids looking nice, bills paid, a kitchen filled with food, and my home looking nice because that's what I had grown up seeing my mother do for my siblings and me. Naturally, I inherited those beliefs from her. Adding a new baby to my life was hard, and I was annoyed that Jeff was not contributing anything to his child. He would pay the electric bill, and after that, he would blow his money in the same ways he had before. While he watched me work my ass off to provide for everyone and take care of all the bills on my own. We had several arguments around the issue, and at times I would reach out to his sisters, telling them what was going on to try and get someone to talk sense into him about what he was not doing. His oldest sister lived in Baltimore and had a successful marriage and lifestyle, and she was different than his other family members.

He often compared me to her, and I could see why. So, I reached out to her to express what was going on. After hearing what I was going through with him, she explained to him how he was not doing his part, and he agreed to do better, but he didn't. I realized Jeff was never going to step up to the plate, and it wasn't in my nature to wait on him. I decided to go and sign up for section eight. I went to a local sign-up meeting and sat through the information session. That day I got placed on the list, and within a short time, they contacted me telling me I was eligible for a section eight voucher.

I went looking for a place and found a nice three-bedroom apartment that was a step up from my current apartment. Shortly after receiving the news about the voucher, My mom found me a private case making twenty-five dollars an hour, and things were starting to get better for me. I moved my family in and went on with my routine daily, not having any issues. My kids had their own rooms, and there was a lot more space for all of us to move around and not feel so cluttered as we had in my old apartment. For four months, I lived with the section eight voucher, and I was annoyed things had not gone the way I had assumed. I took the section eight voucher thinking my rent would be cheaper, but because of the money I made and all the hours I worked, section eight paid one hundred and thirty dollars of my rent, and I paid nine hundred and eighty dollars. I didn't mind because I was making good money, but I would soon learn how the system worked.

One day I got a call from the section eight office telling me I was due to come in for a review meeting. During that meeting, I was informed that I needed to decrease my hours significantly or drop my section eight voucher due to my income. Dropping my hours would have made it hard for me to pay my car note, bills and provide for my kids in the way I was comfortable with, so that day, I chose to break a generational curse and step out on faith. I had watched many of my family members get on section eight and never get off, and I was determined to utilize it as a steppingstone to get on my feet. Once I realized that the only way my rent would be cheap was if I worked less or not at all, I decided God was trying to show me that this was not something I needed, although I thought I did. That day I gave up my voucher, and I started paying the 1,110 dollars on my own every month. During that time, I was bringing home almost four thousand dollars a month, so I took a leap of faith and did what I knew was the best thing for me.

I left Steve Madden after having several run-ins with girls showing up to my job trying to be petty because they had or were interacting with my husband. Shortly after I left, Raye hired a girl who had made herself my nemesis for years, although I was unclear about why. Della and I had been friends for years and grew apart as we got older. During the start of her relationship with her boyfriend, she saw Raye and me out at a party with him and assumed he was interested in me when Raye was the one, he had his eye on. A close friend of mine had invited Raye and me out with him and Della's boyfriend, with whom she was not in a relationship at that time. We all went to a party, went out for dinner and drinks, and parted ways after that night. Della had spotted Raye and me out with her soon-to-be boyfriend and felt upset about the outing.

Neither Raye nor I knew of their interaction, nor were we interested in being anything other than his friend. After that day, Della started hating me and holding grudges for something that had never happened. Shortly after beginning at Steve madden, she had a lot to say about me. So, Raye told me that she made her aware that it was never me her man was interested in. Even after finding out the truth, her energy didn't change, so I was convinced she was feeling away about me because she wanted to and not because she had a reason to. So, I let her carry on with her imaginary beef, and I didn't address it because it was not something I cared about. A few weeks passed, and Raye started calling me, telling me how Della was always asking questions about me, my relationship, and my life in general.

I didn't understand why someone I hadn't spoken to in years would have so much concern for my life, but I kept it moving, telling myself the drama was not a wave I was trying to ride. Raye started hanging with Della and going out with her and her friends and often calling me, telling me how cool she was and how we should squash our issues and go out together. Each time she would make this offer, I would make it clear to her that there were no issues on my part, and I didn't want to be bothered with her after hearing all the things she had said about me. I felt annoyed by Raye's suggestions' of Della and me hanging out. I had never been the type to care who my friends hung out with, but I had also never been the type to link up with people I knew didn't like my friends and had ill things to say about them. In all honesty, I was jealous and didn't want to share my friend with someone who I had known to be messy concerning friendship and sisterhood.

I felt a way about Della and Raye hanging together, and it was simply because I had experienced my fair share of situations with women who were not genuine. I knew it wouldn't be long before things would arise, and people would try to influence me to question Raye's loyalty to me. In my mind, I felt things would not go so smoothly with the two based on my impression of who I thought Della was as a person. I started having flashbacks of my experiences with an old college friend named Samantha. Samantha and I were thick as thieves, and I looked up to her. I met her at a time in my life when I was struggling and trying to cultivate better for my kids and me.

Samantha was older than me, had a beautiful home that was two times bigger than my basement apartment and had her own everything.

I remember looking at her and noticing how she was on her shit, thinking to myself, that's where I want to go. I learned as much as I could from her fast and felt like we would grow to be forever friends. Samantha worked full-time, was a mom of two, and was a full-time student. She was also very religious, introducing me to her spiritual practice and taking my children and me to church with her frequently. She would give me rides to school continually and was always there to support me, or so I thought initially. One day she came clean to me during a sit down at a local hookah bar that she wanted to talk to me about something. A few weeks prior, she had come clean and told me that she used to be a lesbian.

After hearing the seriousness in her voice, I started thinking; I know this girl is not about to tell me she likes me because I have no patience for this today. She sat up in her chair, ready to spill her tea when I interrupted. "Samantha, I rock with you, tough," I said, "but if you're about to tell me you like me like me, I can't take that kind of energy today," I said, still holding my serious expression. Watching as she exploded with laughter, assuring me that I had it all wrong. "No silly, you're not my type," she said. I looked at her, thinking, girl, it isn't that silly because five seconds ago, I didn't even know you were ever attracted to women. "I wanted to talk to you about something else," which made me feel like it was something heavy.

"I think you're an incredible person, and I never expected our friendship to grow so fast," she said, looking at me crazy. As I feared what it was, she struggled to tell me. "I feel like we can't move forward as friends until I tell you something I have been holding back for a while now. I used to date Simon," she said. She left me tongue-tied and mute. "Who is Simon? I asked, feeling like it had to be a Simon I was unacquainted with."

"Your Simon," she said. "My Simon?" I asked as if I was having difficulty comprehending. "Yes," she said. In my head, I was thinking, how is it that I've been around you for two years, and you never told me that you and my current partner were sexually linked in the past. It was giving awkward, but I let it slide, feeling as though she didn't tell me because it was a long time ago, and she wasn't sure how I'd react. So, I moved on, ignoring the situation altogether because it didn't feel necessary. For weeks, a classmate of ours had been taking frequent strolls past our Anatomy and physiology class trying to get my attention.

I would catch his stares and look away, pretending not to notice. One day he worked up the nerve to get my attention in another way whispering for me to come out of class and meet him in the hallway. It was as if he thought we were in high school. Long story short, I stayed put telling my homegirls that I was not interested. He would do this same routine daily for weeks, strolling past my class, asking me to meet him in the hall, and getting no traction. Unaware that I was in the space of feeling like all men were liars and cheaters, I had decided that single life was the only life for me. Samantha would comment daily how she thought he was pathetic and thirsty based on his behavior.

While my friend Tia would reply, stating that she thought he was sweet, determined, and was attractive based on his strong resemblance to two chains. Granny give hallway two chains a chance, Tia said. Laughing while noticing how quick Samantha was to shoot down her suggestion, telling me I should not because he was giving clown vibes. A few weeks later, Samantha asked me to stay at her house for the weekend and given that I had done that numerous times I didn't think much of it. That weekend she picked up my kids and me, and we went to her house, thinking it would be a normal sleepover like all the others. Saturday night rolled around, and Samantha sent her girls away for the weekend. I didn't think much of it and stayed over with my kids after she expressed that she didn't want us to leave, still not thinking anything of it.

That night she appeared to be tired and came into the living room to check on me, informing me that she was going to bed early. I stayed up late binge-watching episodes of the Golden Girls wide awake due to my old acquaintance insomnia. A few hours passed when I watched Samantha get up and enter the living room heading for the door. Seconds later, she reentered the living room with a weird look on her face, followed by hallway two chains. Who appeared to be shocked and uncomfortable with my presence. Although I thought it was strange that she had so much to say about him being a clown and then was sleeping with him, I brushed it off. Telling myself it didn't matter because I was not interested in him, and her being interested in him was not relevant to our dynamic. But oh, how wrong was I at that moment. For had I taken the time to properly observe and dive into what was unfolding before my eyes, I would have gotten it early on. But I was blind or at least pretending to be blind at that moment which I'm sure you all have come to realize was a common pathology of mine when maneuvering my way through relationships.

As I'm sure, you have come to understand that people often showed me who they were and how they felt about me. And for numerous reasons, I often tried to turn a blind eye and play oblivious to the human nature that was often expelled abruptly in my direction. Simply because I had become so accustomed to maltreatments and behaviors, I programmed myself to believe that those behaviors were all I had access to. Therefore telling myself that there was no need to check checkable situations because everyone had shit with them. Although I knew perfection didn't exist, I was overlooking the fact that some forms of imperfection were a choice. Just as friends, baby daddies, and relationship partners were choosing to expel negative frequencies in my direction, I was choosing to accept it. And that was the number one reason these forms of treatment would go on and on and on until I finally stop being afraid to change my narrative and change the people I allowed into my space.

I figured she was too ashamed to admit to Tia and me that she was attracted to him after watching him walk past our class daily, showing interest in me. About a month later, I decided to have a slumber party at my house while my kids were at my dad's for the weekend, which didn't happen often. Leave it to me to be thirsty for a full weekend, unaware that my weekend was about to be an epic fail. That weekend me and a large group of friends got together, and we all went out, came back to my house for drinks, and had a slumber party. Where we all fell asleep drunk and uncoordinated. Landing in random places from the sofa to the floor piled up like drunken idiots. In the middle of the night, I remember waking up to find Samantha storming out of my front door like she was angry.

With my homeboy entering the living room following her departure. Kevin was a Charlottesville local celebrity, rapper, and radio host. Kevin was a ladies' man and had an uncanny ability to make a woman laugh. He often appeared to be more of a comedian than a rapper due to his comedic talent that followed him in every room he entered. I asked Kevin what was up with Samantha as I watched him renter my living room looking suspicious. He hesitated, later stating that he didn't have a clue. "Your skinny ass is lying, so I'm going to ask you again what did you do?"

Assuming he had made her mad with one of his jokes which often cut deep. Disheveling people's insecurities due to his tone-deaf approach. "Man, I didn't do anything," he said again, lying through his teeth, or so I thought. "She was acting like she was feeling me all night," he said as if he had enough meat on his bones for that even to be possible. "And…....?" I questioned, trying to get him to spit it out. "She woke me up and wanted to get me to you know, and I was with it…until she tried to get me to do it in your bed. I told her no, and she was persistent, and I asked her to come with me back to my house, but she started acting weird."

"Weird like how?" I asked as if the sentiment of her wanting to sleep with him, in general, was not weirdly shocking to me. "Man, shorty was acting like she would only do it if we did it in your bed, and I told her no, I wouldn't disrespect you like that, and next thing I know, she storms out the front door." I started fuming on the inside. I couldn't believe what he was telling me. Nonetheless, I knew Kevin was many things, and a liar was not one of them. The following day Raye and her sister came over, and I started debating if I wanted to share what I had been told or keep it to myself.

I liked Samantha as a friend and looked up to her, so I decided to keep it to myself and wait to speak with her about it. Raye had been urging me to be careful after seeing me dive headfirst into my pool of new friends. Warning me how sneaky young women could be after having her own experiences with dysfunctional friendships during her time in college. A hard head makes a soft ass, and I would soon learn how naive I had been regarding my college classmate and so-called friend.

Shortly after Raye arrived, I heard a knock at my door, and it was Samantha. I opened the door and allowed everyone to get comfortable when I decided to see what was going on with Samantha leaving out the details of what I had been told. I started asking Samantha why she had stormed out and not said bye or made anyone aware she was leaving, trying to see what her response would be.

The conversation started typically, and before you knew it, things went left. She started screaming how she was tired of seeing all of the men she was interested in show interest to me, tired of seeing me have everything, and the tears started rolling. The Irony was she had twenty times more than me. I was a single mom of two, living in a two-bedroom basement apartment with no car, a dead-end job, and barely making ends meet. Her low self-esteem had deluded her ability to assess reality. Samantha was smart, attractive, independent, and self-sufficient. She was the girl in class who raised her hand every time a question was asked.

Always dishing out the correct answer each time, displaying her elevated level of intellect. The saddest part about being a woman who has a lot to offer is that you often overlook your own outstanding qualities. It broke my heart to see and hear Samantha acting out in the way she was. There I stood, admiring this woman for her capabilities, trying to learn while having her low-key hate me for my minimal offerings. How was she tired of seeing me get everything when I didn't have much. We were both honors students, single mothers, and women trying to change our circumstances. Yet there she stood, feeling envious of someone who had less than she.

She was allowing envy of small components to cloud how she viewed herself. She talked about how her sisters were always more attractive than her leading Raye and me to see how insecure she felt. Diving into detail about how envious she was of me, her friend, and her classmate. She never recognized that I had a strong sense of admiration concerning her. I glanced over at Raye, who had been planted on her knees in my chair, eating up everything that Samantha was saying. The more Samantha spilled her guts to us about her unhealthy sense of envy for me; the more Raye started acting a fool. Jumping up and down in the chair as if she were in the middle of viewing fight night in a bar.

I glanced at her in the chair, annoyed. "If you don't sit your simple ass-down," I thought as she continued to break my concentration. I wanted to focus on what Samantha was saying, but it was hard to with my best friend jumping up in down in the chair like she was a five-year-old at Christmas, anxious to open her gifts. Anticipating that one gift that outweighed all the others. That day I saw first-hand how it was that a woman could be around you acting as a friend while holding the spirit of a frenemy. Samantha had never shown that side to me and had Kevin not informed me of what she did; I would have never seen it coming. Samantha raged on and on, spilling her guts openly in front of me and two other women she did not know personally. It became clear to me that Samantha was having a breakdown. I didn't know what to say, and I tried giving responses to calm her down and convey to her that we weren't judging her for her truths. But even a blind man could see that everyone in the room, including me, judged her. Although it was an uncomfortable situation, I realized Samantha must have been battling way more than what we all could see prior to that day.

The irony is that years later my outburst at my brother's house party allowed me to understand Samantha a lot more once I had my own encounter with what I feel was an emotional breakdown. As women and mothers, we often carry so much with us every day. Never having those around us consider the mental burdens and restraint that we become overwhelmed with. Samantha was a full-time honors student, a working woman, a single mother of two girls, and struggling with her religious identity based on feeling trapped in a religious culture that she was born into and did not agree with. After assessing my breakdown at my brother's party, I realized life was a full-circle situation. That day I stood in Samantha's shoes emotionally, and I realized how easy it is to crack under pressure when all you have ever done is prevail while in go mode, alone, striving, and struggling mentally to keep it all balanced.

Later I found myself thanking God for that moment of reflection because it helped me to see that most times, the things people do in regard to us that feels so hurtful and premeditated often are not as personal as we would like to believe. Samantha didn't want to hurt me; she did because she needed to feel what it was; she believed she was lacking. She looked at me and admired me just as I looked at her and admired her. But within doing so, she was also analyzing parts of her being that she had been ignoring for so long. The elements of her that felt inadequate, alone, not good enough, and the list goes on. So she made herself believe that hurting me would make her feel less inefficient. Never recognizing that I had my own feelings and issues that involved the emotional rifts that inadequacy creates because I too am human and a woman. What I thought about in that moment is how different life would be if we all learned to do what Samantha did and voice those feelings out loud amongst one another. What would we find? I believe that we would find that as easy and normal as it is for us to pass judgments on statements like those, we all have or do feel similar feelings at times. That day when Samantha left, the conversation amongst Raye and me consisted of how shocked we all were.

Many things that I had overlooked about her started to make sense. Leaving me to realize that although she had made her feelings about me known, they were more so about herself. Her lack of confidence and inability to recognize her beauty and worth. Hating me for the beauty, she felt I had. Unable to see that just as much as she admired me, I was admiring her, trying to learn from her so I could be great in the same ways I felt she already was. We all are familiar with the concept of hate, but we never stop to consider that most times, our haters are a lot closer in proximity to love and admiration than what we would like to believe.

It's interesting to see the places we are willing to go when we allow ourselves to become clouded by the good, we see in others. It's also interesting how it is often so easy for us to see the beauty in our counterparts, yet we look in the mirror daily and fail to take the time to really see the beauty that lies in-depth within our own beings. It makes you wonder why it is that most of us are programmed to operate in such a way? While it also makes you realize how essential self-love is in order to maintain the balance, we all wake up searching for daily. That day we all made a big deal out of what had happened based on Samantha's ill means, but later I realized it was only a big deal because she said it. At the same time, being in the room full of three other humans who were not exempt or as honest in regard to their feelings of inadequacy. If only I knew then at that moment what I know now, I see how that situation could have played out differently. I could have aided her instead of allowing her to walk away feeling broken, embarrassed, and human because we all have a piece of Samantha in us, no matter how much we would like to believe otherwise. The Samantha component of our being is what makes us all human!

I started seeing how fickle and insecure people could be and how they often took it out on the wrong people. I thought so highly of Samantha, and the saddest part about her revelation was the realism behind how poorly she felt about herself. This event made me realize that you never know what silent battles the people around you are fighting. After that event, I started treading lightly with acquaintances, often afraid of giving new women the chance to form a friendship with me, afraid I'd run into another Samantha. When Raye told me she was starting to form a relationship with Della, Samantha came to mind for numerous reasons, but I kept my opinions.

Later I would find out that Della's attempts to find out what I had going on was cultivated after Jeff started having a secret relationship with one of her friends. It explained her constant desire to question Raye about me. One day the phone rang, and Raye complained to me about Della. Telling me, she was on the verge of cursing her out. "I had to tell her girl stop asking me questions about my friend, I don't know what she's doing, and I don't know why you keep asking me about her business" Raye concluded. Although I thought it was odd that Della was so concerned about me, I brushed it off, getting off the phone and glancing up at Jeff as he stared in my face like he had something he wanted to say. "Obviously, Della keeps asking about you because she keeps telling her" he said, walking out of the room.

He wanted to plant a seed in my head about my friend as he did about everyone. I ignored him because he was the last person in the world; I wanted advice from about loyalty. He needed to comment the way he did because he was afraid Della would disclose things, she knew about him to Raye. He hopped in the shower and forgot to take his phone, and just like that, karma showed up biting him in the ass. I heard his phone go off again as I tried to fight the urge to pick it up. I was holding out for as long as I could finally, telling myself that I did not want to be that girl. When your man has been known to be a liar and a cheater, you can't help but be that girl.

So, I picked it up, recognizing the girl texting him right away. The same girl had come to my job when I worked at Steve madden being messy. I felt instantly that his ill feelings toward Raye were simply his way of trying to divert my attention while he texted the very person that was my reason for leaving my job. My mom and my brother had practically been living at my new apartment. Both of them coming at the beginning of the week and never going home. I liked having them there, and my kids did too, but Jeff had always had a problem with it. My guess was he hated my family being there because he couldn't sneak around like he was used to, knowing there were extra eyes on him.

My mom had left for work that day, and my brother stayed behind. Jeff got out of the shower and started getting dressed to go out when I confronted him about all the stuff I had seen on his phone. He pushed me, and I fell to the floor, and before I could get up to say or do anything, my brother Melvin had him pinned up against the wall like he was a small child holding him by the neck. " Don't you ever put your hands on my sister," he said in his normal proper tone; Jeff was quiet and didn't do anything, and all of a sudden, all that mobster East Baltimore shit he talked flew out the window, and I realized he was not about half of the shit he claimed to be. He grabbed all of his things and left, and I didn't hear from him for two weeks. My cousin Christy and my mom had been hanging out a lot, and Christy made me aware that Jeff had been messing with a girl named Devin, who was a few years older than me. Devin was married and had slept with Jeff's best friend before him, so I didn't think the information I was receiving was accurate.

Little did I know him, and his best friend had been known for sharing women. Passing them around like appetizers at the dinner table. Until the drama followed shortly after, and I got all of the facts from the horse's mouth. Devin and her friends had been posting on the internet, trying to take indirect shots at me. Me being who I was, I wasn't having it. We had words publicly over the internet and went back and forth the entire day. After being disrespected, I made it clear to her that when I saw her, I would beat her ass, telling myself that would make me feel better even though I knew it would not.

Later that day, Devin reached out to me and apologized, expressing to me that she was not a messy person and he had lied to her telling her he was single. She claimed she had found out later that he was married. She told me that she was sorry and didn't mean to come at me the way she did. The irony is to this very day Devin has had many entanglements with other married men and men who are in relationships. Apparently, she was a lot messier than what she was willing to admit to me or herself. But that's a story for another day! I'm sure you've come to notice that there was a definite unhealthy pattern going on between Jeff and me. He had made a habit of going outside of our relationship to become involved with other women, and I had made it a habit of taking him back after each affair. I told myself that it was normal for young men to mess around. What I wasn't understanding was that Jeff's level of moral reasoning was low in part to how he had been raised and even lower based on how I continued to coddle him and his poor behavior patterns.

He didn't see any issues with his hypersexual nature, nor did he truly understand its origins. That same day Jeff was back at my door begging me to take him back, giving me one excuse after another about why he did the things he did. Blaming me for working too much, always focusing on my kids, and for not being sexually active with him as much as he preferred me to be. Like usual, I took him back, still not valuing myself, my boundaries, or the path I was repeating that I had seen as a child and vowed never to take part in. That night when Jeff returned, we rested in bed as we usually did. Watching tv until we fell asleep. I woke up in the middle of the night, and the bed surface beneath me was soaked in blood. I got up, rushing to the bathroom as giant fist-sized blood clots began to disperse from my vaginal area.

I screamed, waking up Jeff and my mom as they both ran into the bathroom, noticing the blood flow that would not stop. My mom called the ambulance, informing me that I was having a miscarriage. I didn't know how I could be having a miscarriage when I had no idea, I was pregnant. We got to the hospital, and I passed out from the excessive amount of blood loss. That night I was informed I had indeed been pregnant and suffered a miscarriage. The doctors did a procedure where they had to remove the excess fetal tissue from my wound and gave me a blood transfusion because I had lost too much blood and almost died. As usual, I left the hospital, putting the experience behind me telling myself that I needed to keep going.

Feeling resentment towards Jeff because I felt like the miscarriage was his fault due to all of the constant stress I was under. I would continue going through these types of events, sweeping them under the rug, telling myself that I was ok until the overflow of all the unaddressed issues would finally disperse their way back into my life, leaving me to face each event properly. Coming to the understanding that my experiences were often more daunting than what I had been willing to admit to myself during those days. Jeff started seeing the errors of his ways and often appeared to be ashamed of them in a way I hadn't seen him be before. He started working more hours, yet he still was not contributing in the way he needed to as a husband or a man. I started Noticing how the office manager of my apartment building would give me weird stares as she saw me come in often with shopping bags. She had gone from frequent conversation and compliments to no longer speaking or talking to me at all.

Although I thought it was odd, I didn't mind her much because I knew how fickle people could be. My lease was ending soon, and I had decided I wanted to move after seeing that one of the nearby apartment complexes had vacancies. I went to look at a bigger apartment and fell in love with the granite countertops and apartment details that my current apartment did not have. I got approved for the apartment and paid my deposit. Ecstatic that God had kept me on a path of elevation since my departure from my section eight voucher. That week I went to let the office manager know that I would not be renewing my lease, and I paid the last month's rent. She looked bothered in a way I could not identify with.

Yet I told myself that it was nothing, although my intuition was tugging at me, telling me otherwise. A few days later, I went to pick up the keys to my new apartment so me and my family could start moving in, and I was told I did not have an apartment. The office manager of the new apartment informed me that they would be giving me my deposit back, but they could not allow me to move in. I was confused and shocked and couldn't figure out what was happening. Explaining to them that I had already broken my old lease, packed all my things, and if they didn't allow me to move in, I would not have anywhere to go with my kids.

One of the women working in the leasing office walked me outside after seeing how distressed and confused I was. She informed me that my rental manager had contacted them the previous day, lying, saying that there had been some confusion and I should have never received a good reference.

She told them that I was a drug dealer and that I sold drugs out of my apartment. Also falsely informed them that I was late on my rent every month since I moved there. I could not believe that a woman her age and a mother would be evil enough to lie on another mother in that manner. I also didn't understand why she would say such heinous things about me when she barely knew me. Yet I couldn't help but feel as though my past was catching up with me. No, I hadn't done the things she had stated, but I had allowed Omar to sell drugs out of my apartment in Prospect, leaving me to wonder if this was my Karma for that poor choice coming back to haunt me. I worked more than I slept, so it shocked me to hear that she had told them the caliber of lies she had.

Yet I couldn't help but question what her motive for such an ugly act was against someone who she barely knew. That day I went to the office to confront her, but she was not there. Once again, God was showing up during my times of distress because had she been there, I don't think things would have gone well between her and me. The guy that worked in the office with her had known my family and me for years. I was so angry I was crying as I explained to him what I had been told. He informed me that he was aware of what she had done and had talked with her to understand why she would want to do something like that to a young woman with kids. I had never bothered anyone, and I stayed to myself, only leaving my home to go to and from work and to go out with my kids.

A few days after this, my client died, and I was now on the verge of being homeless, and I no longer had income coming in. It was as if the walls were caving in on me, and there was no stop mechanism available to me at that time. What I didn't know was that the days ahead would go from bad to worse for me. Leaving me to feel like I had reached the end of the road when God would do as he always had for me. Showing up heavy in my life after my period of been through to lead me to a breakthrough of blessings. I knew if I tried to find another place, she would give another false reference, so I felt like I was stuck, and for the first time in my life, I decided to give up. Usually, I would keep going finding a way, but I had been doing that my entire life, and I was tired at that moment.

I had been through so many things in my life, and I was tired of people looking at me and hating me for no reason. When I had first met the office manager, she seemed cool talking to me about things she had been through in her life. Telling me about the degrees she had, and we chopped it up the first week I moved in. Little did I know she was looking at me the entire time, hating me for no reason. Although I had gone through this with other women, I started to become tired of it. What was it about me that made other women feel threatened? Why did people look at me and believe that they could see a version of who I was that was never on display?

What was it about my tarnished little light that bothered other entities so much that they felt they wanted to be harmful and hindering towards me? This would be something I would question for a while until I finally recognized that the answer was not something I needed to be worried with.

I noticed the change in her attitude when I reported my new job and turned in my income documentation. I later started to see how she would give me looks when she would see me walking into my building. Yet I never would have imagined she would allow herself to do something so devious. Later I would find out that Jeffrey had allegedly slept with her oldest daughter. Doing so after this event.

Once again, his actions led me to recognize the hate he indeed carried for me. Out of all the women he could sleep with in the world, he decided to go sleep with the woman whose mother had tried to make his child's mother homeless. I don't know how I was able to endure so much back-to-back as I had. What I do know is all of my trials made me stronger than I could have ever imagined. What I didn't know is shortly after all of this, God would plant me in a space where I would receive abundance in a way I wouldn't believe. I don't know if more occurred while we were living there, and that's what prompted her to do what she did, but knowing Jeffery, there was most likely more to the story. I started to see how he took pleasure in deliberately linking himself to women who disliked me. Mainly Because he shared those same feelings in reference to me.

I shut down and became depressed lying-in bed every day, not trying to find a resolution. Once again, I felt stuck internally. Feeling alone and alone would be the dynamic I would always have because people made it their duty to misinterpret who I was. Watching me walking around with my head held high, making a way for myself. Never bothering a soul because my only concern was building my future, being the best mom I could be, and trying to repair my unrepairable marriage. Jeff had not been used to seeing me shut down, but he was aware that I was tired, and he knew why.

A week before it was time for us to move out, he came to me informing me that he had found us a two-bedroom apartment about two hours away. We moved into the apartment, and although it was not the kind of environment I was used to, I was thankful Jeff had finally stepped it up and provided for us. I felt a surge of happiness because, for once in our relationship, he had taken over and figured something out for us on his own. What I wouldn't anticipate is how the transfer of roles in the relationship would soon become a transfer of power. Leading Jeff to feel as though he was on a high horse. He used his newfound position as the provider to make me and my children suffer. He essentially reminded me why I had always chosen to be self-made and self-sufficient.

For the next couple of weeks, we drove the kids to school in Charlottesville. Jeff no longer had a car, and my car was the only form of transportation we had. We would all get up early, drop Jeff off at work, the kids off at school, and me and my youngest daughter would go to my mother's for the day. After a while, it became too much, so I got my kids enrolled in the Waynesboro school system to save gas and time. Jeff started going to Charlottesville daily on his own, and I would stay home with our toddler. I was now a stay-at-home mom, and at first, it didn't seem too bad. I didn't know anyone in the new area, but later my friend Janelle had decided to work things out with her husband, and she moved five minutes away from me with him, so I was happy to have someone nearby to which I could talk with.

During the day, while my kids were at school, I would spend time cleaning, cooking, and instructing my toddler as much as I could. She had finally started to walk and was getting into everything, so she kept me on my feet a lot. Although I was trying to make the best of my situation, I was eager to go back to work. Jeff was paying all the bills on his own, and although having a break from that responsibility was nice, I realized working was a significant part of my identity. I was not the type of woman who felt comfortable sitting around doing nothing and depending on a man, and that was due to the fact that I had never had a man I could rely on. Jeff could only afford to pay the rent and the electric bill with what little money he made, so my mom would buy our groceries and keep gas in my car, trying to help us out while we tried to get things figured out. I got a part-time private case in Glenmore making twenty-five dollars an hour, and after two weeks of working, I was offered a full-time position.

I asked Jeff to change his schedule so I could accept the offer, and he refused to do so, although he knew more money could help us get on our feet. I soon realized that he didn't want more money because he didn't want me to be the one making it. Although he had no skills, education, or opportunities to make a decent living due to his criminal record, he would rather we struggle than make way for me to get us back on track. That week I left the job and went back to being a full-time stay-at-home mom. Feeling frustrated because I had the resume and the credentials to get better jobs with better pay, but I knew he didn't want that. So, I let him continue to lead. After a while, he started cutting back on paying the electric bill in full, using the money to buy shoes and clothes.

Taking over the new place as if he were the only resident there. Constantly reminding me that it was his place because it was in his name. Hinting at it every chance he got, although he didn't own one piece of furniture, decoration, or morsel of food that was inside the humble abode he claimed as his. He would take me out on dates here and there, and although I hated all of the changes, I didn't complain. Soon we received a disconnect notice, and he reached out to his brother, who was currently incarcerated, to get us the money for the rent to pay the electricity bill with the cash he had. His brother sent him the money, and we were back on track. The holidays had rolled around, and there was no money for Christmas. My mom knew I wasn't working, and she made sure my kids had the big Christmas they were used to having. She bought all of their toys, clothes, and holiday goodies.

She knew I was not too fond of the new environment, so she would come up every weekend and sometimes during the week in the taxicab bringing groceries and spending time with my kids and me to help me feel some sense of normalcy. We would hop in my car and go to Kmart and the Doller tree, where she would give me money to go shopping. Although it was not what I was used to doing, I was grateful for all the help and comfort my mom provided me. I started secretly looking for jobs that I could work that would not clash with Jeff's schedule. I found out that the local warehouse was hiring spinners and offering good pay and benefits.

I applied for the job. Tax season rolled around, and since I had not worked all year, Jeff filed my kids on his taxes. He had promised his brother that he would pay him back the money he borrowed for the rent once he received the money. The day he received the money, he gave me half, and he took half. Naturally, I had planned on using my portion to get things for my kids that they needed that I had been unable to get due to my unemployed status. That day I went to the local Kmart and got clothes for my kids. Then I went to get them all shoes, food for their lunch for school, and personal items they all needed.

I was saving the bulk of my money to sit to the side. Jeff did not contribute to the groceries or anything for the kids, and the same day he left home and came back in a luxury Audi truck with not one dime left to his name. I was furious that he had gone and spent all of his money on an expensive truck, especially after hopping inside and seeing that the vehicle had more miles on it than a prostitute's vagina. I understood how it felt to want things, and I had a few wants of my own at that moment, but I knew we were not in a financial position to be focusing on desires when we had needs that were barely being met. I had just learned about Fashion Nova and had an entire Wishlist of clothes I had saved, telling myself that although I had some extra money, I would keep the money for needs and look past the wants. Yet there he was, sitting in the driveway with empty pockets because he wanted to flex so bad. He was acquiring the truck, hoping it would attract some new thot pockets in his direction.

Who would be mesmerized by the vehicle believing that his financial status was something it was not. In my experience, most times, the young man with a nice car was also the broke man, and the man with the average vehicle is often more financially sound than his counterparts who will flex on an empty tank. The rent was due, and he didn't have a dime to put towards it, so I paid the rent on my own using the tax money I had set aside to do so. A few weeks later, I was hired at the Invista warehouse, and once again, I was back on my grind. Soon after I went to work, Jeff started acting differently towards me, and he was not the person he had been previously since we had moved. He was making it clear that he was upset for selfish reasons.

I was starting to see that he hated seeing me do good and get us out of holes. Although he didn't have the ambition to do so, he didn't want me to be able to either. Two weeks later, I found out from a close friend of my mom's that worked with Jeff that he had been sleeping with a coworker at his new job. I know what you're thinking. Sleeping with someone again? When does this madness stop? Unfortunately, it would not stop until I realized that Jeff was hypersexual due to trauma, selfish, and toxic. But we will get to that later.

She called my mom, telling her that she had always had respect for me. Feeling I was too good for Jeff after seeing him disrespect me in her face. He was leaving the job with the coworker several times on the low. Once again, I was right back in the boat of infidelity; I thought I had finally escaped. I asked Jeff when he arrived home, and he looked me in my face lying like he always did. I was starting to feel like he could only be happy when I was dependent on him and struggling, and that was not a life for my kids or me. So, I started cultivating a plan to leave him.

Every day he would come home and sit outside in his truck that he valued over all things but could barely pay the note on. He was talking on his phone to another woman and thinking that I didn't know. I finally received my first paycheck from my new job, and it was way better than I had hoped. I finally decided to treat myself to my Fashion Nova Wishlist. Telling myself I had earned it for all the hard work and sacrifices I was making trying to be responsible for my family. I then took out money to treat my kids to things, feeling happy that I was getting back on my feet financially and providing for my kids how I preferred to. That day Jeff got home, and I told him I would need his half of the rent to put with my half so I could pay the bills that were about to be due in a few days.

He went off telling me he wasn't paying shit, yelling to the top of his lungs for no reason. He was gaslighting me in hopes of fleeing from his half of the responsibilities. I tried to walk away, telling myself it wasn't worth it because soon I would be leaving his ass in the dust anyway. I walked into my room quietly, trying to avoid any further arguments, when he followed me in the room, pulling out all of my new fashion nova clothes and taking the grease from the deep fryer covering my clothes to the point where they were all saturated in cooking oil. I ran towards him, yelling, trying to see if I could salvage any of my things, but they were all ruined. I was so upset about him ruining my Fashion Nova items because I had waited so long to be able to get the things from my Wishlist. Ironically enough, once I gained the strength to walk away, God would grant me the ability to be able to afford all the Fashion Nova I wanted! He pushed me onto the sofa and started choking me when my oldest daughter came into the living room, grabbing him off of me and throwing him to the ground. He jumped up from the floor, yelling and tossing things around in the house that I had just purchased, breaking up a lot of my new décor items.

My daughter yelled, informing him that she was calling the police, and she did. He stormed out of the house, leaving in his car that he barely had gas in. Soon after, the police arrived, questioning my kids, asking what had taken place, and giving me a temporary restraining order that would need to be extended on Monday morning. That day I went looking for my keys, and they were nowhere in sight. I realized he had taken them with him trying to keep me trapped in the house so I would be unable to leave. He knew I wanted to leave. Who wouldn't have? Given all the things I had been going through repetitively. Later that night, I checked his online banking and saw that he had purchased something at a store in Portsmouth, which was a long distance from where we lived. We had a joined account that I had placed money into.

Although he had never stolen from me, something urged me to remove my money from that account, and I did. That night I opened a new bank account online and transferred my money into the new account he didn't have access to. I had not heard from him since he left, but after moving the money, he texted me right away going off asking me why I removed my money from the account. I figured he had been trying to use my money for gas or cigarettes, and his card declined. That Monday, he returned home as if nothing had ever happened. I couldn't put him out because the apartment was in his name, but I knew I would not be staying much longer. Monday, after my kids had returned home from school, a social worker from child protective services showed up at my house, interviewing my kids about the incident.

My son had confided in his math teacher about what happened, and she had reported to child protective services. The social worker informed Jeff that if he put his hands on me again or made anyone in my home feel harmed or threatened, they would take further action against him, giving him a warning. During this time, I should have realized that things were, in fact, far worse than I thought. My son should have never had to confide in a teacher about what was going on at home because those things shouldn't have occurred. I had lost myself in my toxic relationship, and I was not only failing myself, but I was failing my kids as well. That day I had just gotten the strength to clean my home after Jeff had ruined all of my stuff, and I knew it was nothing but God who had urged me to pick myself up and get my house together because shortly after that's when the social worker arrived. The social worker came to visit two more times before closing the case.

Informing me that she could tell I was a good mom and offering me resources if I ever needed help for that sort of event ever again. Jeff was acting more normal after that, but I was ready to leave and no longer feeling invested in the toxic marriage relationship. I started sleeping in the room with my kids every night, and I would not allow Jeff to come near me. Telling myself all I needed was two or three more paychecks, and then I could leave and get my own place again. One day Jeff stayed out all night and didn't come home. Ignoring my calls when he knew he was my only babysitter for our toddler for me to be able to go to work. I knew he was deliberately trying to make me lose my job, so I packed up my car with my kids and all that I could take, and I decided to leave everything behind and leave him for good.

I stayed at my mom's house for two days. Although she knew I was tired of everything I had been going through, she told me that it did not make sense to leave everything I owned behind. I had worked so hard to get the things I had, but, at the moment, I didn't feel any of it was important. Janelle contacted me telling me that she thought I should not leave my things behind for Jeff's enjoyment. "You really want some woman sitting on your furniture? Enjoying all the shit you worked hard to get?" I had made an abrupt choice to leave; realizing she was right; I worked hard for my things and should not allow someone else to enjoy them.

The next day my paycheck was deposited in my account, and I rented a U-Haul and took all of my things, leaving behind my bedroom set, my living room set, and my tv telling myself that those things would be easy to replace. Jefferey was furious and shocked that I had actually gone through with leaving him. As if he had no clue as to why we had come to the place of no return after all the wrongs he had committed. That day I left him behind, telling myself that I had taken too many losses to continue to allow someone to deplete me in the way he had. I moved into my mom's two-bedroom apartment, and I left my job at Invista, assuming I was fired from not showing up for an entire week. The good thing about small towns is gossip spreads fast even when you're not in the mix, and word had gotten back to my job about the things I had been going through with my husband. They reached out to me, telling me they would love to have me come back, even offering me some time off if I needed it, but I declined. I was no stranger to starting over, and I knew I would find another job in due time, and it didn't seem reasonable to drive across the mountain every day to get to and from work.

CHAPTER 8

The Divorce

$\mathcal{S}$ ix months would go by, and I would not hear a word from Jeff. He never called to check on our child, nor would he answer when I would text him asking for him to get her pull-ups and wipes. He'd read the text and not respond. He felt angry with me for leaving him as if there was some clause in our vows that said I was obligated to stay with him despite his trifling unreliable behavior. I took the hint that he was not going to be present for our daughter like I had always known, and I tried to move forward with my life. I started hearing that allegedly Jeff was in the streets doing schemes and dabbling with counterfeit money, amongst other things. Suddenly, women were flocking around him like he was important, and they all made it their mission to keep me informed in some way or another that they had been interacting with him.

Although I tried to hide it, I was extremely depressed and hurt by the things people were coming to me telling me about his behavior. I had gotten a new job that paid me well and eventually worked my way up to get raises earning eight thousand dollars a month. It was a significant leap from where I had been the past few years, and I used my new income to get on my feet and build a better life for my kids and me. After living in my mom's apartment and having barely enough space, I started looking for my own place again. I found a five-bedroom home in Albemarle County , and I moved in right away. My mom's lease was about to be up, so she agreed she would come with me. Although I knew I had spent a significant amount of time away from Jeff, I knew having my mom with me would be the blockage I needed to keep from allowing him to come back.

My life began to change within the blink of an eye, and I started getting back on track again. I started my own cosmetics line and went back to school, planning to finish an educational journey I had started when I first met Jeff. When we first met, I was in school, intending to get a degree in psychology. I gave up on that goal when I became pregnant with my youngest daughter telling myself I would revisit that goal when the time was right. I flunked out due to all of the stress in my relationship later being placed on academic probation due to my poor performance. I got back in school and worked my way up from my probation status, becoming an honors student progressing steadily through my bachelors' program. I worked eighty-four hours a week, built a business on the side, and went to school full-time. Keeping myself busy, no longer worrying about Jeff or the things I was hearing.

Before I left him, I had dealt with Jeff cheating repeatedly, lying, humiliating me, disrespecting me, and the list of negative components go on and on. I told myself when I left that I would rebuild my life and not look back, but unfortunately, I would look back several times before getting the courage to move forward. Months went by, and I had not heard from Jeff regarding our daughter, and I told myself I would not let that bother me. He had been going around telling people that I was keeping his child from him. In reality, he had not reached out to me once since I left him. I started hearing more gossip about the things he was doing, and it was beginning to appear as though he was enjoying his new life as a single man. He was sleeping with different women and being free from any real-life responsibility.

I told myself that no matter how hurtful it was to see how Jeff had been conducting himself, I would not allow it to penetrate where I was emotionally. So, I held my head high and tuned out the gossip and petty drama attempts from the large quantity of women who didn't seem to mind sleeping with a married man. I focused on my schoolwork and became the kind of student I always knew I could be. My business started picking up, and I decided to pour more into my entrepreneurship goals. Utilizing my new responsibilities as a way to be able to avoid all of the negative sidebar conversations I knew that had been taking place about my personal life. Telling myself that while they all would be gossiping, I would be working. I was specifically working to become a better version of myself and build a better life for my kids and me.

I started traveling more with my brother and friends, going to different places I had always wanted to go but couldn't. I also started taking more frequent trips to Atlanta to visit my brother, using those trips to indulge in much needed me time away from a load of responsibilities that continuously seemed to keep growing. Spending the weekend with my brother was always a great way to help me loosen up, rejuvenate myself, and recenter my depleted body that never seemed to get the adequate amount of sleep needed to be able to function correctly. Occasionally I would visit John, often feeling ashamed of my keen ability only to want to communicate with him when Jeff was no longer in the picture. One weekend I took a last-minute trip to get away and have some time alone. That weekend when I came back from Atlanta, Jeff started randomly contacting me, blowing up my phone back-to-back.

He questioned me about my whereabouts while I was away. He was inquiring if I had seen John during my departure. I ignored his inquiries because I didn't feel I owed him any explanations about my life. When we were separated, and he had been sleeping around with multiple women. He had always had an awkward obsession with mentioning John during the course of our marriage but what didn't make sense to me was why he was concerned about him when we were not together. For weeks people had been coming to me telling me that he had been messing around with his ex-girlfriend, and although he constantly denied it, I knew it was true.

That Sunday, I went to the airport to fly back to Charlottesville and encountered one text after another where Jeff was disrespecting me, calling me bitches and hoes. He was overlooking the fact that he had been in the streets acting as if he was the mascot of the hoes. Accusing me of being with John and going as far as to say that he knew our daughter was not his child. Tormenting me via text saying that he knew she was John's daughter and not his. The irony of the situation was that while he sat texting me insults and lies, he was currently laid up with a girl I thought had respect for me. Finding out later, he had gone to her house and received oral sex from her multiple times over the course of that weekend. Me and her had mutual friends and had hung out many times before me, and Jeff became an item. I didn't understand how he could feel comfortable harassing me .

When he was the one doing all of the things, he accused me of. His narcissism would prove to be unmatched. I ignored the text telling myself that feeding into his disrespect was not worth my energy because I had done that enough. I called Raye in tears as I hung onto his comments about our daughter. Having her assure me that he was a dog, and he used my daughter to get a rise out of me because none of his other attempts worked. "His childish ass is just mad because he sees that you're out here doing good, and he's angry he can't get back in with you. He wishes he could be in that house with you living well, and he knows he can't."

"That's why he's doing all of this," Raye exclaimed. "When are you going to realize that he does this every time you have some form of growth. Girl, it's killing him to see you out here bossing up while he is still in the same spot you left him in." That day he went on and on texting me offensive messages. Telling me how I wasn't shit and wouldn't be shit, but that was a statement I was going to make him eat before it was all said and done. "Yes, you have all this shit your trying to do. You continue to live in that white neighborhood, thinking you're going to get somewhere, but you're not."

"It doesn't matter what you try to do. You are never going to be shit bitch" he texted. While currently sitting on the opposite end of the phone embodying the" not shit" lifestyle for himself. Every argument or disagreement we had was always the same. At some point in the conversation, he'd bring up where I lived, my income, and my attempts to try and follow my dreams—always wanting to instill self-doubt into my head by the end of the conversation. Feeling frustrated because he would no longer be profitable, recognizing that I had finally understood all of whom the fuck I was and had the potential to be. I was at this point allowing his insults and negative curses to go in one ear and out the other.

A week went by, and I hadn't heard any more from Jeff since his last textathon, and I was no longer allowing moments like that to pierce through and ruin my focus like I had done many times in the past. One morning I got up to go to work. I arrived there and worked for nearly two hours when a doctor from the hospital contacted me. The doctor informed me that Jeff had been stabbed. As usual, I left work right away, rushing to his aide to be there for him like he had always known me to do. When I arrived at the hospital, my phone started going off left and right. Every call or text was about Jeff's stabbing.

People had been calling me, giving me several different accounts of what had occurred and who they believed was responsible for the stabbing. My phone rang again, and it was Lanaye calling to inquire about what was going on. Like always, she had gotten the drop on the drama long before the evening news could. She had heard about the stabbing and was trying to get the facts about what had happened from me. Although he had given me small details, his untrustworthy status led me to believe the truth was something I could not be sure of. I explained to her that I had been told multiple stories but that Jeff was not talking or telling the police who had been at fault. Adopting to the Baltimore Street culture way of doing things determined not to be a snitch. "Girl, that is terrible," she said. Soaking it all in and telling me what others had told her. "They are all out here acting crazy over him, but you're the one the doctors called because you're the wife," she said, placing extra emphasis on the word wife. Little did she know that being the wife meant nothing to me because it was not a badge of honor. That day the doctors released him from the hospital under my care, and I let him come back home with me. He had apologized to me for the ugly things he had said about my daughter and me. He was expressing to me that he was finally starting to see the era of his ways after being stabbed. Telling me that he felt like the stabbing was his karma for all of the times he had stabbed me in my back and been unfaithful to me within our marriage.

If he was not good at anything else, he was good at talking some good shit! Telling me what I wanted to hear. And having me play the constant role of the fool who believed what he said. I believed him because it didn't make sense to me that someone could be stabbed and not see the error in their ways. Surely this would have to place things into perspective for him. But it would not because for that to take place, he would have to care about the poor choices he had been making, and he did not. Jeff stayed at my house acting as a present father for about two weeks, complaining and acting as if his stab wound was excruciating.

I never questioned his suffering due to me never getting a look at the damage from under the bandaging. After two weeks of me waiting on him and helping him while he pretended to be in agonizing pain, Jefferey was ready to go back to his old ways of running the streets. Exposing the tiny rupture where he had been sliced on accident when undressing the wound in a rush to meet up with the same friends he had been out with the night of the stabbing. Assuming that he was back locked in with me permanently ready to be abruptly placed back into the same committed relationship he had been in with me and consistently failed to commit to. He went to the bathroom in a rush to get the rest of his outfit together, leaving his phone behind when it rang. I answered that night, not shocked to hear another woman's voice on the other end. Who appeared to be surprised to hear my voice answering his phone.

That night I made him leave my house, determined that I would not get caught up in his web of lies and deceit again. I had made too much progress, and he had made too little. A few months passed, and after being made aware of Jeff's moves, I realized that my marriage had failed, and it was time to let go. I filed for divorce, assuming that Jeff would have no problem signing the papers and getting it all over and done with since I had paid for it, but I was wrong. For weeks Jeff gave me the run-around, telling me he would sign the documents and never did. He even went as far as lying to me, telling me he had been diagnosed with lung cancer, hoping that would deter me from wanting to be divorced, but it did not. I had found out from a reliable source that the girl who had called his phone when I answered was a girl named Tonya he had been sleeping with for a while.

Later the Tonya gossip was confirmed when she started stalking my social media. Sending me a friend request prior to me finding out. Realizing who she was afterward and blocked her after seeing how she tuned in multiple times a day to view my stories on social media. I didn't understand why he wanted to stay legally married when he did not want to be physically married based on how he was spreading himself thin, running around with different women. One day, I drove to Jeff's job to pick up the signed divorce papers after he assured me that he had signed them and was ready. When I arrived at his job, he got inside my car. Sitting in the passenger's seat talking to me for thirty minutes, trying to change my mind.

Telling me how sorry he was for all of the disrespect and "mistakes" he had made during the course of our marriage. I knew better than listening to or believing anything that came out of his mouth because it was usually nothing but blasphemy. So, I let him say what he needed to say, and then I took the envelope and drove home feeling like I could finally close that chapter of my life and move forward. I had never bothered to open the sealed envelope, and to my surprise, when I got home and explored the contents of the envelope, there were no divorce forms inside. He had set me up, and it was becoming clear to me that his motives were selfish. He did not want to be with me, but he did not want to clear the road and allow someone else the opportunity. He would promise to sign the divorce papers week after week and never keep his word.

He had started building a new relationship with Tonya. She had allegedly been aware that he was initially married and entered a sexual relationship with him while he and I were together. I knew if I waited on him to do the right thing, I would never have any form of resolve, so I did what I felt was necessary to get him to sign. One morning I woke up concocting a plan to end things for good. Texting Jeff telling him that I wanted to go to Waynesboro to shop and I needed him to drive me due to exhaustion. He took the bait arriving at my house right away as I knew he would. That day we rode to Waynesboro with him thinking it would be a typical shopping trip. When we started getting closer to Waynesboro, I gave him the directions to the divorce lawyer's office, informing him that I needed to make a quick stop.

When we arrived at the lawyer's office, Jeff was unaware due to the small home-like setup. We pulled onto the driveway arriving at the small house. I asked Jeff if he would accompany me inside, still keeping the details of where we were and why to myself. When we arrived inside, and he figured out where we were, his entire facial expression changed. He looked outraged, and I knew he was upset that he had been set up to do something he had been deliberately trying to avoid doing. Once he was face to face with the lawyer, I knew he would have no choice but to sign, and that day my plan worked. We drove back to Charlottesville in complete silence.

His face still held the same angry expression. From the shock of the way, I had gotten my results. Now Jefferey knew precisely how I had felt being railroaded when he had set me up.

That day when I arrived home, I cried and cried, feeling overwhelmed. It had finally hit me that this would be the end of the road for Jeff and me, and although it was needed, it was hard for me to come to terms with that because I knew he would take out his frustrations on my daughter. And I was right. After I made my move, trying to get my life on the right track, he started keeping his distance, and suddenly it was as if our child did not exist. At times I felt like it was my fault he was absent from my daughter's life, telling myself that maybe I should have just gone along with things as they were just so she would not have to suffer, but I knew that was not the right way to do things.

Jeff was a grown man, and if I had to subject myself to an unhealthy relationship for my daughter to have him in her life, she would have to be okay with just having me because I knew me or her didn't deserve to be subjected to his toxic behavior.

I had learned from my past, and I was making better choices, but those better choices seemed to be equivalent in the hurt department as the poor choices I had made in the past. I would never have imagined that leaving would be as emotionally adverse as staying had been. That was primarily due to my own fear because I knew how hurt and stagnant the toxicity from being with Jeff had left me, but the fear of moving forward and progressing was even scarier. What stung, even more was having my child long for a relationship with a father I knew didn't want to be present unless it was a two-for-one deal, and I was no longer allowing myself to be accessible to him in that way. So, I moved along, putting my focus on the things I needed to do for myself, ignoring all Jeff-related information that would be dispersed to me.

Reminding myself that if he did it while he was with me, it should come as to no surprise that he was doing certain things after my departure. My daughter had Christmas, birthdays, and significant mild stones occur where Jeff was not present, and although I didn't expect that he would be present, it still hurt. The realization was starting to set in that I had chosen a pattern of selecting men who were not equally yoked with me in many areas. I realized I had made a habit of expecting things from partners who arrived at the table in an inadequate form. Never able to give my children or me the things we deserved and desired because these were not things they ever intended to provide. I Recognized that the men I had been in previous relationships with had come from a culture of life where women were expected to give love in its entirety and be okay with never having it adequately reciprocated. The culture of the ride or die chick.

She was expected to go to the ends of the earth for her man while he lied, cheated, and publicly humiliated her. Telling their partners subliminally that "this was how it went." I had told myself that for many years realizing that things didn't have to go that way, but I was allowing it to because I clearly didn't recognize my own worth. Growing up in environments where women subjected themselves to disrespect from men regularly had skewed my perception of who I was, what I was worth, and what I could have. It felt as though my wings had been clipped upon my arrival into the world. Now people were standing around gloating at my inability to fly, this led me to understand that everyone around me often recognized the spirit I had in me. But I had made a habit of being blind to my own true nature. I was growing into an adult woman who still had the exact internal mechanisms from her childhood clinging to her thoughts and emotions.

The imprint of trauma and abuse can cause young women to grow into adults who have no real sense of who they are and what they can do. And for an extensive period, I had been functioning in that way. Reaching a point in my life where I was able to see that many entities in my life had benefited from the broken version of who I was. The people who took pleasure in seeing me down, struggling, hurt, and undervalued. It was one thing to take control of your life back, but it was something significant to do so in a way where you are entirely unapologetic, and that was the road I had chosen. The road that was less traveled and hard to stay on. Simply because it required a level of authenticity and obligation that many don't want to give, I had settled for fake friends, hatred, abuse, and disrespect from so many people in my life.

So, it didn't surprise me that I would leave many bothered by choosing growth. After all, misery loves company, and I had been in the company of the wrong people majority of my life. Feeling the hate people carried for me when their phone calls filled with dialect about my ex-husband was no longer bothersome for me. Noticing the many that watched and talked about my every move as if I had been doing something hurtful. When I hadn't done anything wrong. Choosing to stay to myself and focus on being the woman I had always known God had intended me to be. I was spending my days working hard, building my education, and raising my kids independently.

Often asking myself what it was that I had done wrong that so many people had me on their radar. But the answer was simplistic. What I had done was grow. Grown in a way that no one had anticipated, and no one wanted that for me because the fragmented version of my life was more entertaining to certain people I had allowed in my space. You see, we use the terms friends and family so loosely when building relationships. That we often forget to assess our friends and family in depth . Assuming that the faces they publicly show us are the only ones that exist, I would soon learn that growth would show me numerous hidden faces amongst the people I had referred to as friends and family.

Although I had shared so many of my hardships with the people around me, none of them wanted to see me prevail. As a woman, I could never take pleasure in another woman's pain, and I realized that people weren't around during my hard times because they supported me, but they were there because they celebrated my mishaps. So, I made the necessary cuts after evaluating my circle and continued to progress, telling myself that alone was a space I knew all too well. And it was not a place of discomfort for me because I had not had much help through the things I had experienced. I placed the bulk of my trust during challenging times in my life in God and my own endurance. So alone was where I would sit until the right people came along that valued me in my entirety. I decided to remove myself from all of the under-cover haters that were not as undercover as they thought they were.

I removed myself from the man obsessed with my qualities as a woman and hated me for those same qualities. Because I could not be controlled or fooled in the ways, he had desired. And lastly, distancing myself from family members who barely knew me as a person and took pleasure gossiping about my hardships when they were going through worse. The only difference was that I was not hiding the content in my life, so it led people to believe they could use my shortcomings against me. Waking up realizing one day they had me pegged inaccurately, and I was indeed growing into a woman that no one saw coming. That woman would ruffle a lot of feathers unintentionally just by continuously rising above the bullshit life would throw at her repetitively. Showing a level of growth, faith, and resilience that many hated to see.

Ending relationships with people I had known for years based on their inability to respect the person I was. People were doing things out of spite to try and get a rise out of me and feeling bothered when they could no longer bother me with their petty attempts to rattle my cage. A real friend who no longer receives a phone call or a text from you will always make an inquiry about what's going on. No investigations were being made during my abrupt exit from these relationships because I was walking away from people who didn't really like or care for me to begin with. People who knew I was aware of the shady things they were saying and doing behind my back. I felt the peace that was taking over once I took the initiative to end the toxic insincere relationships, I had been letting weigh me down.

CHAPTER 9

Thou Shall Snatch Wigs!

*D*ays turned into months, months turned into weeks, and finally, I had reached an entire year of being a divorced woman who had engaged in zero contact with her ex, and it felt good. I had not gone on a date since my ex-husband, and I decided it was time to try and give it a shot. I had taken an interest in a new guy, which had not been something I had experienced in a long time. We had known one another since high school, and we clicked instantly. Like me, he had also been married before and had experienced the disappointment of a failed marriage. We talked for weeks, and he seemed like a very easy-going and respectful person. He never pressured me for anything. He conversed with me frequently and respected the boundaries that he knew existed without me having to disclose them to him.

I researched gardening and decided to plant a garden in my backyard, getting him to agree to help me with the project. One afternoon I went to Lowes to pick up the supplies and headed back home to work on my garden. I was working in the backyard, struggling to shovel, when my kids alerted me that someone was at the front door. To my surprise, it was none other than the devil himself, Jeffery. Standing in the doorway dressed in brand new everything looking as if he were fishing for some form of attention he didn't deserve. He had popped up to see our daughter, and although everything in my spirit wanted to turn him away from the door, I knew she would be happy to see him, so I allowed him in. Usually, I would sit and monitor his visits, but I had no desire to be in his presence, so I left him in the living room with her, and I went back out to my backyard to continue to dig.

A few minutes after his arrival, he made his way to the back yard where I was pretending not to feel his being standing behind me. "What are you doing? "He asked as he watched me struggle with the shovel. "What does it look like," I said, not turning around acting as if I was not interested in any conversation with him. "It looks like you're fucking up the yard," he said, laughing, trying to be playful, hoping to get something in return, but I gave him nothing. "What are you trying to do? Start a garden?" He acted as if the container of plant food and seed packages were not clear indicators." Yes," I said, still giving him no conversation in return. "Aren't you supposed to be here to see your daughter?" I said. While he stood behind me, ignoring his phone as Tonya called him back-to-back, he ignored her calls. Finally, picking up the phone, trying to seem inconspicuous, leaving out the details about where he was. He hung up the phone and grabbed the second shovel and started helping me. Under normal circumstances, I would have objected, but the way I had been struggling with the digging before his arrival, I figured what the heck.

If I can let him drag me through the dirt during our marriage, the least I could do was let him dig up some dirt and help me with my garden prep. Before you knew it, I was sitting on the patio furniture, relaxing like I had nothing to do while I watched him do all the work. I wondered how he would explain it to his girlfriend when he arrived back at his house covered in debris. I secretly got a kick out of his desperation. Jeff was not one to play about his shoes and clothes, and getting them soiled, especially when they were new, was not like him. But it's something about being in the company of an untouched woman that will make a man forget about his prior preferences and obligations. So, I watched as he dug and planted seed after seed, never lifting a finger to help him.

We started conversating and catching up. I figured it wouldn't hurt me to talk now that he was doing all the hard work, and I was sitting doing absolutely nothing as I should have. He started talking to me, asking me personal questions he assumed he already knew the answer to. Only this time, I had some tea for that ass, tea he did not see coming. Tea that was extremely hot and unexpected. He started inquiring if I was dating anyone. Being fake, asking a question that usually would have been no, but it was a little more loaded than he anticipated this time." I'm not dating anyone, yet" I said with a petty smile on my face.

Gloating as I watched his entire disposition become bothered. "Yet what do you mean yet?" "Well, I'm not dating anyone, but I am talking to someone." Talking to someone? He asked with a puzzled look on his face. "To who?" He tried to figure out how it could be possible.

As if he has somehow chalked me up to be the virgin Mary herself since I departed from our relationship. " Probably one of these bum ass nobodies from here," he said. As I waited for the proper moment to make him completely miserable. "He's no bum;" I said, still sitting happily in the pool of anticipation as he kept cultivating my garden and digging for details about the mystery guy; he was shocked to find out existed. "He has a good job, is a professional boxing teacher on the side, and a perfect gentleman," I said, glowing as my Capricorn pettiness seeped through my pores. "So, you're sleeping with him;" he said, shaking his head.

Because in his world, a woman only thought highly of a man if they were being intimate. "Nope, I said "I Haven't even been around him or had any contact outside of phone and Instagram conversation. But I plan to go on a date with him." I watched as he began to unravel. I was getting a kick out of the frustration and lack of focus he now had after getting a hold of this new information I was purposely divulging to him out of spite. After planting the last of the seeds, he put the shovel down and made his way to the patio table to take a seat. He was unraveling at the seams, immediately informing me how he had been messing around with Tonya and lying to me about it as if I didn't know that before our conversation.

He lit the marijuana he had in his pocket while I continued to rattle his cage effortlessly. He started disclosing to me how he had cheated repeatedly because he was struggling with seeing me in positions to build our family when he felt like as the man that was his job. I listened to him, ignoring his words because his actions were all I could replay in my mind. I expressed to him that I was always the leader, not because I wanted to be but because I had to be. I also knew that everything he was saying was a load of bullshit as per usual. He always had the ability to step up and take the lead. He never did because he was lazy and weak. Unwilling to do anything that required dedication or new skill sets.

He always took the easy way out because it required no sacrifice or fundamental footwork. He watched his partner act as the man and the woman in the relationship while he acted as a leech. Draining all that he could and speaking to his shortcomings anytime he thought it would change my mind once I walked away. The next thing I knew, it was like he was suffering from word vomit, excreting age-old secrets and lies coming clean to me about things he had lied about for years. Telling me how he thought about me all the time, even when he was with Tonya as if that was something I didn't know. I listened to him spill his guts, not taking a word of it seriously. Because I knew if Jefferey was breathing, he was lying, and that was not something I wanted to gamble with ever again. I was still holding onto feelings of love for him and fighting off those urges daily because I knew he had been a horrible untrustworthy partner. But like any unhealthy pathology or desire it is always easier to remain clean and uninterested when you are not around those desires. Our connection could easily be severed when we were distant. But as soon as that distance was voided, we would always find ourselves gravitating back to the very space we knew we needed to stray away from.

So, I did what any self-respected divorcee would do in this situation, and I pretended to listen and believe—allowing him to remind me of how his tongue game was still undefeated. He went on and on with his usual genre of lies and broken promises. Shortly after, I would find myself lying in bed receiving grade A oral sex and lies. Allowing him to use his tongue game to satisfy me in a different way. I know what you're thinking… Girl but you were just giving him the cold shoulder… and doing so good… and now…. your… letting him….I know, but in my defense, I was initially only trying to release some much-needed sexual frustration I had been building up due to my elongated relationship with celibacy. Making him explode within seconds and feeling proud of myself for reminding him of what he was missing as I prepared myself to throw him out right after.

I listened to him as he allowed the grip of my untouched vagina to skew his thought process. As he lay in bed telling me how he wanted his family back. The family you completely shitted on, I thought to myself. I was ready to give him a taste of his own medicine the next day when I ignored every call or text he sent. While he returned to Tonya telling her the same caliber of lies, he had told me when he was cheating on me with her. It was petty and tactful, and at the moment, I didn't see anything wrong with objectifying him in the same way he had done to so many women, including myself. But revenge is a poor sport, and I would learn that karma would pay me a visit for my poor choice soon enough.

Sure enough I would find myself planted back in the very puddle of mud I had escaped after allowing myself to become engulfed in the same toxic pool of bullshit. Looking back on these days, I wish I could have approached the old me and shaken some sense into my fried skull. Sure, Tonya was wrong for sleeping with my husband but was I any better than her for sleeping with him deliberately trying to show her my capabilities? I wanted revenge, but why? Tonya was not the first or the last to engage with Jeff, so what was it about her that annoyed me? It was simple; I was annoyed because she thought she would be different. Constantly trying to portray her status in his life as something it was not and stalking my social media accounts.

Asking questions about me to people and talking about me amongst others when she had never laid eyes on me, let alone had a conversation with me. She had become determined like so many others to be in the know about me. Silently making me her competition as if Jefferey was some sort of consolation prize. His mother had initially disliked Tonya as well. She constantly threw me in her face when she got irritated. "You hate his daughter's mother because you know you could never compare to her," she would say in a rage whenever she got tired of seeing Tonya and Jeff become serious. Jeff had informed me that his mother consistently tried to hurt Tonya's feelings by exploiting her feelings of inadequacy concerning me. This was something she often tried to do to me as well concerning the women he had cheated on me with. But it never worked because I knew none of those women compared to the woman I was. Specifically based on the many components that altered their ability to be good women.

and mothers in general. You can't compete where you don't compare and they didn't compare but, neither did Jefferey but I was missing out on that key fact altogether. Only to have Roberta turn around and switch teams once she realized Tonya being a fool for Jeff also made her a fool for Jeff's mother. They got her to do, be, and give anything they desired. While they both secretly held onto the fact that they knew Jeff did not have genuine intentions with her. Tonya often tried to influence Jeff and his dynamic with me. Her biggest fear was losing him to me because she knew that he was longing to be back with me despite his behavior and lies. Although my reasons for wanting revenge made sense from an emotional standpoint, it was not my style as a woman. And the universe had other plans for my scheming ass because my plan to leave him in the dust afterward would not be what occurred. Due to my feelings popping back up abruptly, allowing me to recognize that I still loved and wanted to be with Jeff despite all of the horrible things he had put me through.

Clearly, I had drunk a considerable glass of hypocrisy and was unaware of it. Why didn't I see the power I was giving this man? Diving into a fling with him trying to prove who he was to someone who deep down inside knew who he was. Because she had become enthralled with him under these same circumstances. Hadn't I, too, at one point thought that things with me would be different? Hadn't I been warned and told about his behavior? Who was I to judge Tonya when I, too, had been her numerous times with this man?

The only difference was I had been playing the role of stupid as his wife and child's mother. And she had been playing the role of stupid under the role of his long-term certified side piece. Who desperately wanted to be the main thing. Never caring if he did her wrong because she would rather be played by him while with him than not be with him at all. Clearly, someone should have come along and smacked the shit out of both of us. But that is an acknowledgment for another day. The next day we woke up late, sleeping our way through breakfast and waking at lunchtime.

My youngest daughter was happy to see her father there, assuming he would be there to stay, and I made it clear to her that he would be going home to his mother's house sooner than later. "You hungry," he asked as if he had ever inquired that and heard a no. "Why don't we go get some wings" he said, baiting me in, knowing I would never turn down free wings. We were headed out the door to go pick up the wings when our daughter started begging to ride with us. I agreed, telling her she could come. Expecting the trip to pick up the wings to be short. We got a short distance away from my house when we pulled up to a red light.

I noticed Tonya's car going past us as if she were headed in the direction of my house. I glanced over at Jeff, trying to see if he was going to pretend not to notice what I had. "Is she going to my house I asked," although I knew the answer? "No," he said as I looked at him, trying to understand how she knew where I lived. "For your sake and hers, she better not be," I said as anxiety began building up on the inside. We continued making our way towards the wing restaurant when we noticed her riding on the opposite side of the road along with Jeff's mother on the passenger side. I hadn't noticed her the first time I spotted the car, but it now made sense as to how she knew where I lived. I began to feel furious trying to figure out why Roberta, my daughter's grandmother, would bring someone to my home and disrespect me in that way. Suddenly, the practical, sensible version of Nina went out the window, and I started preparing myself as I watched Tonya's car follow us as we pulled into the parking lot of the wing restaurant.

Jeff stopped the car, letting down the window looking as if he did not care about being caught up. "What are you doing?" Tonya asked with a level of sternness in her voice that I found hilarious. "I'm going to ask you again, what are you doing?" It was ridiculous that a woman would cheat with a married man and then play oblivious when it was her turn to get cheated on. I guess her mother never told her that if they cheat with you, they will cheat on you.

She looked at Jeff, acting as if she was utterly shocked by his actions. "Getting food," Jeff replied as he exited the car and entered the restaurant as if he didn't have a care or concern for her and her questions. She sat in the front seat, going off loudly as if she wanted me to hear, not realizing she had no clue what type of woman she had been playing with. Making subliminal comments as if she thought I was not going to speak up. While his mother sat in the passenger's seat, eager for an explosion of drama to erupt. As she tried to kill two birds with one stone, silently praying that the event would leave us both angry enough to finally leave Jeff alone so we could move out of the way for her selfish desires to control her son in the ways that were easier if there was no permanent partner standing in her way. Tonya kept talking her shit, unaware that the hulk was on standby, ready to explode out of me as I heard her talking shit that I could look at her and tell she was not about.

"What was that?" I asked after hearing her make another slick comment. "Nobody was talking to you," she said. "But I'm talking to you," I replied. She went on and on, running her mouth, gloating about how she had been sleeping with him while we were married. I started talking my shit in response to her petty digs. Expressing to her that no matter what he said or did, nothing would ever change the fact that I would always be the "baddest chick" in his life. Reminding her that I could take him from her anytime I wanted.

That comment infuriated her because she knew every word that rolled off my tongue was all facts, and that was a hard pill for a woman to swallow that had been waiting patiently on the sidelines. What I should have understood at that moment or sooner is that the stature of the woman I was didn't matter to him. So, I should not have used it to over exemplify where I stood in his life as opposed to other women. Why talk about how significantly important I was to him when he lacked the ability and desire to notice that for himself. There I stood, allowing myself to go back and forth with other women about a man I knew didn't have the ability to care about anyone outside of himself. I was standing there recognizing Tonya's stupidity while deliberately overlooking my own! Feeling as though it was understandable for me to hold this position due to our child, the marital aspect that was now voided, and my awareness of Jeff's internal hardships.

" Bitch I will fuck your ass up," she said to me, not realizing she had given me the reason I had been waiting for the entire conversation. As I exited the car abruptly, begging her to try it. Reaching my arm through the driver's seat window pulling the wig from her head, exposing her hair. I slammed the wig in her face aggressively in poor taste trying to get her to exit the car and "fuck me up," but she did nothing. I looked at his mother as she watched everything unfold. Shaking her head as if she wanted to come out and say, "it's a damn shame you let that girl pull your whole wig off and throw it in your face, and you didn't do anything."

As I stood there ready to pounce after hearing her disrespect me repetitively. Telling myself, she deserved my aggressive response after having the Gaul to disrespect me. There I stood, acting violent and stupid, trying to signify my position with a man that didn't even value me. Only able to see what I brought to the table internally and externally when it was convenient. Under normal circumstances, I would have handled myself differently, but I hated coming across women like Tonya. I didn't understand how she had the audacity to have so much anger and hatred towards me when she didn't know me, and she had been sleeping with my husband and making it hard for my family.

She was confused as to who was in the wrong. Jeff ran outside, grabbing me, trying to get me to get back in the car as he heard us go back and forth. He disclosed to Tonya how she had violated pulling her stunt when our daughter was in the car. She calmed down, instantly apologizing, telling us that she did not realize our child was in the car. I didn't care about her apology, especially after realizing she had her daughter in the car as well. After seeing how scared her child was, I felt terrible for pulling off her wig and being aggressive, wishing I would have controlled my anger. She approached the car, asking Jeff to give her the copy of the key he had. He handed her the key, driving away as if he was unaffected.

He knew in the back of his mind that he could go be with Tonya anytime he wanted to despite what had just occurred. Apologizing to me for the role his mother had played in the situation. "You didn't have to do all that," he said to me, shaking his head. "Do all of what?"

I asked. "You know what I'm talking about, Nina. You didn't have to do her like that," he said again, looking like he felt bad for her for the embarrassment I had caused her. "Well, she learned a lesson today. Don't tell me you're going to fuck me up unless you really plan on fucking me up…period." I said in a petty tone, trying to ignore the fact that I knew he was right.

But who was he to tell me about my conduct when he had been worse for years. All the lies, the physical abuse, and disrespect. After all, the event was only happening due to him being him, trying to be in two places at once. Lying to two women about their significance. When in reality, no one was significant to him, not even his own child. It was just like a libra to be indecisive, and Jeff would prove that he was the king of being unsure.

My conduct had been horrible, and I knew there was a better way I could have responded. But hurt people hurt people, and after all I had been through with her intruding in my marriage, her wig being snatched seemed fair. I knew she wasn't to blame for my marital issues before the divorce, but it felt good to blow off steam. We arrived at my house prepared to eat our wings and salvage what was left of the day when I heard the doorbell ring. I opened the door, annoyed to find Tonya on the other side of the door. I prepared to give her the ass whipping she had dodged previously. Had she truly returned for an episode of wig-tossed part two?

Or was she returning to apologize? "I'm not here to start any trouble; she said, looking crazy as hell. While still trying to go through with this weird-ass Barbra to Shirley moment. "I wanted to come to talk to you and get your side of the story because I realize he's been lying." I looked at her trying to understand her way of doing things as I looked in the car, noticing she had her four-year-old daughter with her again. This time leaving her in the car with some girl while she pretended to have a woman-to-woman moment with the very woman she didn't care about hurting five seconds ago. But now, since karma had paid her and her wig a visit, she wanted to talk.

I invited her in, telling myself that if she got out of line, I was going to drag her from the kitchen to the living room and send her on her way. Jeff looked shocked when he watched me renter the kitchen with Tonya following me closely behind. She sat at the table, making me aware that she had been sleeping with him for two years. Telling me that she knew about me, and he had told her awful things about me. He talks about you terribly, she said, placing emphasis on it like she wanted it to penetrate its way into my emotions, but it did not. "Girl show me, someone he doesn't talk about," I said, appearing unscathed by the remark. "He talks about you too, telling me that he met you one night in Prospect when you and your friends were riding around acting like some thirsty hoes looking for men," I said.

I waited for Jeff to interrupt, but he never did. "He also told me that he never took you on a date until about a month ago and that before that, it was just sex." She looked at me, confirming everything he had told me, leaving me to wonder if maybe her elevator didn't climb all the way to the top. As she sat down, trying to continue with the side chick intervention she had orchestrated in her head. She started informing me of the pillow talk sessions they had been having, telling me that she knew it was too good to be true. I looked at her trying to understand how it was she was so comfortable with divulging her simple way of thinking. Of course, it was too good to be true dummy look at how you got him, I thought silently to myself as I let her continue. She went on and on, saying he told me this, and he told me that.

My mom arrived home from work, walking in on the tail end of the event and soaking it up like it was an episode of Jerry Springer.

Entering the kitchen, standing in the doorway of the fridge pretending to look for food as she kept her ear to the entire conversation. Exchanging looks with Jeff and me insinuating that something was off about Tonya. Overlooking the fact that clearly all of us were half damn crazy! I watched as Tonya kept her eyes on Jeff, looking as if she wanted to murder him in the middle of my kitchen. I explained to her that he only talked about me so viciously because he was mad; I left him and didn't look back. I explained to her that Jeff telling her all those things was simply him being him. Passing the time with whoever he could when he could.

After realizing he had been lying to her, I thought it would end there, but it didn't. I apologized to her for pulling off her wig, expressing to her that at that moment, she had made me gravitate to a place I didn't want to be. She accepted my apology articulating to me that she had been through things like that many times in her past with her children's father and other women. Making the conversation about her children's father. This led me to recognize that she was not over him or the experiences she had been through because of that relationship. She told me how he had gone and started another family and she went into details about their dynamic, which had nothing to do with me. But had everything to do with her conduct as a woman.

At that moment, I recognized that what she was making herself believe she felt for Jeff was not real. She was sitting in a desperate place in her life, feeling like she wanted to have what her child's father was having with another woman. Making it clear to me why she wanted a child with Jeff so badly, although she was aware that he was not present in his daughter's life. She saw Jeff's inability to completely let me go, and she equated it with him being my ex-husband and my child's father. Telling herself that if she could get a marriage and a kid out of him, she too would have that dynamic with him as I had. She was unable to recognize how antagonizing that dynamic had been for me and all of my children.

It was all starting to come together for me the more I heard her speak. I could look at her and see how easy she was to take advantage of. Listening to the key indicators, she unconsciously divulged to me. I could see how Jeff and the people around him had been benefiting from this lost, hurt girl. Who was clueless as to what she had gone and stepped into. She had been clinging to him out of desperation for a man since her ex's departure, and he had been clinging to her because she was like fresh play-doh in his hands. Anxious to be molded into whatever he wanted; she didn't mind the negative drawbacks that came with who he was.

She was encompassing a desperate nature that he recognized and utilized for his benefit. Tonya was a piece of fool's gold waiting desperately in plain sight. Although she was a lot less problematic due to her lack of standards and common sense, Jeff was getting bored. Having someone that was willing to let him do what he wanted when he wanted was no longer looking as appealing to him as he had assumed it would be. I couldn't help but feel sympathy for Tonya. Despite how we had previously been acquainted, I looked at her and saw my former self. A young mom, alone, hurt, lonely, with a dire need to be loved.

I could tell by the way she conducted herself that she had no support system, and that was also a reason why she was an easy target for men like Jeff. She went on to disclose to me how she had been living in Waynesboro and had recently relocated to Charlottesville after Jeff convinced her he would move with her. She arrived to find him reluctant to do so, making her trip unwarranted. I knew Jeff could be messy but what I didn't understand was how he could sit and listen to the things she was saying and not feel like shit. He had hurt so many people and never stopped to evaluate himself or his actions. I looked at Tonya, seeing firsthand that she was not a bad person. She had been hurt, and, in her mind, it felt good giving that same hurt to another woman because it had been done to her.

She didn't feel as though she was wrong for intruding in another woman's marriage but what she didn't know was that God would never bless her with the happy ending she wanted with Jeff because of her methods. Nor would she ever have that based on the person Jeff was as a man and partner. She had been allowing herself to believe that I was standing in her way of a happy ending with Jeff. Listening to him paint me as a bitter baby mama who was stifling his ability to be a dad. Later learning that Jeff was a liar, and the only thing standing in the way of their growth was his dire need to have multiple partners. A few minutes later, she started begging him to leave with her in front of me, and my mom and I couldn't believe our eyes. I had never seen a woman conduct themselves in this way, and it was mind-boggling to me.

This served as a reminder that Jeff was indeed the master of manipulation. The boy wasn't worth a damn, yet there we both stood battling for his broke-ass affection. I started unconsciously studying her as she kept talking and giving him a strange look. Insinuating silently that if he didn't come along with her, she would divulge something to me that she knew that I did not. Jeff stood still for an elongated period of time as if he did not understand what it was, she wanted from him. When my mother, who had been standing in the kitchen the entire time eating up the drama-filled episode, spoke up. "Jeff, she wants to know who you chose," my mom said in a sarcastic tone making a mockery out of the question.

"I'm sorry, but I'm still in love with Nina," he said, shocking both me and her at the same time. There I sat low key happy to hear those words with my dumb ass! It's okay; I knew this was going to happen," she said as she stood up, removing herself from the table, thanking me for my time as she left out of the door as if she was exiting a job interview. There was a small part of me that felt happy hearing him say those words, but there was an even more significant part of me that felt for Tonya because I could Identify with a lot of the things she had gone through and was going through. My mom closed the door behind Tonya making her way back to the kitchen in a hurry. "All I want to know is where in the hell did, he find that fool?" As if there was not still a fool present in the room. The fool she had given birth to.

My mom stood there shaking her head as Jeff stood in silence. "I feel bad for her; she actually seems like she is a sweet girl. But that's what she gets for sleeping with other people's husbands," my mom said, contradicting the sympathy she had appeared to have for her. "That has to be a hurting feeling but, karma is a bitch!" She continued. "Imagine helping a man-dog a woman and his family only to have him turn back around and do the same thing to you," she said in a petty tone. She was clearly trying to make Jeff feel uncomfortable. "I guess somebody should've told her that how you get them is how you lose them."

"And you're just standing here looking half simple, while she looked like she wanted to jump across the table and kill you, and we should have let her," she said as she laughed hysterically while exiting the kitchen. Anxious to go call my brother Gavin and fill him in on what had taken place. Within the blink of an eye after our Jerry Springer moment, I was back knee-deep in a relationship with Jeff. I know what you're thinking…clearly, Tonya wasn't the only dummy …. But let's save our judgments for later as I continue to fill you in on how things transitioned, or so I thought they had. Jeff started having honest, in-depth conversations with me that were significantly different from the previous discussions we had in the past. Informing me of all the lies he had told me in the past. Dating back to lies he had been carrying since 2014.

We started doing more with the kids and one another, and it finally felt as though he had recognized what he had lost and was trying to earn it back the proper way. He started staying at my house on the days and nights I had to work and helping my mom around the house. Facetiming me during my long shifts and staying on the phone until he or I would fall asleep. He was going to work frequently, never missing a day or so, I thought, but that would come to the surface much later. I started spending more time with him, and that included going to his mom's house, although she never liked me and was never respectful unless it benefitted her in some way. She would say shady things to try and get me to feel uncomfortable, but it never worked.

Despite her efforts, I always stood my ground, making it clear that I could not be moved out of my position unless that was a choice, I made for myself. I could tell that she didn't like me, and I knew it was simply because of who I was and who I wasn't that made her want to see my child and me long gone. She saw what I was about but given what and where she came from to her, that was nothing. Speaking on my ways, frequently telling Jeff that she felt as though I was "too much "for him. Always making it clear to him and me that she didn't feel as if he was on my level. I always took her comments as a form of disrespect because they often were. Later realizing that some of what she said held a lot more truth to it than what I may have wanted to admit to at that time in my life.

I understood that she did not like me because she could not relate to me. So, I made myself comfortable with that dynamic, as awkward as it may have been at times. I hated being at Jeff's house when his mother got drunk because she would always make it her duty to start drama with me, and as much as I may have wanted to respond, I didn't believe in disrespecting people's parents. No matter how deserving of it, she could be at times. One day we went to Jeff's house to pick up his mother to give her a ride to the store. After picking up everything she needed, she got back into my car, ready to start the drama for the day. Jeff drove because, like usual, I was too tired to drive after working long hours that week and spending the remainder of my free time studying.

I often utilized Jeff as my designated driver, so he was used to it. But for some reason, his mother, Roberta, was not feeling the idea of him driving me anywhere. "Why are you driving her car like she is disabled" she said. While we both ignored her. "You are so damn needy you act like you can't do anything for yourself," she continued, referring to me. As I ignored her simply because I knew, and she knew that Nina White was many things, but dependent on others, especially her son, was not the case. So, I continued to look out the window and say nothing as she went on and on in the backseat, trying to rattle my cage.

Not recognizing that the only person who was bothered by her statements was her son. "You are stupid as hell, and everybody is laughing at you with your dumb ass. You got it going on, and you're out here still walking around with his ass like a fool," she continued as she let the alcohol do the talking for her. "You don't need him; you need to just go on and do all the stuff you want to do. You don't need him to do that. Dumb ass! Making all that money and running behind him, and for what" she concluded.

As if money was the key answer to a woman's happiness. As I continued to sit in the front seat, silent. Desperately awaiting her drop-off. "Mom cut that shit out," Jeff yelled. "Ain't nobody got time for your shit today," he screamed. Silencing her shenanigans until we arrived back at her house. We entered the house helping her to bring in her groceries when she sat down looking angry, trying to hold back her frustration after being cut off by Jeff. "And you're stupid as hell, too," she said, glaring up at him.

"She doesn't want your ass; look at you. She's got all that going on, and you don't have shit. She's just playing with you," she continued. I didn't understand what it was about our dynamic that made her so angry. Often wondering how it was, she could like every hood rat, hoe, schemer, alcoholic, deadbeat mom, etc., he brought around. Yet a real woman who was caring, hardworking, and a great mom she had so many issues with. I later realized she couldn't like me because she couldn't understand me.

We weren't relatable, and the way we did things in relation to children, a household, and relationship criteria were significantly different. In order for her to like me, I would have to lower myself in ways I was unwilling to. So, I stayed in her disliked category, trying not to let it bother me. She continued prying at Jeff's self-esteem, saying ugly things picking and prying at the both of us. Usually, Jeff would say nothing in return and allow her to go on and on until she tired herself out. But that night was different. "I don't understand what it is she has; why you don't leave her ass alone."

"She ain't for you! "You don't even know what you're talking about," he said. "And you sound crazy; that girl has never done anything to you for you to dislike her." He acted as if he had not contributed to her behavior with the frequent lies, he had told her in reference to me anytime he couldn't get what he wanted from me. "And it doesn't make sense to be so worried about another woman. "That bitch ain't shit!" she yelled as if she didn't want to hear any of that. "Take your drunk ass in there and sit down somewhere." I was so used to her disrespecting me when she felt like it or got drunk that this type of behavior was not bothersome for me as it should have been.

"Look at how you're conducting yourself in front of your granddaughter," he said. While he watched her go on and on, still being as disrespectful as she had originally been when she first started out. At that moment, I thought about the story he told me about his late father. Sharing with me how he would often lock her outside when she was intoxicated and acting a fool. I could see how locking her outside was a great resource. As I listened to her, go on and on as if she had no pause or stop mechanism. "When are you going to see that it's not her?"

"I did that; I imprinted on her," he said, leaving his mother and me both silent. I had witnessed her be this way over the years on numerous occasions, I always felt angry with Jeff when he never stood up for me. That night I was shocked that he had said anything in response to her allegations at all. For the first time, he made me feel like he was not okay with his mother disrespecting me. Was he really turning over a new leaf? That night we talked, and the next day, his mother attempted to be moderately respectful to me despite her true feelings. He had talked with her expressing to her that whether she was a fan or not, we were moving forward with our relationship.

Things kept moving forward, and Jeff started staying at his mom's on the days I had to work after feeling uncomfortable with my mother conducting herself in a similar manner just as his mother had been.

My mom would say things while being on the phone with her friends, trying to talk loud enough so that he would hear and feel uncomfortable and leave. Although he appeared to be making significant changes, all of my family members were convinced he was a fraud. And they made it no secret to him or me how they felt in regard to us rekindling our failed relationship. Things were going really well with Jeff and me, and despite the trust issues I had, he was slowly making me feel more comfortable with him when he was absent. The only person who supported my choice to reestablish our relationship was Raye. She liked hearing me give good reports, warning me to chill and still be vigilant. Reminding me that it didn't matter what anyone else thought as long as I was happy.

CHAPTER 10

House Party

$\mathcal{S}$ ummer rolled around, things were still moving along smoothly, and there hadn't been any hiccups. My brother was flying into town for his birthday and started badgering me to let him have a birthday party at my house. I was not a fan of many of his friends, and I didn't understand why he wanted to have a gathering that included family members we had no relationships with. My mom's family could be messy and drama-filled, and one of the main things they liked to engage in was gossiping about their family members, so it was a no for me. After having him express how important it was for him to celebrate his birthday, I agreed to the party. I informed him that I would not be present because I had recently suffered a miscarriage and my body felt exhausted. The day of the party had arrived, and my brother and his friends started working on the décor early in the day.

My brother had never been a fan of Jeff since the start of our relationship. He was often making it his business to pass judgments on my relationship. He felt as though he was suitable for doing so after being informed of details from his friends about Jeff's secret counterparts. He never extended me any grace or understanding because, like most people, he didn't understand why I was choosing to put up with Jeff. On the day of the party, my brother and Jeff appeared to be getting along relatively well compared to previous occasions. My brother was being friendlier, often engaging in conversation with Jeff. Even going as far as bringing Jeff a plate of food which made me question if my eyes were playing tricks on me.

Jeff never felt comfortable amongst my friends and family, but I often deduce that to be a result of his guilt for all of the harm he had caused me. I understood his lack of comfortability amongst my loved ones, just as I understood their dislike for him. They often felt annoyed when me and him were back in a good space. I continually wanted them to join me. I was never respecting their feelings. Like most women, I felt as though my family should have been supportive of me and Jeff's rekindling. I never understood that I was asking for too much. I had gone to my friends and family every time he hurt me, lied, cheated, abused, and improperly used me.

Me choosing to forgive him did not mean my family had to share the same fate, and they would precisely clarify where they stood. My family members started to arrive on the day of the party, and I was shocked by all the people who came.I realized my brother's idea of a handful of people was completely different from my definition of a small gathering. I entered the living room stunned by the tall banners that hung from the ceiling with my brother's picture on them. The cardboard cutout that overwhelmed the dining room area. It was as if he had been running for senate, and no one informed me. The kitchen and dining room were overwhelmed with loads of food and refreshments.

Turning thirty was a significant milestone, but I knew that this would not be a party filled with fun and good memories alone. I hated being a skeptic, but people's behavior patterns are often entirely predictable. And I knew tables filled with Hennessy bottles were not a good combination for a family that was equivalent to strangers, my brother, who was known to be an aggressive drunk, and my ex-husband, who was known to be a huge topic of discussion for all of his wrongdoings. I entered the kitchen, speaking to everyone while they looked at me in confusion. Trying to figure out why I was not dolled up as I usually would be. As they assessed me in my oversized sweatshirt and sweatpants, looking as bad as I felt. I explained to everyone why I would not be present, making my way back to my bedroom to lay down and get some rest.

Getting rest turned out to be a lot harder to do once the music from the party started penetrating its way through my bedroom door. The party went on for hours, and everyone seemed to be enjoying themselves. Jeff began feeling anxious and desperate to smoke the marijuana in his pocket. He asked me to escort him outside to his car to do so. I went with him to the car, where we sat and talked while he smoked. Blowing off the anxiety that I could tell had been present since his arrival at my house before the party. I heard a tap at the window of Jeff's truck, letting down the window to greet one of my cousins I had not seen in a long time. "What the hell have you been up to?"

He said as he looked at me, trying to figure out why I was not inside. "Not much, just working, as usual," I said. Exchanging a few words with him before he walked away from the truck, leaving Jeff and me to continue with our conversation. My cousin returned to the window a few seconds later, tapping again. I rolled the window down, expecting he had returned for more conversation." Do you know where I can get some tt from?" He asked. As I looked at him, confused. Tt? What? Before I could finish, Jeff intervened.

"That's powder," he said, making me annoyed instantly. "Nah, man, we don't know anyone," Jeff said, watching as my cousin walked away from the window. "Is he serious? Who the fuck walks up to people randomly inquiring about crack?" I asked. Leading Jeff to laugh. "That's your people," he said, trying to be shady. I'm so over this. "We have a house full of people eating like it's the last supper, but not one of them had the decency to bring my brother a birthday gift."

"Then we have his ass in the cut, walking around looking for crack," I said as I joined Jeff in laughter as we continued to talk about all of the crazy things we had noticed.

Jeff finished smoking and prepared to go back inside when we noticed a rush of people exiting out of the front door. My brother and several of his friends walked past Jeff's truck, and it appeared that there was some form of argument going on. My brother's friend Alexis approached my window, alerting me that my brother had drank moonshine and Hennessy and was in the midst of a dispute with one of his friends. I knew better than to try and calm him down when he was drunk, and I didn't have the mental or physical energy to try, so I stayed put. My brother approached my window a few minutes later with his drunk disposition taking over.

He could barely stay focused on his conversation with me, and it was clear he had something he wanted to say. I let the window down, annoyed at how intoxicated he was. "I love you, sister," he said about five times in a row until I replied, telling him I loved him too. "You are a dope ass woman and a dope mom, and you don't need anyone to validate you," he said, glancing at Jeff with an evil stare. Giving us both a clear indication of where things were headed. "I know," I replied as I watched him start to converse with Jeff through my window. Informing him that he felt they needed to talk. Jeff agreed he would come in to talk with him man to man. He understood that there had been an elephant in the room for a while now that needed addressing.

I exited the car with Jeff as we walked to the door. Thinking to myself, who tries to have a heart to heart when they're drunk, but Gavin. When my brother started yelling abruptly out of nowhere, trying to charge his way toward Jeff, and just like that, the Hennessy monster had erupted, as I knew it would and he was ready to knock Jeff's head off. I stood in the middle, asking Jeff to step back while I attempted to calm my brother down, who a second ago seemed calm and drunk. I watched as the entire room full of friends and family stood around, allowing me to try and hold my brother back on my own while no one interjected. After hearing me yell, numerous times, my mom's family members stopped standing around. Soon after, they decided to charge Jeff along with my brother instead of helping me calm my brother down, who was clearly the only threat in the room.

I couldn't believe what was going on. My brothers' friends tried to intervene, but they couldn't get him to calm down either. And all of a sudden, it was like we all had bought VIP tickets to fight night. Jeff had not said a word or made a move appearing to be just as shocked as me as to how things were going. My youngest daughter ran to Jeff when she saw what was happening while I continued to try and diffuse the situation—feeling overwhelmed by the entire house full of family members charging at my daughter's father while my three-year-old was at his side crying and afraid from all of the chaos. One of my mother's sisters started charging Jeff, adding fuel to the fire pushing him out of the door, and causing my daughter to fall to the ground.

Jeff saw his daughter on the floor, feeling overwhelmed with anger. He yelled and became just as aggressive as the crowd of strangers rushing towards him despite them seeing that my brother had initiated the confrontation. I would have understood if my family had been conducting themselves in this way if we were close, we had an actual relationship, or Jeff had disrespected one of them, but that was not the case. I watched as my mom's sister shoved Jeffrey sending me into a rage. Although I didn't have much of a relationship with my mom's family, I was shocked at how they were conducting themselves. "Don't you put your hands on him," I said to my aunt, yelling at her as if she was a stranger. I watched as her eyes became big and engulfed with shock.

As she assured me, she had not touched him when I had watched her with my own two eyes. Jeff picked up our daughter, making his way out the front door while my family continued to yell and be aggressive as if they didn't notice my three-year-old crying and scared. I was not one to disrespect my aunts and family, but it was something about their conduct that had sent me over the edge. Their behavior made it impossible for me to control my anger. It disgusted me to see grown women act as they were and especially in the presence of a child. I couldn't believe they had the audacity to disrespect my home in the way they had, making me furious. Suddenly, the calm Nina I had been all day was now the Nina from Orangedale Ave who was comfortable with letting the hulk out. Everyone was yelling and talking over one another while Jeff stood in front of his truck holding our child.

I made it clear to everyone that no one would be placing a hand on him. As I stood in front of my house, ready to go toe to toe with any family member that went against my wishes. I knew deep down inside that Jeff was long overdue for a good beat down due to things he had done. But I also knew he had made changes and didn't deserve what was happening. "I don't even know why you all came," I said. "This is precisely why I didn't want to have this party here. Look at the neighborhood we are in," I said as they all looked at me quiet, waiting to see where I was headed. "This is not the kind of shit we do," I continued.

That's when I heard someone scream out, "but this isn't just your home; it's you and your mom's home. You all bought this house together." Typical, I thought to myself. Of all the things to worry about at the moment, they were worried about the logistics of how it was we had made our way into the new neighborhood. She was speaking on facts that were not accurate. "This is my home and my mother's home, and you will not disrespect it." I did not understand why any of those details were significant to them. "You all shouldn't be here anyway. You all don't talk to us, and none of you like my family enough to have a relationship with us ," I continued. My aunt Sheryl was the only aunt present that I felt genuinely had a relationship with my mother. The rest of them only called her when they wanted to be nosey, gossip about another family member, or ask for money. I watched as everyone stood shocked and silent. No one spoke up to say I was wrong because they knew they couldn't.

"You all think I don't know what you say about my mom and me and my brothers." I said, focusing on the growth we had exhibited over the years. Majority of them hated us for our ability to prosper despite our many unfortunate circumstances over the years. They constantly held outside conversations about us that were filled with hate. None of them could honestly say what or who we were because none of them truly knew us . The irony is after yelling at my aunt, I would find out that she had allegedly gone on to have a secret affair with my mom's ex. This served as an accurate indicator that some of my mom's family members had a horrible idea of what family and respect consisted of.

At that moment, I recalled the many sisters who had allegedly slept with my mom's husband—smiling in her face afterward. Becoming the catalyst that created my mother's inability to trust others. My mother often assumed or feared the worst being done against her because it was the only dynamic she had ever known. Can you imagine having numerous siblings violate your trust in this manner? My mother shared stories about the many ugly behaviors she was subjected to from people who came from the same wound as she. This was alarming to me. It made me understand why she had always raised and encouraged my brothers and me to be close.

Encouraging us to look out for one another strongly due to the fact that it was a dynamic she had never known for herself. Watching my mother endure the many unwarranted hurtful actions from family members made me want to formulate a different kind of family for myself. I was always trying to show up for my siblings and my children in the best ways possible, deliberately trying to break generational curses that had befallen my mother. I hated the dynamic, she came from because she deserved so much more than what she had been given. I Understood how that very dynamic alone was and still is the reason God continues to bless her tremendously before the very people that set out to harm her consistently. A few of my cousins pulled me away after seeing how upset I had become. As my anger and aggression continued to pour out in a transparent format.

They had all heard every word of the conversation and knew I was stating true facts about my observations of our dysfunctional family dynamic. I graced my entire family's faces with shock as they tried to understand how I could say those things to their faces.They recognized that I was many things, but blind to their true feelings and nature of messiness was not one of my characteristics. My cousins walked me down the street, trying to calm me down. "Look at you. You need to calm down; you're supposed to be a leader and look at how your acting. Are you a leader, or are you a fake?" She asked. While standing in my face being the epitome of the things, she was inquiring about from me.

She was running a business that preached about woman empowerment while she talked about all of her friends, family, and whoever else made the cut in a cruel and disgusting way. Hating on anyone and everyone she felt was doing better than her. I had no problem taking advice, but, at that moment, I was not going to let someone talk to me about leadership who knew nothing about it.

"Since when were leaders not allowed the ability to get upset?" I questioned. "You all came here for a party at my house and disrespected me. Instead of calming down my brother, everyone chose to go along with the drama, hurting my three-year-old, trying to attack my man, and bringing negative energy into my home. Me being a leader has nothing to do with me standing my ground and not tolerating disrespect because if it were you this happened to, you'd feel the same way."

" I just had a miscarriage, I'm tired from vomiting all day, working crazy hours, and I am overwhelmed from trying to get a book completed, and I'm now behind with everything else going on in my life." I wanted to get The Diary of Janay Wilkerson out of my head and onto paper . But I could not due to the numerous stressful components in my life. I kept listing all the reasons I was tired and fed up with people's bullshit as my tears began to fall . At the same time, I began to bleed heavily again from the miscarriage. My head was pounding, and I felt dizzy and drained. Yet I stood still, screaming, and crying like a crazy woman.

I was allowing myself a moment of vulnerability. I realized they hadn't heard a word I said after mentioning the book. I noticed they looked shocked, looking at one another, trying to figure out how it was; I could juggle all these things. Little did they know juggling, my relationship, and life was depleting me more and more each day. I walked away, realizing I was wasting my vents on people who could not relate—making the contexts of what I was saying about everything but what I was saying. It had become clear to me that I was having a breakdown at that moment. I was tired of trying to do my best when my best kept being met with drama and chaos that I did not desire.

After I started venting and speaking my truths to the people, I felt needed to hear them. It was like a force had taken over my spirit that could not be suppressed. I started sending everyone away, shutting the party down. Telling everyone they needed to get the fuck out when I heard my brother's friend Kelly respond with a rude remark and an eye roll. Unconsciously making it her turn to listen to some true facts next. "Put the plate down and get your ass out of my house," I said to her in a rage. As she looked at me like she was shocked. "I know you're not talking to me," she said as if she was blind and deaf.

Leaving me to clarify who I was referring to in an even more aggressive tone. "Yes, I am talking to you, and I dare you to do something about it. You shouldn't be in my house either, knowing you don't care for me, and you have had many conversations about me that my brother is not aware of," I said, leaving her tongue-tied and mute as she left my kitchen, making her exit. She got in her car, ran into a neighbor's car, and damaged it. She was trying to flee the scene when the police stopped her, catching her in the act. I felt terrible for how I had conducted myself. But I felt like I had been pushed to the edge and left with no choice.

The truth was I had not intended to give so much rage and aggression to all of them. I had been piling so much inside for the longest time they simply became visitors to a show of outrage that was initially not intended for them. In other words, I broke giving them a little of what they rightfully deserved while giving them a little of what they did not. I would later realize that they all had their own opinions of who 'Jeff was, and they all felt like he was long overdue for a good ass whipping. I would later regret not allowing my brother to get to him that day but doing so wouldn't have helped anything. I changed a lot over the years, developed new mechanisms that worked for me, and kept my energy aligned with positivity most days. I had always had a temper since I was a child, but I had learned how to control it over the years.

I focused very closely on how I reacted to things and people sent to destroy my peace. Although my conduct during the party was not my finest hour, I said many things that I felt I needed to say. I never worried about who didn't like me for my expression because the truth was the majority of the people who came had already had a substantial misinterpretation of who I was. I often told myself it was better to stay secluded than to form familial relationships with family members who gossiped about one another, slept with each other's men, and hated to see one another do well. I often felt left out when I saw all my cousins gathering and hanging out—wondering why they never included me. Until I grew up and realized I had not missed out on anything.

The cousins that were so close and hanging out were also gossiping about one another, doing shady stuff behind each other's back, and encompassing the same generational jealousy as the parents who gave birth to them. I realized I had chosen the right path by not engaging. Although this was my way, my mother and youngest brother felt differently. Shortly after the party, they would disappoint me by engaging with family members I had tried to warn them about. After the party, things were significantly awkward between Jeff and me, and I could tell he was holding something in, but I was unsure. He kept bringing up the party repetitively, and I felt like he was using it as a veil to conceal something else. My brother Gavin started a business selling handmade fragrances.

After the party, my mom's family started commenting on his social media in excess and buying from him consistently, making it clear to many viewers that they were trying to make me feel a way. They wanted me to question why they were supporting my brother after five seconds of being in business when I had been in business for over two years and had never received support from any of them. I didn't let it bother me, especially after reading them for filth at the party, so I figured this was their clap back. My brother started eating up all of the fake love and fake support, taking on the opportunity as if he didn't know what their motives were. I didn't blame him because business is business. It would have been selfish and foolish of me to expect him to not engage or respond to people who were supporting his endeavors. I sat silently watching everyone's conduct, reminding myself that I had too many things to focus on than to let petty attempts get to me.

Frequently my mom would be hanging with my cousin and engaging with family members along with my brother, who they knew weren't genuine. But Karma has a way of fixing insincere intentions. And I was no stranger to the fact that vengeance is the lords. So, I sat back, waiting for God to show up and shut down all the bullshit in my favor. Showing them what I had tried to show them before. My brother called me, informing me of all of the people who supported his business from my mom's family, and he noticed the fake vibes. While my mom joined him in unison, sharing the exact details about the shade, she saw people throwing subliminally after the party. This went on for weeks until, finally, people got tired of being fake, especially after seeing that I was unbothered.

The same people showing my brother fake love started pulling back after his business started booming. He soon after opened a brick-and-mortar location in Atlanta, and the hate pilled on even more. The excessive comments and support died down instantly because my mom's family could no longer take the blessings growing in front of their eyes. This led me to recognize how easy it is for people to support you in the beginning stages. Especially when they don't think you're going to get somewhere with your endeavors. But as soon as your blessings arrive, their support flees instantly. I released my first book like I had intended showing no signs of worry about anyone's path but my own.

I had been full of anxiety after releasing the book. I felt nervous after having no prior knowledge of marketing a book properly. I started putting myself out there, similar to how I had with my cosmetics business telling myself that faith without works is dead reminding myself that God would eventually provide me resources to move my book and my writing goals forward as long as I kept going and didn't give up. Within weeks after releasing the book, things started moving fast, and I saw progress. I was able to get the book on the shelf in popular retail locations such as the Nubian bookstore and Malik's books. The book was also on the shelf in five local public library locations, schools, and my first billboard in Georgia.

I reminded myself that my blessings would come as long as I did the work, kept my energy positive, and I continued to walk in my purpose no matter what adversity came my way. My family dynamic was still very messy, but I didn't let it bother me. My intuition was nudging at me, telling me Jeff was keeping something from me. I watched as he spiraled into deep thought patterns frequently. Leading me to wonder if what he was keeping from me had anything to do with Tonya's nonverbal communication during our encounter. I sat Jeff down one evening when we were cooking out for the kids in the back yard noticing he seemed a little off. I approached him in my usual manner, being straightforward, getting down to business.

Inquiring what it was that had him so distant mentally. He struggled with a reply leading me to realize that I was absolutely right about what I had deduced from his behavior. So, I led the conversation telling him that whatever it was, we would get it figured out and still move forward in the same way we had been for months. Jeff sat me down, informing me that while he had been in a relationship with Tonya, he had cheated on her with a woman I had asked him about in the past. Telling me that he had contacted the woman after not hearing from her for a while and found out she was pregnant with his daughter. There are so many red flags that I should have considered at this moment, but as usual I was ignoring things I shouldn't have. I didn't know what to say after hearing a bomb of that magnitude being unloaded, and it made sense to me why he was acting strangely. A few weeks after we had gotten back together, the girl had made it her duty to stalk my social media frequently heart liking statuses trying to get my attention.

I didn't pay it any mind finding out later what her attempts were about. She was younger than me and had six kids with six men who weren't present, seeing her child with Jeff as an opportunity to have a different storyline. Based on the false imagery he presented to her about the kind of father he was to our child. Jeff led the story by disclosing that she had been around as if he had not. He told me that he didn't think the baby was his. He disclosed to me how she was known to dabble in sexual activity with numerous men, making it possible that the baby could have been anyone's. It pissed me off that he felt like talking down on her was a way to make what he had done less hurtful.

I always knew eventually someone would end up pregnant because he had been doing too much for it not to have happened. I didn't believe his stories about her being promiscuous because it was predictable. It made sense to me why Tonya had been looking at him in the way she was. Trying to remind him of the fact that he had another child, assuming I would not want to be with him if I knew that. Instantly I inquired if he had seen the child before. He informed me that he had gone behind Tonya's back and visited the baby girl shortly after she was born. Holding her for his entire visit and feeling no connection.

"That is the stupidest thing I have ever heard. Do you really think holding a baby can help you to determine if it's yours or not? "She's not mine," he said again. "And how do you know that?" I asked. "Because she doesn't look like me and our daughter looks just like me." At that moment, I had never been so disappointed with how stupid he was. How could he use our child in comparison to another to determine if the child were his or not? I made it clear to him at that moment that I was not going to handle things in the way Tonya had.

It made sense to me why she wanted his child so desperately. Yet she watched him father two children. One of which he created during the course of their relationship and was not present for either. I wondered why women like Tonya were so naive. Wanting a child with a man who had several, he was not present for telling themselves that the same man who abandoned his first and second born would do differently with their child. I made it clear to Jeff that I could never be comfortable with him neglecting a child. Telling him that his "it isn't mine" stance would not be permissible if he wanted to be in a relationship with me.

I urged him to set up a time to see the child and undergo a blood test. He appeared to be shocked by my reaction, low-key offending me. Children don't ask to be here, and I knew firsthand how it felt to have to be responsible for kids on my own. I had never been the side piece or the fling and had conceived two kids before Jeff with men I was in long-term relationships with. Bearing their first children and watching them neglect their child while I suffered and struggled on my own. It didn't matter to me at that moment how the child was conceived or when. All I wanted was for him to do the right thing. Letting him know I would have his back and treat his daughter as if she were mine. As commendable as that was, he was not jumping to the occasion to do the right thing, although he tried to make me believe otherwise.

For weeks he went on and on with pretending to reach out to his potential child's mother and having no luck, claiming that she would never reply to his attempts to reach out. And when she did, she would give him the runaround. Never agreeing to a time or date to get a DNA test. What didn't make sense to me is why a woman with six kids and no help would turn down potential help from someone reaching out attempting to do the right thing. Although he kept this story going for some time, something in me told me it was not the truth. I decided I would reach out to her getting no response back. A few days later, Jeff informed me that the child's mother had gotten locked up for shoplifting and would be unreachable for some time. I continued to try and encourage him to reach out to family members and friends to try and get some form of resolve, but there were no results. I didn't know if it was because he was not trying or if the mother had made things as difficult as he had told me. I found it hard to take his word alone because I knew how consistent he had been with making me look like a bitter baby mama every time I left him. Spinning the narrative to all that would listen. Lying and telling people he was not an active parent because I would not allow him to be. Still, I kept my mouth shut despite the many rationalities roaming around in my head about the situation, I didn't realize that it made no difference if I was trying to be a standup woman if my man was not going to try and truly be a standup man.

A month later, I started feeling sick and unable to keep food down. So much had taken place I hadn't noticed that I had not had a menstrual. I realized that my former arch-nemesis, Hyperemesis gravid arum, had come to visit me. I started having dizzy spells at work and vomiting nonstop to the point my client started inquiring if I was pregnant. That day, I ordered a pregnancy test utilizing door dash and getting multiple tests delivered to my job within ten minutes. I took the first set of tests, getting a positive confirmation within seconds. Ripping the second box open aggressively, trying to get a different verdict. Producing the same positive results. That night I laid down on the sofa at work feeling overwhelmed. Although things had been going well with Jeff and me, I did not feel as though things were solid enough to be welcoming another child into our lives.

The next day, I talked with him, disclosing that I was pregnant and having him feel excited right away. He threw me off course because I didn't know what to feel. We had no updates on his potential second child, and I didn't know if he was fully prepared to commit to parenting a new child when he had failed to do so with the kids I already had. I was still living the lifestyle of a single mom. Taking care of all of my children on my own, and Jeff was not contributing anything as usual but a bunch of promises of what he was going to do differently. Day after day, he started going to work, working extra hours, and appearing to be preparing to do better. Although that should have offered me some form of solace, it did not because I had seen him do that several times and not be consistent after he got tired of putting up appearances for my sake. Although I felt sick, the sickness started out more tolerable than it had been in the past. So, I tried my best to tough it out, telling myself that I could still do everything I was doing while pregnant.

I started mapping out my schoolwork load and getting most of my assignments done early, designating days to work on my writing, and spending more time with my kids doing lax activities on my day off. Telling myself that if I took it one day at a time, I would be ok. Although I appeared happy, I felt miserable from the sickness, and I was starting to feel anxious. I thought about how I had done things in relationships to make my partner happy and gotten no reciprocation. I silently reflected on previous pregnancies with Jeff and realized that none of them were successful accept my youngest daughter due to stress. I secretly feared that he would utilize my pregnant position as a way to lock me in. Shortly roaming off into the realm of no good as he had done in the past. I had experienced firsthand how fickle men can become when a woman gets pregnant. They feel a sense of safety as the woman's belly becomes engulfed with fluid and a fetus. Telling themselves that the coast was now clear to run wild. Because, after all, what would a pregnant divorcee do after a fourth child and another failed relationship? These were the negative thoughts that consumed me as I continued to get sick trying to focus on so many things and people at once while no one focused on me.

Burnout had become the permanent cultural component of my lifestyle, and being bloated, pregnant, and alone in all of my daily tasks were in no way making me feel better. Jeff started to get comfortable. As I knew he would. No longer spending as much time on the phone with me during my work hours. He was no longer present in the same way helping my mom out while I worked. And he stopped staying over, finding excuses to stay at his mother's house, leaving our daughter behind. Instantly I felt like he was back to his old ways. I was constantly waiting for the ball to drop. He started exhibiting so many ups and downs emotionally it was hard for me to tell who was pregnant, him or me. I decided to take my next day off and have a much-needed girls' day out with Raye. She had been going through a lot that week, and so had I, so I figured what better way to approach my frustration than to have some good food and shop with my best friend. That day we went out to our favorite restaurant and indulged in steak and lobster and girl talk. Afterward, we headed over to a local store that was going out of business to stock up on clip-on earrings that we both were addicted to. We made our way through the store, picking up every pair of earrings we could find, leaving the shelves bare in the clip-on section.

As we approached the register, I got a phone call from Jeff inquiring about where I was. I told him that I was out shopping and was headed across town to the beauty supply store to pick up some things for my mother. Asking him how my daughter was doing because he had taken her with him when he left the house. He told me she was doing good, informing me that he would be headed back to my house soon. I didn't question him hanging up the phone to check out my items. Me and Raye hopped in the car to make our way over to the beauty supply store. As we pulled past the gas station prepared to enter the parking lot of the beauty supply store, I saw Jeff sitting in his truck, looking like he had seen a ghost. He pulled up fast behind my car, following me into the parking lot, pulling up on the side of my vehicle abruptly as if he had just caught me doing something out of the ordinary.

He started acting strange, instantly yelling for me to come to him. Leaving Raye and I both confused as to what was going on. I got out of the car and walked toward him, trying to understand why he was so upset. As he acted irate, yelling in the parking lot while everyone outside looked at me as if I had just been caught cheating in the middle of the parking lot. His mother sat in the passenger's seat, looking as if she were unamused by Jeff's antics as she watched him gaslight me publicly, hoping it would throw me off of the trail of suspicion. He continued to act aggressively, yelling, and causing a scene. I looked over at Raye as she glared out of the passengers' window with her lip dragging the floor. Utterly shocked at how Jeff was conducting himself. His mother rolled her eyes, looking out of her window, trying her best not to engage while he continued to make a fool of himself. I glanced in the back seat, noticing my child was nowhere in sight. Coming to the instant conclusion that he was acting like he had caught me doing something in hopes that he would distract me long enough for me not to smell the stench of sneaky that was flowing through his veins.

"Where is my daughter?" I asked him after being calm for far too long. He ignored me, trying to overtalk me and act as if he did not hear the question. So, I asked him again, this time getting even louder. I became furious that he had tried to gaslight and humiliate me when as usual, he was the one up to no good. I asked again, this time letting my anger flow freely throughout my tone. "Where the fuck is my child? "She's with her aunt. Why is that a problem? "He said calmly, trying to play it off. "Yes, it's a problem; I said since when do you drop my child off somewhere without alerting me. You know that's not the way we do things,"I said, prepared to give my spill as to why I felt he had done so before he sped off. Raye looked like she was more confused than I was as I made my way over to the car, too distracted and angry to go into the store. "What the hell just happened? "He acts like he just caught me and you sleeping together in the back seat," she said, shaking her head keeping the bulk of her opinion to herself. However, I knew without her having to say it that she was thinking the same thing as me.

"Why do you think he did all that?" She asked again, curious to see what my theory was. "I think we just caught him and his mother coming from Tonya's, and that's why he was doing all of that. I believe he dropped my daughter off with his sister and was coming from or on his way back there." Do you really think he'd go over there with his mother with him? Yes, I do, I informed her that Jeff had made me aware that his mother had been reaching out to Tonya, telling her that we were having arguments trying to get Tonya to come to her house and try to get back with him. "Girl, no, she was not," Raye said, finding it unbelievable as I filled her in on more details as to why I thought that was what was going on. "You need to go pick up your daughter and go home. You are pregnant and don't need this type of stress. Let his ass be dumb and do whatever he wants to do. Because in the end, it will be his loss."That evening I dropped Raye off at her boyfriend's shop, and I went to pick up my daughter from her aunt. I hated thinking negatively, but the thing about small lies was that they always lead to even bigger lies. When I arrived in the parking lot, I noticed Jeff's truck sitting in the distance.

I retrieved my daughter and went home, telling myself that as much as it hurt to admit it, I was living in a realm of insanity, going through the same motions repeatedly. Looking for different results, I would never get. That night Jeff came back to my house begging and pleading for me to give him a chance to explain himself. He tried to make me believe he was not doing anything wrong, but I felt differently. Jefferey had a way of building you up to a place of high hopes and significance, only to turn around and drop you on your head, disappointing you faster than you could ever anticipate his ability to do so. My faith in him started to flee, and I felt the same hopeless, unhappy feelings I had felt before me leaving him.

He left my house for work the next day, and I went to work scheduled to work a twelve-hour shift. A few moments after he arrived to work, he face-timed me informing me that he was on his way to the ER to get his hand checked out after injuring it on the job. He expressed that he was in tremendous pain, telling me he had cut his finger badly. I didn't question him as he showed me his hand covered in a bloody bandage that covered his entire right thumb. He spent the majority of his day in the ER. Greeting me the next day, informing me that he was in tremendous pain. A few days passed, and he was still appearing to be going through it, and I was overwhelmed.

I was feeling burnout from the many things occurring in my life at that time. Jeff had never been anywhere, for the most part, other than Baltimore and Virginia, and he had always expressed a desire to go on trips. Coming to me abruptly, informing me that he wanted to do something special for me. He was throwing me off, making me wonder what had prompted him to want to do so suddenly. He contacted me at work, letting me know he had booked plane tickets for us to go to Florida to Fort Lauderdale. A vacation was just what I needed after all of the things that had been overwhelming me at that time. Jeff had never been on a plane, so I thought it was great that we were finally going to be making memories together.

The kind of memories I preferred. When we arrived in Florida, we went straight to the house I had rented, prepared to relax, change, and start our day. But after getting settled, Jeff didn't appear to be as excited as he was when we had left. We got changed and went on a boat ride. We were touring Fort Lauderdale when we got some history from the tour guide about the wealthy homes on the water. I sat on the boat listening to the history lesson wondering how all of the well-known wealthy individuals had gotten their start. Wondering if they had found entrepreneurship to be as tricky as I had.

I was daydreaming about what my future held once it was finally my turn to have what God had intended for me. We left the tour, went to dinner, and headed back to get some rest and watch movies. When we arrived back at the house, Jeff started acting as if he was in tremendous pain after viewing a message on his phone , popping Tylenol back-to-back. Pacing back and forth in the room, making loud noises complaining in a way he had not for days since his alleged hand accident. At that moment, I couldn't help but wonder if there was more going on with him than what he had disclosed to me. That night Jeff took off the bandage, and I was able to see that his thumb was not hurt in the way he had initially told me. My observation of the cut and the hand it was on led me to believe he had slit his thumb deliberately. He was right-handed so I didn't understand how he could cut his right thumb. After all I had never seen anyone prepare food and cut with their insufficient hand.But I kept my observations to myself.

I would later find out that he had done so, went to the emergency room, and then later over to Tonya's. Feeding his dire need to have multiple sexual partners due to his issues that had never been appropriately addressed. He had a small cut of skin that looked as if it hadn't gone past the first layer of the dermis after initially telling me that he was missing a chunk of his thumb. I knew something was up, but I tried to overlook it. Lying in bed trying to replant my focus on something else. While he lay in bed, falling asleep. I started trying to formulate my about me section for the back of my debut publication.

Typing the paragraph repeatedly, unsure what to include and what to leave out. I read the section over and started overthinking the description. And I started comparing who I was to who Jeff was—focusing on where I was trying to go in my life and where he was. I recognized that where he was at that moment was where he had been since the day, I had met him. I analyzed my poor choices, trying to make sense of the rocky road I kept coming back to. Asking myself what it was that I was looking for. I had wanted love, commitment, and trust. Trying to build a life with someone I could count on in the same capacity that they could count on me. But I had never received any form of reciprocity from Jeff.

I thought about my kids and the child I was currently carrying, trying to understand what I gained from staying with Jeff. The answer was simple I was gaining nothing while he was gaining everything. I constantly felt the sting of disappointment from continually coming to his aide, paying bills he couldn't pay, paying for truck repairs for a truck he could barely afford, and giving him the utmost care and respect while he gave me nothing but lies and high hopes. I knew at that moment I was now recognizing my pattern of poor decision-making. I had given up my goal of obtaining a Ph.D. when I got pregnant with my youngest daughter. How was I going to have a new baby, work, go to school, and be an entrepreneur?

The answer was simple it would not be possible unless I had adequate help. And I did not. My daughter was now four years old, and he had done nothing to help take care of her and help provide. What would be different this time? I had been the woman to bear children with men who wanted them. Putting aside my dreams and desires for my relationship and my children. Telling myself, it was what had to be done. But I now knew that was not the case.

God had been showing me that I didn't owe anyone anything, and I could do, be, and have whatever it was I desired without always having to sacrifice my being to do so. So, at that moment, I decided to keep that in mind while I silently gambled with hard choices, I knew I would have to make sooner or later. The next day we went out for lunch at a nice restaurant we had come across while sightseeing. When we entered the building, there was no one of African American descent insight. I didn't feel bothered due to me and my brother being certified foodies, always venturing out to nice restaurants, and having had occasions where we didn't see people while there that looked like us. Jeff looked uncomfortable, so I tried making conversation to help loosen him up. Within a few seconds after doing so, he started squirming around in his seat and making disturbing noises again, trying to pretend he was in pain. He was making us the center of attention.

I felt so embarrassed and mostly annoyed because it was evident to me that he was purposely trying to sabotage my experience during the trip, and I didn't understand why. A huge part of me felt like he might have been back talking with Tonya behind my back, and he was doing so because he felt guilty for hurting her. I didn't know what to make of his behavior, but it was helping me to make my choice of what was best for me a little easier. We left the restaurant abruptly, returning to the room. He knew I didn't have much to say to him after his shenanigans in the restaurant, so I showered and got in bed. He continued to pace the floor, pretending to be in worse pain. Trying to keep up with the act. I ignored him and watched as he took more Tylenol and eventually fell asleep.

Never disclosing to him that I had seen his thumb and knew he had lied about it. As I lay in bed trying to focus, something kept nudging me to check Jeff's phone. Although I had graduated from being that person, I knew my suspicions were starting to feel well warranted, especially after he had ruined the trip that was supposed to be a rejuvenation trip for me. I picked up the phone after being unable to shake what my intuition was telling me. Opening up his social media platforms and finding him conversing with several women I knew. Having inappropriate conversations and some of which involved me.

Lying to one of his exes, making her think that the dynamic of our relationship was something it was not. Making her believe that I had been moving foul and doing things to him that he was currently doing to me. He communicated with women on social media platforms where women requested cash app payments in exchange for inappropriate pictures. The thought of him paying for freak poses while he watched me pay for everything concerning our child made me furious. There I was providing every meal, shoe, clothing item, and resource for our child's care while he squandered his money on hoes, fetish photos, and his own desires. My eyes felt like they were burning with disappointment as I looked at him lying in bed asleep, trying to understand his cognitive mechanism. Wondering what kind of person told the caliber of lies he did without feeling any empathy.

I wondered why he was leading me on in the way he was when he had no intentions of changing for our kids or me. I texted Raye telling her what I had seen after being unable to sleep. Trying to process the weeks since his return wondering why it was, he had been pretending the entire time. Raye called me instantly after receiving the text. Telling me that I didn't need to let his actions make me doubt myself because who he was had nothing to do with who I was. I knew that was true, but how do you not find flaws in yourself when your partner keeps conducting themselves in such a way. I often felt like there was something wrong with me.

What was I not doing right in our relationship? Overlooking the fact that no matter how satisfied or unsatisfied he felt regarding me, this was who he was as a man. I felt like a fool. Investing in a man that had let me down numerous times only to have me awake each time more hurt, fragile, and humiliated than the time before the last. I sat in bed that night, assessing the previous six and a half years of my life, trying to understand how it was I had become this person. Looking for someone to give me something they couldn't even offer to themself. Wanting a man to provide me with the proper love who had never seen it or known it for himself. Waiting on him to step up to the plate and be an active father and take care of his responsibility when he failed to take care of himself.

He was relying on me to do that for him and using our child as a pawn to keep a hold on me, my resources, my finances, and my heart. While he played me for a fool. Never giving a single fuck about his child or me. I had made the mistake of bringing children into bad situations. Doing it all on my own and seeing how my single-parent status scarred my children psychologically. Leaving me to be the provider, the parent, and the therapist all on my own. I knew I should not be foolish enough to walk down that road again, so I cultivated a plan to do what I felt was right for me.

The day we returned from the trip, I contacted the women's center and set up an appointment to have an abortion. I told myself that although it was wrong, it was the best choice for me, my children, and my future. I realized Jeff was not happy about me being pregnant because he wanted more kids and was ready to be an adequate father. He was only trying to trap me with another child, hoping it would be the unfortunate glue to keep me planted by his side even when he didn't deserve for me to be. I had played that game with him for many years, and I was now sure about what I needed to do to prosper internally and externally starting with ridding myself of dead weight. The next day I went to the appointment lying on the table, feeling anxiety overwhelm me as I prepared for the ultrasound.

I requested to have the screen face the doctor the entire time because I did not want to forge an emotional connection with the baby. Since ultrasounds had always been a considerable connection resource for me during pregnancy, as it is for most women, I tried to block it out. Afraid I would have second thoughts and go through with the pregnancy. That night while at work, I face timed Jeff informing him of my choice, acting as if my only reasoning were how sick I had been and how a child would affect everything I was doing and trying to do. He agreed, telling me he understood and acted as if he didn't have a problem with it. What I didn't know at the time was that Jeff was only pretending to agree, assuming he would be able to sway my choice. The next day I prepared myself to go through with the procedure. I kept the appointment to myself, leading Jeff to believe that this was something that would not take place right away.

This made him believe he had time to influence my choice and change my mind, but he did not. For by the time that would occur, the pregnancy would already be terminated. I went through with it and got a birth control implant the same day. Telling myself, this would be the last time I would find myself in that sort of situation with Jeff. That day after the procedure, I called Jeff to come to pick me up after being instructed that I could not drive myself home. When I got in the car, I could tell that Jeff had an awkward disposition, but I didn't pay it any attention. The crazy thing about Hyperemesis is that once the fetus is no longer in the body, the sickness goes away instantly. I had not been able to consume food for days and was ready to eat and rest.

I ordered food for my kids and myself and fell asleep after consuming two small bites. Thankful that I no longer felt the urge to vomit. Jeff laid in bed fidgeting around the entire night, appearing to have a massive chip on his shoulder, but I didn't pay any attention. I told myself that if I didn't feed it, then it wouldn't grow. But how wrong I was. For overnight, it had grown and grown until the vines started penetrating their way out. I woke up the next day not surprised to find Jeff fuming hot with anger. I was still weak from all of the vomiting and the procedure lying in bed, trying to find some form of normalcy, when Jeff started picking petty arguments.

I got up out of bed to grab something to drink when I came back to him, going off running his mouth about how I had killed his child. I didn't understand why he was so upset about a fetus when he had a living, breathing child he neglected to take care of. I tried to understand why he felt he was in a position to have another. Especially with a woman he gaslighted, disrespected, and cheated on fluidly. Under normal circumstances, I would have objected to standing my ground debating why my choice was right for me, but I was too weak to engage. I turned to walk away when I felt Jeff's hands around my neck choking me. As he shook my body viscously, screaming to the top of his lungs about how much he hated me.

Yelling repeatedly about how I had killed his child as if he hadn't encouraged me to have abortions in the past. Never caring about them but somehow placing significance on this event as if it were any different from the others. It was not in my nature to allow a man to harm me, and I not fight back. But that day, I was significantly weak and in no position to attempt to defend myself. My oldest daughter ran into my room after hearing the incident watching as I tried to get his hands from around my neck, but I could not. Shortly after, my youngest daughter ran in, joining my oldest in tears as they begged for him to stop, but he would not. I felt like he was trying to kill me as he elevated the firmness of his grip, lessening his grip and then tightening it up again.

I felt his hands get tighter and tighter. When he finally threw me to the ground. Rushing towards my oldest daughter, grappling with her trying to grab my toddler from her arms while my toddler screamed, yelling out to us that he was hurting her. I ran to him, trying to remove his hands from my daughter, when he grabbed me again, choking me as I tried to get him off me again with no success. I reached for a coffee mug that sat on my desk that I kept all of my pens in. That read Malcolm, Harriet, Martin, Maya, and Fredrick. I Swung the mug aggressively with no accurate coordination.

I realized later that my ancestors would most likely not approve of my utilization of the mug. I hadn't realized that the cup had broken on his skull. I was still swinging with his hands wrapped around my throat. Never taking notice that all that was left of the mug was the handle as I grasped it tightly, still swinging it, carving his face with every swing. Finally, freeing my neck of his hands. When he looked at me, "What are you doing? Why are you doing that?"As if he had no recollection of him attacking me. The mug had given him a concussion.

The meat from the center of his nose was hanging, and he had blood in multiple areas pouring out from different places. He grabbed his nose, rushing to the door. When my daughter followed behind him, locking the door and calling the police. I stood frozen in the middle of my bedroom, feeling numb, weak, and in shock. It was as if I were that traumatized little girl all over again. Only this time, I was not trying to save my mother, but I was trying to protect myself.

My bedroom floor was covered in glass shards, pens, and all sorts of debris that had flown around during the event.

Blood splatters covered multiple places on my bedroom wall and area rug. My daughters were crying, and I felt as if I couldn't move. I looked at my left arm, noticing I had a long laceration that was deeply penetrating through my dermis, with blood flowing out aggressively. I changed my clothes and tried to clean myself up as much as possible.

I then sat in the recliner above the stairs awaiting the police's arrival. Judging from the severity of his injuries, I assumed I would be going to jail. I had been manipulated for so long I was no longer thinking clearly.

How would I be going to jail when I had simply tried to defend myself? A few seconds later, my phone rang, and it was Jeff's mother. I answered the phone frantically, informing her of what had happened. Crying uncontrollably as I tried to express to her how I didn't understand how he could do that to me and in front of my children. I could hear the happiness in her voice on the phone as she told me verbatim, "you don't need him; go on with your life." Appearing to be happy to hear the dynamic of the incident, praying this would be enough to keep my child and me away for good. Little did she know it would be, and despite her hatred and hidden agenda, she was right.

I needed to let him go and move on with my life, so that's what I did! The police questioned my daughters and me, and after hearing their story and recognizing that it was congruent with mine, they proceeded with pressing charges and implementing a protective order. In the past, I had dropped the ball, allowing the protective orders to expire when Jeff had broken my wrist and during other incidences when he had attacked me as well embodying the typical abused woman mental mechanism. I told myself that I didn't want to see him in jail. Not recognizing that I was now the very woman I never wanted to be, carrying the generational curse of allowing abuse. Allowing it to penetrate my cognitive process, my emotional state, and my physical wellbeing. While also allowing it to compromise who I was as a woman and mother.

I understood at that moment that I had to break the cycle and do better for the sake of my children. I had called Raye after the incident when she rushed over to my house to see what was going on. The police had taken my statement, urging me to leave in the ambulance to have my injuries addressed. Alerting me that I would need stitches, but I did not go. The shame of what had occurred was resting in my lap. As I tried to figure out what my next step would be. The police officer urged me to stay away from Jeff, expressing to me how dangerous it was to have someone around that was willing to harm me in the way he had after the stress I was already encountering due to Hyperemesis, an abortion, and dehydration.

The paramedic looked at me with pity filling his eyes. As he handled me with care, telling me that it was ok to cry, noticing that I was trying to hold back my emotions. Stressing to me that I didn't deserve to be handled in the way Jeff had and I needed to go through with the protective order. During my entire relationship, I had never allowed myself to feel as though I was a victim. I often told myself that I was strong and always fought back, leaving my mark that I was not a victim of abuse. I Understood that the physical abuse and mental strain had seeped so deeply into my being, I didn't recognize my reflection. As I looked at my mirror image, seeing my mother, my cousins, aunts, and grandmother all staring back at me.

Finally, letting it seep into my brain that I was a victim of many things and had been for a long time. The police officer left to go to the hospital to arrest Jeff. Assuring us all that Jeff would be getting a good helping of Thanksgiving turkey while sitting behind bars for the holiday that was approaching in a few days. Jeff had been texting me the entire time after his departure playing as though he was the victim. Telling me that he was not going to press charges on me as if he even had the option after attacking me in the way he had. Even after me leaving him in a horrible physical state due to self-defense, it still hadn't occurred to him what he was doing. He was counting on his ability at that moment to manipulate me in the way he always had, hoping there would be no ramifications for his actions.

But he would soon find that this time he would not be so lucky. He had gotten away with hurting my children and me consistently. Never paying the toll for the hurt he deliberately inflicted. When all I had ever done was try to help him recognize that he could be better and have better. But I had finally learned that growth was a self-decision. Jeff had never grown while with me because he didn't care to. That's why he always gravitated towards the type of woman he did as soon as I would turn my back.

Because he found comfort in those spaces with those sorts of people, I had requirements, standards, and goals that he could not identify with or understand. And as much as he liked me for my qualities based on who I was as a woman and mother, he also hated me for them. Often feeling inferior in my presence because I was always trying to do better while he tried to do absolutely nothing. We were not nor had we ever been equally yoked, and we both were aware of it despite our lack of transparency around the idealism we had cultivated of what we felt we wanted individually and together. The police officer returned to my home, informing me, Raye, and my oldest daughter that Jeff had been arrested. The officer was a middle-aged white man who was one of the funniest yet slightly ghetto officers I had ever encountered. He had an upbeat spirit and made us all feel comfortable with him despite the stress of the incident. I lay in bed with my bonnet on my head, feeling terrible.

The officer walked upstairs, entering the room, making Raye laugh right away. "Well, I went over to the hospital, and I got to tell you, you fucked him uppppp," he said, making Raye burst out in laughter. "He'd be a fool ever to try and do that again," he said. Looking up to the plaque on my wall and reading it out loud. Work hard, have fun, no drama, he read aloud. Well, I guess two out of three aren't bad, he said, making the entire room laugh as we assessed the irony for ourselves. I overheard you talking with the other officers, and you sound like you are an intelligent, hard-working young lady, he said, ready to give me a word of much-needed advice. "I'm not here to judge, but I'm looking around, and you have some beautiful children, a lovely home, and people that care about you."

" Leave this guy alone; you can do better. Especially if you take that tire off your head," referring to my bonnet as we all continued to laugh with him. "You know us police officers aren't all that bad; despite what's going on in the world right now, there are still plenty of good officers roaming the world," he said. As he made his way out of the door after instructing me how to extend the protective order. My youngest daughter ran down the stairs hugging the officer before he left. Despite the culture of police negativity, my four-year-old was a huge police and firefighter lover. Often telling me that she wanted to do both when she got older. Jeff had sent a picture of his face to my phone, trying to make me feel guilty for defending myself before he was arrested.

After hearing the officer's comment, Raye asked if she could see the picture. I showed her the image, and she was shocked. "Damnnnn …… you're in here crying, but you look fine compared to him. Cheer up, girl," she looked at the picture a second time and placing significance on his injuries, making joke after joke trying to cheer me up, but I only felt worse. "Your sitting here feeling bad, but his ass deserved it. I told you a long time ago I didn't see how you put up with him because a bitch like me would've fucked his ass up a long time ago for all the games and disrespect." Raye continued on trying to make me realize that I had no reason to feel ashamed or bad, but nonetheless, I felt horrible. I had spent so much of my life engulfed in violence.

From street fights to relationship brawls graduating from that culture of life and trying to avoid situations that cultivated the Nina who was with the shit. Dealing with Jeff had brought me back to that rendition of myself more times than I could count. I knew this time had to be the last because next time, one of us might not make it out alive. My family had always warned me about Jeff telling me that he seemed like the kind of person that would eventually kill me if I continued to let it get as far as I had. My mom had warned me several times. Often calling me when she heard a heartbreaking story about a young girl being killed or strangled to death by her partner, telling me that she feared I would one day share the same fate if I didn't leave Jeff alone. It was at that very moment when he choked me that I saw how things like that took place with women. Seeing how a man could accidentally or deliberately kill a woman understanding why it was vital that I remove myself from the never-ending saga immediately.

A few days later, after the incident, child protective services sent a social worker to my home. She interviewed each of my children individually, then me trying to see if there was a need to take further action concerning my children and their wellbeing since the incident happened while they were in the home. I was familiar with the protocol due to the previous event. The children all interviewed with her, and after the initial visit, she sat down with me, offering me resources for counseling. Telling me that she could see my children were living comfortably and in good hands. She left that day and never returned, essentially closing my case with child protection services assuring them that my children were not in any potential risk or unsafe environment. As usual, I rested in the solace of God's favor.

Taking notice of how quickly things were halted that could have affected me, my children, and my mothering. I was thankful that God had shown us favor because I knew many women who were not so lucky after involving child protective services. My children had always been my center. Acting as my motivation to strive, grow, and prosper even when I felt like my energy was internally depreciating and I didn't know if going on was possible for me. I made a choice on that day, vowing that I would see the entire process through to have Jeff pay for his actions, removed from my life, and removed from my children's life. The following week I was contacted by a victim advocate that was provided to me by the courts. I had gone through with extending the protective order and was now preparing to go to court to ask the judge to extend it for two years.

That week the victim-witness advocate asked me what I wanted to see happen with Jeff. The options were he could go to jail, or he could undergo probation, family abuse counseling, and a psychological evaluation that would require him to follow through with any treatment that would be requested for him. I thought about his life timeline. The drug addiction he had witnessed in his household that he had told me had affected him, being placed in foster care, and taken from his mother, the sexual abuse from his foster mother, early teenage incarceration, and being in solitary confinement in prison for an extended period. It had always been evident to me that Jeff needed help, and, at that moment, I did what I felt was best and would get him that help that had been a long time coming. I told her that I didn't want to see him in jail, and I felt the psych evaluation, probation, and counseling would benefit him. For weeks Jeff had been violating the restraining order by texting my phone, calling, and plaguing me with redundant messages out of fear of the consequences due to his actions.

Although I had been seeing things through, I still did not have the proper boundaries with him. I alerted the victim's advocate that Jeff was still violating the order. She informed me that she would pass the information along to his lawyer to see if he could intervene and get him to stop. A few days before court, Jeff's mother contacted me. I answered the phone, not recognizing the phone number. She informed me that Jeff had been acting strange, and she had encouraged him to go to the hospital. Telling me that if he tried to contact me to get him out of the hospital to, ignore his wishes. "He needs to stay in there and get his head checked because he has not been right in the head ever since you hit him with that coffee pot."

I could tell that her call was contrived and intricate, and I made it clear to her that she would not play me or insult my intelligence. "I never hit your son with a coffee pot. "Well, whatever you hit him with, it fucked him up, and the boy hasn't been right ever since," she said. I responded back, letting her know that before me defending myself and hitting him with the mug, Jeff had already had mental inabilities. Most of which stemmed from her lack of rearing and the environment he came from. She got angry, knowing she could not argue with facts or play me for a fool hanging up the phone abruptly. A few seconds later, my phone rang, and it was Jeff calling me from the hospital.

He sounded strange as he started talking in a low tone, sounding like he was Michael Jackson's long-lost twin. The tone was so quiet and soft I thought it was someone playing on the phone pretending to be Jeff, but it was not. "How are you doing?" He asked in a whisper tone. I'm doing good, I said, trying to understand what he wanted. Are you ok? He asked? "Am I ok? Are you alright... you're the one calling from the hospital," I said. Trying to understand what kind of stunt he was trying to pull. I've just been worried about you, he continued. "I can assure you I am fine, and you don't need to worry about me."

He started talking in circles, going on about how he was a good person and he never hurt people. Telling me how he was so tired of everyone leaving him. Bringing up past traumatic events from his childhood trying to trigger my sympathy response. Hoping I would feel some form of care for him. He Talked about how he never had anyone to have his back, which was why he didn't know how to treat me. As if he was telling me things that had not been obvious to me. I started telling him that I understood that hurt people hurt people.

Telling him that he needed to seek help so that one day he could learn to love properly so he would not continue with his current pattern of inflicting hurt on good people. Making others pay for the trauma they had not imposed on him. While not holding the people accountable in his life that had. He started to get frustrated after not gaining the results he had hoped to with me. Becoming aggressive and yelling to the top of his lungs. The nurse came grabbing the phone, telling me that she felt it was best for him not to talk on the phone because it was triggering him and causing him to get upset. I agreed with her hanging up the phone. Waiting for ten minutes before I called the hospital back, and the nurse informed me that Jeff had left the hospital right after our conversation.

Old habits die hard, and he had gone to the hospital to call me and appear to be in distress, hoping it would make me retract from going through with court and the order, but I did not. That day I Thanked God for my strength at that moment because had I allowed pity to take over my thinking process, he would have played me again. The following week I went to court prepared to give my testimony. Jeff arrived at the court with his mother accompanying him. The victim witness advocate accompanied me taking me into another area of the court so that I would not have to look at Jeff. When we entered the court, the judge asked us both a series of questions. I responded to each accurately and calmly while Jeff stood across the room, interrupting me as if he had never seen a single episode of law and order.

The judge warned him that he could not interrupt me when giving my testimony. Letting him know he would have his time to speak. During the entire event, Jeff was angry, disheveled, and telling one lie after another as I assumed he would. I kept my composure, reminding myself that although it was hard for me to go through with things the way I was, God was on my side. It came time for me to describe the event, and I couldn't without letting my emotions chime in. I tried my best to stay strong and hold my tears in as I started shaking and feeling anxious. Feeling ashamed to have to disclose what had occurred in a room full of local strangers.

The judge granted me the two-year protective order alerting Jeff that he was not to come near me or any of my children for the remainder of two years. Informing him that if he were to text, email, call, or do anything to try and contact me, he would go to jail. Sure, enough I left the courtroom that day with Jeff still texting me. I informed him that if he continued to violate the order, I would report it. Which I later realized I should have. A few weeks later, he called me telling me how he had been seeing a therapist and had been diagnosed with a mental disorder. Apologizing to me for all the bad things he had done to me and telling me how he had changed and become a new person. I congratulated him, feeling sure that most of what he had said was untrue and telling him that despite his growth or lack of change, I was no longer accessible to him. Listening to him as he went on about how he was not with Tonya anymore and he wanted his family back.

Telling me that Tonya had lied to him, telling him that I had been sleeping with her ex-boyfriend's cousin. I knew that if she had told that lie to him, it was only because she was afraid of losing him to me. Not understanding that I would never allow that to be an option for him ever again. I made it clear to him that I did not run in the same circles as Tonya or any of the people she knew. Making him understand that I was no stranger to rumors, and I didn't care about petty lies being told about me. I exited the conversation feeling proud of myself for not letting up. After this conversation, he left me alone for a few weeks before trying his hand again. One night I woke up to a call late in the night answering it.

I kept saying hello and couldn't hear anything. A few seconds later, I could hear Jeff arguing with Tonya sounding extremely aggressive. Disrespecting her, with one horrible comment after another. I could hear her trying to calm him down as he continued going off over and over. I hung up the phone, thinking to myself how he was still being the same person only now he had changed victims. Counseling was doing nothing for him. The phone rang again, and I picked it up, hearing him going off as I heard a loud rummage in the background with Jeff telling Tonya he was taking his things and leaving with her begging him to stay.

I hung up, realizing he was calling my phone, purposely hoping I would take pleasure in hearing him mistreat Tonya. The way she had when he mistreated me and ran to her, but that was not who I was. He called my phone asking me to come and pick him up, going off saying things about Tonya when I interjected. Had he lost his mind? Why would he assume he could encourage me to pick him up from Tonya's? After all that he had done to her and me. But it was simple; he thought that way based on the previous behavior I had exhibited.

Allowing him to harm me over and over. Always welcoming him back into my space as if nothing happened. I was subjecting myself to countless disrespect. I was serious this time, but he had no real way of knowing that based on all the other times, it appeared I was serious and was not. I expressed to him that it was disrespectful for him to call me trying to place me in their relationship spat. I would never disrespect another woman by picking up her man from her house. Letting him know that he was still being the same ole Jeff.

I inquired if her children were home while he had been disrespecting her. Explaining to him that his blessings had been blocked due to his endless misconduct and disrespect towards women. He got silent, unsure of what to say in response to my comments before saying he would calm down, and I hung up the phone and went back to bed. I wasn't sure what Jeff's reasoning was for calling me and letting me hear him and Tonya's drama, and for all I know, she could have been in on it, but I was determined to keep looking ahead and making progress. Leaving him and all of the events he had caused in my past. Jeff continued to try his hand, often utilizing our child as an entryway, but I made it clear to him he would no longer be able to use her as a pawn. Breaking old habits telling myself I could make things easier by approaching the issue differently than I had in the past.

Counting on the lessons, I had learned from my relationship with Omar to help me approach co-parenting properly with Jeff. Offering to have a sit down with Jeff and Tonya so we could talk and cultivate a plan to co-parent. Have our kids meet and let my daughter get to know Tonya so she would no longer feel like I was a factor in her and Jeff's situation. Doing so would also help him to understand that he needed to let me go and focus solely on his daughter for once, but he declined. Coming up with every excuse in the world as to why he didn't want our daughter around Tonya. Proving to me that he would always be the same Jeff using his child as a one-way ticket into my world where he knew he did not belong. Always having a strong desire to be in my presents anytime I made it so he could no longer have the privilege.

Never valuing me or what I brought to the table when I was present. For a month, he would send me messages that I would ignore, trying to get back in with me. Where I would experience a moment of weakness here and there, questioning if it were possible, he could be being sincere. Before coming to my senses and reminding myself that he would never change in reference to my children or me. I had allowed too much disrespect, manipulation, abuse, and deceit to occur during our relationship. I Informed myself that, in reality, those would be the only components he would ever be willing to give me because those were the only things, he felt I deserved from him even when he knew I did nothing to deserve those maltreatments. After the incident with Tonya showing up at my home, I started silently evaluating myself. Recognizing that I had become a person I did not want to be. Thinking back on the many incidences that had occurred with me and random women who felt a desire to make their relationships with Jeff known to me.

Recollecting the many friend request, I had received from women I had never met. Accepting them initially, believing it to be of no importance. Later watching as numerous subliminal posts popped up on my timeline instantly becoming obvious to me. Later asking Jeff about suspicions and having him deny having knowledge of who each woman was. Later finding out he, in fact, knew and had dealings with all of the women I had inquired about. I wondered what made women feel as though I was on their radar when they engaged with him. I never bothered anyone, stayed to myself, and never cared about anyone he was involved with when I was not with him.

Yet I was always a topic of concern and convo amongst women I should have not been. I later learned that Jeff made it his duty to talk about me to women he engaged in relationships with. Wanting them to feel as if I was of some form of importance. As he dangled my name, personal business, and achievements in the faces of many misleading them to believe that I was significant to him in ways that I was not. Listening as stories came back to me, he had shared where he had changed our relationship dynamics, making our status appear to be one that was not accurate. Leading women to think we were engaging during time periods when we were not. While also painting himself to be a father who provided and took care of his child when he had not done so since the birth of our child.

I Felt infuriated by the drama, he always steered in my direction. While I tried to keep my head down, hustle, and get my life and my kids' life in a better position. Feeling frustrated that Jeff preferred putting me in his drama with women more than he preferred being an adequate parent. I thought back on a time period when we had not been together. One day logging online to see an abrupt post he had made labeling me his woman crush Wednesday. Posting my picture along with a long-drawn-out post of why he appreciated me. The post was odd due to the fact that a few days prior to the post, he had been texting me, accusing me of men I barely knew. Calling me bitches and whores while I ignored each message.

Feeling absolutely nothing in regard to his accusations because I had experienced similar behavior from him numerous times. A man could not like, comment, or share a post of mine without Jeff feeling as though we were intimately linked. This was not based on my behavior or previous behavior but his own guilt from how he conducted himself. He could not put this type of behavior past me because he could not put it past himself. He had made a habit of finding women through his social media, so he had to believe that I would or was doing the same.

Each time finding out shortly after that it was, he who had been involved with someone. This time was no different than any of the others. I initially assumed the wcw post was his way of trying to get back on my good side after being so disrespectful.

Yet I didn't think much of it, ignoring the post never acknowledging it due to my belief that he did not mean a word of what he shared via social media. A few days later, I got a friend request via Instagram from a girl named Brit. Accepting it after seeing she was a Charlottesville local and psychology major. She had followed my business page and had made inquiries about some of my products, so I didn't think she was anyone associated with Jeff. A few days after her last inquiry, that all changed. Brit in boxed me, explaining to me that she had been seeing Jeff and wanted to know if he and I were together. During this period, Jeff had been contacting me daily after the wcw post, hoping to get me to give him another chance, but I declined.

I explained to Brit that me and Jeff were no longer together, and I was in the process of trying to get him to sign the divorce papers. She expressed to me that Jeff had initially informed her that we were divorced, but after seeing the wcw post, she started doing some digging. Finding out from one of her friends that he had lied and was not divorced after all. She couldn't understand why he would flaunt me on social media after expressing to her that we were no longer an item. I explained to her that he was simply using his number one marketing strategy. Dangling me in the faces of his many constituents. Hoping to strike and grab a hold of a new woman by using me as the bait.

He did this constantly, trying to make other women feel inferior to me. Using it as a way to bait them in. Oddly enough, it was a tactic of his that always seemed to work. During this time, Jeff had also been reaching out to me, expressing to me how numerous women I thought had respect for me were trying to get with him. One day naming names and going down the long list as if he wanted me to feel bothered. Shortly after stating that allegedly Lanaye had been in boxing him trying to get her slice of the community penis, he had been dishing out everywhere. Making comments about things she had stated in relation to me.

I couldn't believe that she would do that to me, but I told myself that if he was telling the truth, it didn't matter. He had failed to get me back, so he was now trying to use a new method. Constantly bringing up Della and Lanaye, hoping to bait me in. But what he didn't know was I did not care. I couldn't wrap my mind around why he thought this would make me feel a way about those women and not him. What he didn't understand is that if any of my old friends, enemies, or anyone in between was currently trying to get with him, it was simply because of his conduct. They all knew he was messy, didn't turn anything down, and lived for opportunities to try and hurt me.

And those were all petty components I did not have the time or energy to focus on. We constantly hear stories, where men will go after a woman they know, has been around. Viewing their attempts as an opportunity to get a piece of what everyone else is getting. Never recognizing that women are capable of doing the same thing. I had been through so many events with Jeff messing around with women in my small town. Bringing hateful energy in my direction because they all operated the same way. Soon as they started their entanglement with him, it was common behavior for them to start trying to attack me.

He had done this with strangers, friends, ex-friends, and family members. Shortly after all of this, I would find out that he had slept with one of my cousins, who I thought I was very close with. Having her stop speaking and talking to me. As if she had the right to be angry after she had decided to sleep with my ex-husband. These events started making me realize I had done the right thing by letting Tonya have him. Brit told me that she started scoping me out after seeing the post because her initial thought was, I looked attractive, and she wondered if we were still being intimate in some way. I explained to her that I had no desire to be intimate with someone who was doing so with other people.

She went on to give me a more in-depth understanding of why she was reaching out to me. Unlike most of the women I had encountered from Jeff's life, Brit was respectful and reasonable. She explained to me that she had been stalking my social media, contemplating if she should reach out to me or not. She told me that she had been dating Jeff and thought he was a sweetheart in the beginning. Later taking notice of his ability to lie consistently with no regard. She told me that she had been giving him rides to and from everywhere he needed to go. Allegedly she had also been paying for things for him and those connected to him often feeling as though she was being used. She shared with me that she had started to see a pattern with him that she did not like or respect.

Slowly disassociating herself with him after feeling like he was not bringing anything to the table. Sharing with me all of the things he had shared with her about me that sparked a few question marks as to what his motives were. He had been known to talk me up to women sharing details about my life in reference to my earnings and endeavors that never made sense, being that he always attacked those components of my life. Leading me to feel like he used me to try and make other women feel away, and in my opinion, it was lame. Brit shared with me that she noticed that and was reaching out to see what was up. The irony was Jeff started texting me in the middle of our conversation. Going in about how he too had been celibate.

And had no interest in any other women. Clinging on to his usual dynamic of "wanting his family back." I ignored his text, still conversing with Brit on the phone, soaking up everything she was telling me. As she alleged that his mother had talked about me poorly to her numerous times. As if I was shocked when in fact, I didn't expect to hear anything different. Oddly enough, when I would finally get the courage to leave him for good, his mother would try contacting me numerous times. And I would ignore all of her attempts.

I allowed Jeff to text and keep going making a complete ass of himself before I told him what I had just learned from Brit. First, he responded by calling me, saying he didn't know anyone named Brit. Waiting for a few minutes before calling her, trying to go off on her for contacting me, accusing her of trying to ruin his family dynamic when he himself had already had the pleasure of doing so. Later that night, he phoned me coming clean about his relationship with Brit. Equating it to being "just sex." Trying to go in about her as a woman expressing to me that he had slept with her on the first night he met her. Wanting to make her look bad to me when in reality, all it did was make me question who he was. Later accusing Brit of being a lesbian telling me that she was trying to fill my head up with content about him because she was interested in me.

I had been through so much at the hands of Jeff's lies and poor conduct, and I had finally learned to let go of all that he said. Making him aware in that moment that I didn't care if what she said was true or false because I knew him. And even if she had stretched the truth, which I don't believe she did, he had still proven himself to be unworthy of my affection a long time ago. So, I kept looking ahead, ignoring all attempts to give him another chance to ruin me as he had so many times in the past. Britt turned out to be a real woman, and despite how we had become affiliated, she gave her apologies for involving me in her and Jeff's messy relationship. A few weeks later, I was booked to do a vendor's event to sell my products, and she showed up. Coming to the table showing support to me and my brand.

Purchasing products and allowing me to take her photo with her items and post it to my business content from that day. Somehow Jeff got word that she had come and contacted me going off.

Making it clear to me that he did not approve of me being friendly with her. This was based on the fact he had always managed to spark drama with me and other women, and this time he was unsuccessful. Because unlike the list of previous women he had been involved with, Brit, had standards, was intelligent, and she had class. So, arguing about a man who had wronged her was not her style. I ignored Jeff's temper tantrum, hanging up the phone because I knew why he was enraged.

For once, he had met a woman who could not be programmed in the ways he had hoped. Brit was not on the let's hate my baby mama train, and due to that, he lost interest in her quick. Her psychology background had given her insight into Jeffery's world of flaws and poor behavior in reference to women and how he treated them. She would show love to me on social media sending him through the roof as he contacted me consistently accusing her of being a lesbian due to her keen ability to think and respond for herself. The day of the vendor's event, I had many women who had been in some form of relationship with Jeff after me show up to my table making inquiries about my business. Some of them even purchasing products. Although it was extremely uncomfortable, I would give myself silent reminders that I was walking in my purpose, and I would not let any form of messiness take me away from that.

Although I stayed progressive throughout this time period of my life, dynamics like this created a lot of social anxiety for me. I was Constantly walking out into the world, running into numerous women who had been intimate with Jeff during and after the course of our relationship.

Having women stalk my social media, show up to places where I worked, or was doing an event. Finally, allowing the behaviors of messy, insecure women to ruin the sense of security I had. Feeling as though I no longer wanted to go out, fearing I would run into entities from my past realm of hurt triggering emotions I was trying to lay to rest. I started working out less, being less mobile, and lacking a quality sense of self-care in general, shortly after gaining a significant amount of weight, feeling as though I was now losing myself physically. I had unconsciously stepped into a state of depression because no matter how hard I tried, I could not escape Jeff, the scars he had imprinted on my life, and the environment full of people who knew my personal business based on his public displays of disrespect. As much as I tried not to look back, there were times when I felt like it didn't matter if I stayed or left because the trauma and lack of comfortability would follow me no matter what.

This, my friends, is the psychology of a broken abused woman. We tell ourselves that nothing we do will matter because that, in turn, becomes our mental reality. What I was not understanding is that I was only being dragged in such a manner because I was allowing things and people to penetrate their way in. When in reality, I had the power to change my dynamic. So that's what I did. I started trying to tackle my insecurities in regard to my weight gain by showing up for myself in the way I always had. Trying to look good, recognizing how that made me feel better.

I would constantly receive invites to attend outings from people I knew were not positive authentic entities in my life. Often, I would try to break away from the long-term relationship I had established with anxiety, fear, and hurt and find the detachment process to be unsuccessful. Many people were reveling in the negative components of my life. It was very emotionally distracting to recognize that there were so many people praying on my downfall. But what God allowed me to realize is that component of my process did not matter as much as I initially thought it did. Although I could see the pointlessness in allowing my emotions to get the best of me. I was still struggling with emotional control. Nonetheless, I would look in the mirror daily, engaging in positive self-talk while changing my eating and exercise habits and seeing some resolve. Thanking God for the small changes I produced while still going after the bigger changes that I felt I was in dire need of. Something I had possessed throughout my entire journey was the ability to pause, reassess, and conquer anything I set out to. Finding it easy to focus on cultivating and conquering my goals during my times of distress. Deeming myself a true Capricorn because there was nothing that would stop me from putting in work and gaining results no matter what happened.

Jeff would be off doing him with any and every one he saw fit, never caring about our child or me. Spending all of his time, money, and ambitions on the things he wanted for himself. Never offering me a hand while he watched me bust my ass day in and day out. News began to spread about my come-up as people watched me acquire a bigger home, a second vehicle, and an overall enhanced quality of life for my children. Leading Jeff to feel as though he now felt interested in his daughter. Utilizing his position as a father to try to get in where he didn't belong or truly desire to be for the right reasons. Raye would always take notice of my elevation, urging me to keep Jeff away.

Telling me that she felt as though he did not genuinely desire to do the right thing. I feel like he is only trying to come back around because he wants to sabotage what you have going on. She was right. How many times had he tried to throw me off track with my business?

Hating when he walked into my kitchen, seeing me blasting my music as I compounded handmade skin and hair products. Feeling the euphoria of innovation running through me. As I combined my love of science with my love of cosmetics.

Bringing to life a vision that I had since 2009. Yet there I stood in 2019, failing to see how I was finally walking in my purpose and allowing negative entities to knock me off my game. What I didn't realize was that I was blocking my own blessings, keeping people around that God had showed me numerous times were not for me or about me. One evening I lay in bed trying to write when I received more texts from Jeff trying to do what he had always done. Play me against other women and cultivate drama. While trying to work his way back in with me. I decided to end the games I knew he never got tired of playing. In boxing Tonya via social media and asking her to get him to stop violating my boundaries.

Sending her messages of Jeff's texts where he denied their relationship, telling me he didn't want our daughter around her and begged me to take him back. I explained to her that I had no ill feelings towards her and felt like we all had allowed things to go on that shouldn't have for far too long. I Expressed to her that I didn't want him, and I didn't want to be an issue for her security. Taking initiative to do what should have been done a long time ago and stop the culprit in his tracks. She agreed, thanking me for my honesty telling me that she assumed I had still been dealing with him although I was not. I knew she would never leave him alone, but that was not my focus. I wanted her to keep him away from me. Never really grasping the concept that she had less pull in reference to him than I did.

He didn't care if she knew what he had been doing because he knew she was a different type of woman. Unwilling to fight against his maltreatments because to her, it didn't matter what he did as long as he did it and continued to be with her. I didn't owe her that respect because she didn't give it to me initially as his wife. But I knew he was only moving how he was because he had been allowed to for far too long. After hearing the things, I had told Tonya and how serious I was about wanting to be left alone, he paused for two weeks before trying his hand again. Making me realize he didn't care about the two-year restraining order or care about me reaching out to Tonya because he didn't value that relationship either. So, I blocked him from my phone, all social media networks, and blocked everyone who was an extension of him.

Setting boundaries with him and others in ways I never had, trying to make it clear to him that this was the end of the road, and he would no longer be able to infringe my space of peace and happiness any longer. Days turned into weeks, and weeks turned into months, and before you knew it, I was no longer having to deal with him contacting me, hoping to get results. My conduct had shown him more than any words I could ever speak, and it was becoming clear to him where I stood. Jeff stopped reaching out to me, and I started moving forward. Putting all of my time and effort into working on myself and my children. Trying to right countless wrongs in my life in regard to how I had failed to take care of myself. Taking vacations from work to spend time with my kids. Going places and doing fun family activities.

Where I would cultivate conversations about the traumatic things, we had been through. Trying to help everyone to talk and express any and all things they felt in regard to the past and the future. Learning that my kids had felt the same disappointing feelings I had as a child after watching me endure things that I shouldn't have. Although I was free of the drama and stress of Jeff after removing myself, the weight of all that had occurred was still taking a toll on me mentally and physically. I was still working long hours, going to school full-time, and authoring books in my spare time. Unable to sleep due to insomnia. Telling myself I would be ok now that Jeff was gone, but in reality, Jeff was not the only change I needed to make.

I started getting multiple phone calls from people after it was clear that I was not looking back and making strides in my own personal growth. Calls that consisted of information about Jeff, other women, and things people were hoping would bother me. Telling myself that these individuals no longer needed access to me. Realizing it was my job to protect the peace that had taken me a long time to cultivate. Blocking numbers, interaction, and overall contact with anyone who showed me they were not a genuine entity in my life. Noticing the irritation from people who desired to move my spirit with negative content and no longer could. Telling myself that moving forward, I would only allow good energy in my space.

And if that meant I had to make drastic cuts from my life, then that's what I was prepared to do. I started to recognize how my level of consciousness was elevating now that certain aspects of life and human behavior were being revealed to me. I came to the realization that my lack of self-awareness, self-love, and loyal behavior was holding me hostage in multiple spaces. The thing about life is that it never stops serving you bullshit. But bullshit helps you to learn and grow and I was now reaching a level of awareness that was helping me to break away from life's unhealthy bondage. I started the severance process and it was contagious. I realized there was something to the whole self-love dynamic Afterall. Knowing who you are and falling in love with that person creates a higher frequency internally and externally. Once I started loving myself properly, I was no longer willing to accept half-ass renditions of love, value, and respect from the people around me. All of a sudden, the woman who never made cuts due to her unrealistic sense of loyalty to others started making cuts left and right. And let me be the first to say that watching people take in my new valued sense of awareness was a cringe-ass situation. All of a sudden, the gaslighting, and emotional abuse were depreciated and removed without any question. Once I reestablished myself and made it clear to those inflicting psychological abuse upon my being that I was aware and done based on these unhealthy components. If you could have seen some of the facial expressions I encountered once I made it clear that I was no longer willing to accept the fake shit and the fuck shit you would have been at a loss for words.

I started to take notice of the fact that my good heart and loyalty had been used and abused by many around me. I had been locked into so many long-term relationships with people who didn't value, respect, or even like me for the most part. These people liked my giving spirit, drive, and intellect but only when it was convenient. I was so tired of people looking at my being and feeling threatened and expelling out unnecessary hatred in my direction. But life's lessons have a funny way of molding you. Once I recognized who I was and what God had instilled in me I realized I would never be able to stop malice, hatred, inaccurate perceptions, persecution, manipulation, and the list goes on. But what I could do is recognize foul energies and take heed to recognizable behaviorisms so I could shield myself from previously uncomfortable situations in regard to relationships. The responses I received from people once I confronted them with my feelings in reference to their fake love, and affliction were priceless. Each and every one of them responded in a way as if they wanted to outwardly come out and say who the fuck does she think she is? How dare she recognize my gaslighting and emotional manipulation! How dare she recognize my strategic ability to try and instill doubt into her being! How dare she recognize that I too have an agenda! This my friends is when I knew I had leveled up mentally and was truly ready to step into my field of study. It's a beautiful thing to be able to recognize the flaw and psychologically skewed behaviors of strangers and approach all components adequately. But it is an even greater reality when you are skilled and honest enough to do so with yourself and the people around you. Life had been hitting me from all directions but I was finally taking in the realism behind the ideology that every hardship leaves imprints of emotional, and psychological scars. That is deeply embedded into the human psyche against our will. Those imprinted scars all leave behind a blessing and a lesson that grants us a higher level of consciousness if and only if we are willing to accept our truths in their flawed forms.

Day after day, I had begun to struggle with anxiety more and more. Often feeling the weight of panic flair up in my chest, making me feel as though I was having a heart attack when I was not. My body started communicating to me that I needed to slow down, and for a while, I was ignoring all indicators that I was overwhelmed. Constantly pushing myself to keep going telling myself I could prevail. Later listening to my body as it indicated to me that prevailing was no longer an option because I was tired and emotionally drained. Pushing through one traumatic event after another.

Never allowing myself time to process one event before another popped up on my radar. One day my hot water tank stopped working, and I contacted my landlord, hoping to get it fixed. Informing her that there was no hot water and hadn't been all day. She agreed that she would send a handyman over to look at it later that day. She sent the handyman over, and he looked at the tank, informing me that it needed to be reset. He hit the reset button, alerting me that if the water did not get hot after a while, I would need to reset the water tank. Instructing me on how to do so. I waited two days, and the water did not get hot, so I went in and hit the reset button as the handyman had instructed, but there was still no hot water.

I contacted the landlord, asking her to send out someone professional telling her that the tank was still not working. She gave me the run-around and dragged her feet for almost an entire month. Leaving my family and me to have to take cold showers until we got to the point where it was too uncomfortable, and we started staying in hotels. One morning I got up prepared to reset the tank to try and get the hot water working again. I was tired, and after doing my assignments, it slipped my mind to reset the tank. My mom yelled for me to go downstairs after informing me that she smelled a burning sensation. We called the fire department, and they came right away.

I told them how I had been hitting the reset button, and they assessed the tank. The firefighter informed me that had I gone in and reset the tank like I did usually and had planned to that morning, I would have died instantly from the large voltage coming from the tank. I was flabbergasted and relieved that God had spared me that fate that morning. After becoming overwhelmed, I reached out to the landlord again, requesting that she have the tank fixed or I would be unable to pay her the rent for the month. Due to unlivable circumstances, we were now in. She started being aggressive, and after having her disrespect me several times and insult my intelligence, I hung up the phone. Deciding that since my words were getting me nowhere, my actions would.

It was ridiculous to me that she was charging over 2,000 dollars a month for a home she didn't want to fix things in. Thinking about how inhumane it was for her to expect rent when we had now been without hot water for a month and paying for hotel rooms. That day I started looking for homes right away. Finding a bigger home for me and my family that had a better quality of appliances. Upgrading from the five-bedroom home that needed work to a six-bedroom home that had been recently built. That day I took the new landlord a check securing the deposit and two months' rent after splitting the cost with my mom fifty-fifty. Coming back home to call my current landlord and let her know that I was no longer renewing the lease and would be moving out within thirty days.

She sat on the other end of the phone, shocked, trying to clean up the situation, telling me that I had somehow misinterpreted her intentions when I had not. She thought that if she handled me aggressively, I would pay for the tank replacement due to me and my mother having made many upgrades and paid for repairs in the past, but she was wrong. I was no longer in a space where I was allowing people to take advantage of me, and I was not going to sit in a situation that I knew was not compatible for my family and me. I thanked her for her time and told her how I was going to miss the house hanging up and leaving her in a distressed state. She didn't care about disrespecting me because she had somehow convinced herself that I needed her when I did not. Counting on that need as a way for her to take advantage and mistreat my family and me. When I never paid her late and had upgraded her home significantly with my mother's help paying for new appliances and repairs that she was responsible for.

I had become so tired of people thinking they had more leverage than what they did in reference to me, and I was drawing lines and implementing boundaries with everyone, and it was now her turn to see how much God favored me and mine. Long story short, I got my family and me out of there asap, and I didn't look back. She called, trying to convince me that there had been some form of miscommunication, but me and her both knew that was not the case. I thanked her for letting me rent the house for four years and made it clear to her that my mind was made up and I was no longer interested in staying there anymore. Although I had found a fast and more comfortable solution for my family and me, I could still feel the stress of anxiety and tachycardia happening frequently. My body was communicating with me heavily, and I was ignoring it. Telling myself that slowing down was not an option for me.

Due to my load of responsibility. But the truth was I was afraid to slow down. Allowing myself to believe that if I didn't continue to grind harder, my lifestyle, goals, and progress would somehow depreciate. Losing can feel like a curse because we want so many things to go right. Craving the solace of stability. But in my own reality, I was starting to see how winning felt like an even bigger curse. Simply due to the fact that I had lost the ability to live in the moment of every blessing I had received. Fearing that something would happen, and I would experience a loss and hardship like I had so many times in the past.

Preparing for the worst when God was showing me so many signs that the worst had already come to pass. Sure, I had experienced hardships and had to start over numerous times in my life. But what I was overlooking was the fact that during those times, I was living wrong, stagnant, and dependent of relationships and people who were not dependable. Lacking the true understanding that it was those very incidences that had morphed me into a woman with wisdom, intuition, ambition, and agility. God had helped me through a million and one hard hurtful events because it was this very season of life, he had been preparing me for all along. A season of transformation, clarity, and strength. Allowing me numerous breakthroughs. Leading me into a space of purpose where I could use all of these unfortunate events to heal, help, teach, and lead others to know that there is always something better waiting on the road ahead.

I had been so busy going after my future that I was overlooking the many accomplishments that lay gracefully in my present.

Overlooking the generational curses I had broken as a parent. The lifestyle I offered my kids was better than the one I had known. And the peace I had stepped into after finally having the courage to leave a marriage and relationship that was filled with toxins and abuse. Black women are often molded to be strong upon their arrival into the world. Being taught by society that they are not as valuable as women of other ethnic backgrounds. Constantly being made to prove themselves even in situations where the proof has already been laid out on the table.

I had come from a culture where women were taught that abuse is normal. Looking at the many women around me who endured it so gracefully as they stood by their man, acting as if their pain was not present. I had also come from a culture where the man did not protect the women adequately. Leaving her in many instances divorced, vulnerable, and alone to raise and provide for her children. Naturally, I walked into some of the same events as my mother, telling myself that this was simply how things go. But God was now showing me that this was not how it had to go for me. Yes, some of the same curses my mother and grandmothers had faced had befallen me, but I had handled them differently.

Standing up and owning the very strength that so many were trying to strip from my being. Showing my oppressors that the force they hated that resided in me was unmovable. And it was for that very reason I decided to stop letting my trauma from my past hold a place in my present and future. I started taking a long hard look at myself. Recognizing internal components that were not homeostatic. Understanding the space I was sitting in as I chased dream after dream. At the same time, completing one responsibility after another.

Only to realize that I was tired. I had been through so much in my life. Never taking the proper time with myself or my issues. Telling myself that my hurt and anxiety didn't matter because I needed to keep my focus on being a mother and a go-getter. But my mind and body would soon take the lead conveying to me that slowing down was now the only option I had. I started dropping the ball in so many areas of my life. Long days and early mornings were the only lifestyle I had known for going on five years. Working long hours at my job, studying while being a full-time student, and pouring into my writing ambitions. While my body was indicating to me that it was tired of being improperly handled.

Ignoring the jittery feeling I had numerous times during the day. While getting no sleep and standing on my feet daily for long periods trying to unpack and get our new home set up. I had encompassed this overwhelming feeling of always wanting to show up for the people around me while no one showed up for me. Telling myself constantly that I would get through my feelings of burnout as I always did and be ok. But this time, God had other plans for my hardheaded ass. My grades were dropping, my house was still not unpacked, and my contract agreements were not being met. Like usual, I started feeling panic manifest as I began to fear failing myself by not having these things executed in a timely, adequate manner.

I started working hard to play catch up and keep up. Dishing out as many assignments a day while trying to unpack and get my home in order. I had developed an extreme case of OCD as a result of my childhood trauma. My OCD had made it impossible for me to function or produce in spaces where there was no cleanliness or organization. My home was always organized and clean to the point you could eat off of the floor if you wanted to. As you can imagine, boxes piled to the ceiling and dust everywhere was not my idea of structure. Day after day, I juggled with adding to my manuscript, getting schoolwork done, and unpacking.

Feeling as though no matter how hard I tried to get back on track, things were not moving at an adequate pace. I had been on my feet so much trying to get things done my feet started swelling. My feet had become so engulfed with fluid I was unable to wear shoes for two months. Walking around daily in a pair of fuzzy night slippers because I could no longer fit shoes. I started suffering from headaches and dizziness, still telling myself that this too shall pass, but it would not. One day I started feeling dizzy and decided to lay down and get rest. I had been due to go into work and do a twelve-hour shift that day, so I figured a little rest would rejuvenate me.

I managed to sleep for a few hours before waking up, realizing that if I didn't get going soon, I would be late for work. That night I got to work, and I felt extremely different. I felt dizzy, and I was still suffering from headaches along with blurred vision. I sat on the sofa, propping my swollen feet up. Trying to get back to my studies still trying to get my grades back where they needed to be. I started feeling sick, and my heart started to beat fast as if it was trying to push its way out of my chest.

Tachycardia had once again taken over, and I felt as if I was having a heart attack. The accelerated heart rate was followed by weakness and vomiting, and I started to fear that something was wrong. I made it through my shift getting up the following day, noticing that the swelling had now become present in my hands as well. That morning I rushed to the hospital where I stayed. The doctors did labs and ran several tests concluding that I was suffering from burnout from being overworked, anxiety, and my weight gain was contributing to minute health responses that could be reversed with the proper intervention. I waited to hear that something significantly serious was wrong. Not understanding how I could feel so terrible and have nothing major going on.

In denial as to how it was, I had befallen this state of feeling drained. For two years, I had been urged to undergo weight loss surgery after becoming overweight after my divorce. I had been overweight for three years, and it was now becoming clear to me that I needed to make a lot of hard changes in my life to get to a state of homeostasis. The doctor expressed to me that the road I was on was deadly, and I needed to get my body back on track before I developed a more serious aliment due to the lack of care, I was offering myself. That week it was as if I had been scared straight. I called and got set up with a therapist, I contacted the bariatric health clinic and planned to move forward with weight loss surgery, and I started slowing down significantly. I had become so wrapped up in making good changes to try and reverse how I felt I was no longer concerning myself with other people. There was no one who didn't need or expect something from me at the time, and I told myself that my next move would clarify who was for me and who wasn't.

Everyone around me knew my circumstances. Watching me work my ass off with no help. Attending to my kids alone and it was clear that self-care had fled so far away it was no longer visible to me. I stopped hearing from everyone, and I tried not to let it bother me. Taking each day slowly as I made a daily list of what I needed to do. Checking off every meal I consumed, making sure I only ate healthy, checking off my assignments, often reminding myself that Rome was not built in a day. Therefore, leaving things unattended that I normally wouldn't.

Reminding myself that sleep and peace were more essential to my wellbeing than any degree, entrepreneurial endeavor, or need anyone else had for me to fulfill. The more I put myself first, the less I felt people were starting to hold a place for me in their lives. I realized I had cultivated many relationships that were only conducive as long as people felt I was on their time doing things they wanted. But what they all had failed to realize is that a woman who can't depend on anyone but God does not feel as though she needs anyone but God. I made the needed cuts after looking at the poor dynamics amongst my circle, and although some of them were hard, I kept moving. I had been the person that friends and family came to for advice, relationship issues, parenting issues, money, and the list goes on. Always showing up and helping out in ways people desired.

Often going out of my way even when they didn't deserve it. Showing up and being dependable for people who never seemed to extend that back in my direction. It was as if no one understood that my life was different from theirs, and I, too, needed support. I had three kids who all depended on me and me alone. Working more hours in one week than most people worked in two to three weeks while trying to keep my grades up and my head above water. Often finding myself repeating my list of life requirements and responsibilities to others when they lacked understanding of where I was as opposed to them. It was becoming a frequent thing with me to have people upset that I wasn't as available or on their time as they wanted me to be, and it was starting to piss me off.

I realized I was surrounded by selfish people who knew my story and knew the load I was carrying. Yet none of them were willing to handle me with care gloves. Often expecting me to go out of my way for them devaluing my time and my load because no one was concerned about me. Everyone was looking at me, expecting me to give and give and do and be. Watching as I neglected myself. Watching as I carried a heavy load, never offering to lesson it for me. This dynamic only existed for me with my people because it was one, I had allowed for so long.

That people now had no other way of being with me if they could not hold onto old ways that suited them and not me. I was disposable to everyone if I was unwilling to be a doormat and a resource. God was allowing me so much discomfort in so many different areas because he wanted me to realize that it was time to make changes. Changes I had been avoiding for far too long. I was starting to see how no one ever lent me a hand. Even when they heard my cries for help. The only response I ever got was to drop this, lose that, or stop this.

Because I had been surrounded by people who would rather see me lose than help me win. Never wanting to offer me the same aide they did others around them. Because it was me, and they were too afraid to lend me a hand because they saw what I did with no help and no resources. Often fearing where I would get if they extended a hand or a resource in my direction. For as much as I had uplifted, helped, and influenced the people around me, most of them felt like they would rather try to exceed me or discourage me than help me. Secretly wishing that my increase would decrease. Or my drive would no longer be as consistent as they had witnessed.

I was seeing this dynamic with friends and family. Recognizing the frustration people had every time they watched me prevail. Listening to people's selfish comments when I showed a need for help. Often hearing responses that revolved around phrases like I can help you with that later, but first I need you to help me with this or that. Or I never stepped in because you didn't ask; when they had stepped in with everyone else, they saw needed a hand without being asked. Watching as people emulated my goals, claiming them as theirs after seeing me be innovative in certain areas. Convincing themselves that I was now their competition instead of owning that I was their inspiration. When we walk into a grocery store, we tend to walk down every aisle, noticing that there is plenty of every item we are looking for.

Often considering that although there are multiple companies selling the same items and doing the same things, they offer different mechanisms that make it easier for us to select who we prefer. As we make our choices and watch others make theirs, it never matters to us who selects what brand because all of those brands coexist. Residing on the same shelves as one another, not seeing one another as a threat, an enemy, or a roadblock. Because God has made room for them to all be able to succeed within the same realm, I started feeling as though people were hating me and mishandling me due to my change and progress. I was no longer entering the room as the teen mom. In those days, being introduced as so and so's friend with the baby. I was no longer the friend or family member who was struggling financially in the ways I had for so long. And I was no longer Jeff's wife that was being cheated on and played for a fool.

I had become a force of change, transition, and growth. Evolving before some of the very people that never saw it for me. Causing then frustration as I continued to reach and grab and stride while the tides of life brushed against me vigorously, still trying to throw me off course.

I decided the only thing for me to do to progress was to distance myself from it all. Focusing on making health transitions to improve my mental and physical health. I started attending therapy sessions every week with a therapist. Adapting to the awkwardness that comes along with telling a complete stranger your innermost thoughts, feelings, and life events. Discovering a lot about myself, the people around me, and my unaddressed trauma. Eventually, understanding that I had developed anxiety from adopting the strong black women myth that had been handed down from one generation to the next.

The myth that made me believe there was no time to focus on my hurt and issues because I had to be strong for the people around me. The myth that had me believing that slowing down was no longer an option after making a significant amount of progress. The myth that had me believing that I was alone when in fact, there were abundant resources waiting for me that would come from the universe's faith and belief that I could heal from everything I needed to. While the people I knew, loved, and cared for offered me nothing but awkward looks, fake love, and low-key hatred, resenting me for the changes I had made that they had not anticipated. Helping my choice to remove myself from their space easier than what I had assumed.

I was starting to understand why people left their original environments after they began to elevate. Change is good, but it is not always greeted amongst the people you start your journey with. Some people come into your life to grow with you. While others enter your life to assist for a season. My problem was I was ignoring the vibes. Trying to overlook people's seasonal dynamic believing everyone had come to stay. When I had been shown by several that their time in my life had expired a long time ago, and that is a hard-ass pill to swallow. Especially when you look around and see that more people are going than staying, but I knew more spring cleaning amongst my circle needed to be done for me to have the internal peace I deserved, so I took heed to what was being revealed to me based on people's behavior, and I acted accordingly.

Only this time, I made my cuts silently. I told myself, there was no need for me to explain to people why I had removed them from my life. They all were aware of their pessimism. They were also aware of the things they had been saying and doing behind my back. An explanation was not needed, nor was it deserved. I was tired of explaining myself to people who didn't deserve my energy. So, I made my exit calmly, ignoring people's attempts to reenter after realizing I had become aware of their conduct. I started divulging more to my therapist, still feeling anxious every time I became emotional.

Allowing myself to break in ways I hadn't before. Listening as she paused, assuring me that I was in a safe space where I could let out everything I needed to. Each time I wanted to retreat. Wondering if I was indeed in a safe space to divulge. Allowing my anxiety to make me feel like I was unsafe to do so. Noticing at the end of each session how internally lighter I felt just from talking and addressing elephants that had stood in the room with me for years. Untouched and unclaimed. Clinging to my being, waiting for the moment to be acknowledged properly.

I had come to understand that therapy was essential if I wanted to step into my new season successfully, conquering my fears and anxiety from the scars of my past failures. I had not heard from Jeff, and he was finally respecting my boundaries after realizing he could no longer penetrate his way through them. It hurt to see that he was proving himself to be a nonexistent father, but I had finally accepted the fact that he would never be present for our child if he could not have access to me and all that came along with that access. So, I moved on and made peace with my truth. I had gotten rid of one thorn from my past, unaware that another was ready to pop up.

CHAPTER 11

Baby Daddy Drama

M y son's father had been released from jail for months and hadn't reached out to him. Nor did I expect him to. I had received word while he was in jail that he was waiting on a settlement check from a car accident he had been in. During the span of twelve years, I had not received support for my son, Christmas gifts, or even a single call to say hello to him. Since a lean had been placed on him due to unpaid child support, I was informed that the settlement would be garnished and sent directly to me. I didn't give it much thought because I knew Omar would do everything within his power to make sure that my son or I never saw a dime of the money. Shortly after his release, one of his family members reached out to me, telling me that Omar had received the money.

She wanted to know if my son had received anything from him. I explained that he had not given my son a dime or a call. His family member then expressed to me how allegedly Omar's mother had been paying Ashley's bills for the entire duration of his incarceration. Allegedly Omar was supposed to pay his mother back the money after receiving the settlement and did not. His family member went on about how his mother was upset with him due to not hearing from him after he had received the money. She informed me that his mother had suggested that he give me a portion of the money for my son because he had never helped me take care of him.

I didn't know if what I was being told was true, and I didn't care. I had made peace with what Omar hadn't done for our son a long time ago. Feeling in the moment that my name was only being suggested because everyone was upset that he had not given them any of the money. Oddly enough, I started receiving calls from family members of Omar's inquiring if my son could go out with them and their children for family events. I declined feeling two things. One that my son would never want to be around strangers because that wasn't his way. Secondly that these attempts were revenge-fueled attempts to make Omar annoyed.

His family had never reached out to me about my son, yet now that they were angry about money and mad at Ashely, they thought they would try to use my son as a pawn to be messy. I was not having it at all. I declined using my son's asthma and covid as an excuse because he would not be attending what I knew was a messy situation. A few weeks later, Omar started reaching out to my mom via social media, with her choosing not to respond for apparent reasons. A week later, Omar reached out to me, inquiring if he could come to see my son. My son had made it clear that he was not interested in seeing Omar. Filled with resentment and distrust for the way Omar had handled him his entire life.

Although I understood why he felt bitter in response to Omar, I knew that they needed a sit-down. It had been far too long, and I thought there was a possibility Omar had changed. So, I talked my son into it, praying there would be some resolve and they could potentially move forward. My son had disclosed that he did not want Ashely involved expressing that he felt like he and his father needed to have one-off with no one involved, including me. I agreed and reached out to Omar, informing him of my son's wishes. Omar had promised to bring Christmas gifts with him when he arrived, and it seemed like things were set in motion, and it would all roll over smoothly. The day of the sit-down, Omar messaged me asking me if Ashley could come in with him.

I had promised my son that it would be him and Omar only, and that was a promise I was not going to break. I explained to Omar that he didn't know our son and he was a different kind of kid. He was not one to try and communicate with anyone other than the people in his household. Never feeling comfortable around a lot of people, people he didn't know, or people he didn't trust. I told Omar he needed to feel like he could trust him and me and that going against his requirements would not be a good start. I tried to figure out why Ashley would even think her being present would be appropriate. She didn't have a relationship with my son, and as far as everyone was concerned, she had played a considerable role in Omar's choice not to be present.

When Omar arrived, I opened the door noticing Ashley in the driver's seat, I said hello to her to try to be polite when she rolled her eyes and sped off aggressively with a raging attitude. It had been twelve years, and she had not changed at all. She was still harboring hatred for a woman who she had wronged. She was upset at her inability to have control or input in a situation she didn't respect or want to evolve. My son had always been a threat to her, and I never understood why. Omar looked at me, looking embarrassed by Ashley's pettiness.

"Why does she have to do all that? Were grown women, and it's been far too long for her to be still that bothered. "

Omar started responding quietly, appearing to be in agreement with me. He walked through my front door, took one look around at the inside of my home, and his energy started to evolve into something else instantly. He started saying how Ashley wanted to be involved with my son when he and I knew that was not the case. I looked at him immediately, remembering the day he had given me the confirmation that Ashley did not want him around my son. As he entered my tiny basement apartment running from the police after damaging someone's property with his new girlfriend's vehicle. I remember asking him why he never helped me with my son but always looked out for Ashley taking care of her child that was not his. "She's not like you, man."

"I know that you're going to be ok because you're willing to go out there and get it on your own, but she's not like that. I was hurt by Omar's behavior. And even more offended by his response. "Is that why you don't try to be consistent with my son?" I asked in a petty manner. "Because you know she doesn't want you around him. The girl feels like she should've come; first," he said. He shocked me, as he implied that Ashley felt like my son shouldn't exist. When I was the one in the relationship with him, when she came along already pregnant with someone else's child. I did not understand how she had the gall to feel that way, nor did I know why he thought it was appropriate to defend him being absent in the manner he had.

I snapped out of my thoughts, leading Omar, and my son to the kitchen, leaving them alone to talk. After a significant amount of time had passed, I went into the kitchen speaking with Omar informing him that my son was having some trouble in school with not following directions, etc. I was trying to get him to talk some sense into him from a male's point of view. Overlooking the fact that Omar was not the right male for the job. He started talking stupid about how the white man has a way of doing things and how they want you to conform because they think education, degrees, and money means something . "You have to suck it up and follow their rules, man," he said. The subliminal shade was thick, and I could tell he felt annoyed, but I ignored his terrible advice. Afterall white men were no longer the only educated beings on the planet so I didn't understand his basis for the stupid, biased remarks he was trying to highlight. During his first father to son chat.

I decided to chime in, reminding my son that in order to be something, you had to do the footwork. I could tell that Omar had been shocked walking into my home, seeing where I was living and how. That day he left, promising my son that he would move at his pace and be more present. Never giving the Christmas gift he claimed he had for him. During that visit, they exchanged numbers, and I started inquiring if Omar had tried to reach out since his visit, but he had not. Later I received numerous complaints about my son's lack of participation in virtual school, and I decided to reach out to Omar to see if he could give the father-to-son advice another try. I asked him to call and talk to his son about his lack of participation.

Omar read the message that day, responding days later, telling me he would give him a call. Days went by, and my son never heard from him. Nor did he ever keep his word and contact him as he had agreed. After that, I realized Omar had not changed at all regarding my son. My mom and my brothers were furious with me, telling me I had dropped the ball, allowing Omar to come over knowing he would not be active in our son's life. I had tried to do what I thought was right, hoping there would be a change, but there was not. Four months had passed, and I had not heard from Omar nor had my son.

My mother had informed me that he watched her social media stories daily. She would post things about my entrepreneurial endeavors as well as content about my son purposely. Trying to let Omar see that although he had been a coward and not done his part, my son was living a good life. In return, Omar started posting his own content, causing her to be just as watchful as he had been. She began seeing posts where he would post his large quantity of new shoes, pictures of him holding money, and new items he would get consistently for his other children. Causing my mom to be upset as she questioned why he felt comfortable providing for some of his kids and not my son. Omar kept tuning in to see what my mom posted on her stories, occasionally liking a picture of my son here and there until she became fed up with his presence and blocked him.

One day Omar reached out to me via Facebook, being rudely aggressive telling me that my son's way of doing things would not work for him. I didn't understand what he was referencing, but I waited as his messages continued to come through back-to-back. He started saying that he had been trying to call and text and gotten no response, and I knew that was not true. I had checked my son's phone regularly as well as asked and had been aware for months that Omar had not kept up his end of the bargain as usual. He appeared to be combative, going on about how he would take me to court again if he had to. I could tell he had a chip on his shoulders, but I could also tell that it had nothing to do with my sons' way. He started telling me that he would rather pick him up and have him spend the night at he and Ashley's house. He wanted to introduce him to his half-siblings he had never met.

Making it clear that he had a desire to do things the way he and Ashley wanted to. I made it clear to Omar that I knew nothing of him or Ashley's lifestyle, nor would my son ever feel comfortable doing things their way. "I am not the one making these choices," I told him. "He is old enough to express his emotions to me and make it clear what is comfortable for him and what is not. And you can't just pop up and require that he do things your way when you are the one that failed him." It would be disrespectful and tactless for you to try and force a child into an environment and a way of doing things with which they are not comfortable. I couldn't believe that he thought picking up our child and taking him to meet siblings who had known the comfort of their father's love and support and throwing him into a group setting with strangers abruptly made sense to him.

I felt like Ashley had something to do with his request, but I let him continue. I started telling him that his son had trust issues due to his lack of rearing and that it would not be good for his well-being to throw him to the wolves. Me and my children had our way of doing things. And I was not going to dishonor my son by making him uncomfortable because my care and stability were all he had ever known. He depended on me to be a woman of my word. Relying on me to take his care, feelings, and emotional wellbeing into consideration so I would not abandon that for anyone. Especially not Omar or Ashley.

I had dropped the ball with my children so many times unconsciously while being in a relationship with Jeff, and I was no longer oblivious to my flawed areas in relation to parenting. After ridding my life of my ex-husband, I vowed to always show up for my children in the ways that were most beneficial to their wellbeing. I knew the only way to do better in regard to my son was to honor his preferences because he had suffered silently for a long time due to his father's lack of care. I explained that phone conversations, starting out, and home visits were what our son preferred. Eventually, hoping they could have outings together alone and then work their way up to him meeting his siblings and being able to come to him and Ashley's home. Omar started getting rude and disrespectful, appearing to want to argue with me, which felt odd. Based on the fact that we were equivalent to strangers after not having had any contact for years.

I didn't know how to argue with him even if he wanted me to. Because it seemed baseless. During his messaging spree, it became evident to me that he was hoping I would engage negatively with him. I had made a massive transition with how I responded to things sent to destroy my peace. Still, within doing so, it was becoming a commonality that people were longing for the Nina white from Orangedale Ave. The Nina that was with the shit and didn't hold back. But that version of Nina had been suppressed for so long regarding Omar it felt like a joke that he was longing for her presence. The culture of the baby mama drama was one he clearly preferred, but it was not one I would ever have made assessable to him for many reasons.

I was no longer bitter in response to him and his actions. Because I had made my peace with all of my experiences, including those concerning my fatherless children who had deadbeats who never saw the value in rearing because they had never known what that was like based on their own experiences. I expressed to him that his threats of taking me to court held no weight. He had done that back in the day, trying to be spiteful, but I assured him that based on how he did not follow that agreement, my full custody status, and my overall character in comparison to his, he would never be able to do what he had in the past. I had rebuilt my life from the ground up, furthered my education, and provided my son with a great lifestyle, and there wasn't a judge in America who would allow him custody of my son based on who he was and wasn't. I was not the little twenty-year-old girl he could threaten and toy with anymore, and he read my responses feeling furious because he could see that all of what I was saying was true.

"I'm not trying to make it hard for you to build a relationship with your son because I would never deprive my son of something I know he needs and deserves. I reached out to you four months ago about our son, and he never heard from you." Now today, you wake up wanting to start drama with me for what? "When I knew you hadn't been contacting him," I said, letting him know I was aware of the lie he had told. "Why don't you stop acting like a white woman and let me see my son" he said. Trying to rattle my cage with more disrespect. "Why am I acting like a white woman to you? "

"Is it because I'm speaking to you as someone who has knowledge about her child's mental health and trauma due to his father's lack of parenting? Or is it because I've changed, and I'm educated and using my words to communicate like an adult instead of cursing you out and making threats like I did way back when? I don't know why you are trying to project your misery onto me or my son, but I don't have time for it. I have worked too hard on myself and my son to allow you to enter my life fucking up what I've worked hard to build. The requirements I gave you were never mine; they were his. And if you can't respect the boundaries, he has established due to his pain and lack of trust for your abandonment, you don't need to be around him anyway." I don't need a therapist; he said I already have one."

I ignored his pessimism, letting him know that I had spoken my peace and was getting back to work. There is something about taking the high road during an argument that pisses people off even more. He wanted me to be the old Nina he had been acquainted with, but I could not because there was no care or concern about anything related to him. I had healed from the hurt he had caused in my life and my child's life. And forgiven him a long time ago so I could genuinely establish peace in my heart. He read my messages, not responding, leading me to think the childish spat he had conjured up was over, but it was not. A few minutes later, he started sending me paragraphs giving his recollection of the past that was not accurate.

Telling me that he knew he had not been present, but he was in and out of jail. I made it clear to him that his memory was not accurate. Long before he had gone to jail, he had spent years not being present. "If I could have been there more, I would have," he said. "What kind of man abandons their first child," he asked as if he really wanted the answer? In my mind, I thought You! Man! But I kept that response inside and read through his false accounts before shutting his fake memories down. Reminding him that he always seemed to come around when he got into a relationship with a new girlfriend.

Picking our son up and being consistent until he ended the relationship with whatever new victim he had at the moment and would go back to Ashley, stopping his fathering altogether. At that moment, I recalled an incident from the past. I sat on my sofa, prepared to relax, when I received an inbox message from Omar's new girlfriend, Maya. She wanted to know if I had seen Omar. Unaware that me and Omar barely communicated due to his lack of presence in our child's life. "He has my car and has had it for two days," she said. Instantly I read the message understanding the dynamic of their relationship.

"I am due to go to work soon, and he won't answer for me to bring me my car. Could you please call him for me?" She asked desperately. I didn't understand why she was reaching out to me, but I figured she had no other hopes in contacting him. Assuming my baby mama status with him could offer her some help. I could look at her and tell she was a kind girl, young and naive, just as I had been many times in my life. I asked her for his number, telling her I would try my best to get a hold of him for her. Feeling confident that Omar would avoid bringing her back her car until he felt he had made all the drug runs he could.

I called the number, getting an answer after the first ring. Omar was surprised to hear my voice. "Maya has been calling you and getting no response," I said." You need to get your ass up and take that girl her car before she loses her job." It baffled me that he was so careless. "I know, man, I'm going to take her the car," he assured me. Low key annoyed that Maya had involved me. "You need to grow up and take your ass back home to Ashley and those kids," I said.

" Man, I know" he responded like I was his mother telling him something he didn't want to hear. It disappointed me that Omar was doing Ashley the same way, if not worse. Making me question why he was choosing this immature path. Ashley now had multiple children with him, and he had numerous new relationships during the course of their relationship. I didn't care about Omar not being there for my son because I had done it alone for so long that, at times, I forgot about his existence. Recognizing that all of the poor choices he had made in regard to our child helped me to prosper. For years he had hidden behind the lies he told, making people believe I was stopping his parenting when he was never present because he didn't want to be.

That day, he left my home after seeing my son thrown off by my progress. Feeling guilty that he had not done my son right while still allowing his ego and pride to hinder him from fixing things properly. He kept going on and on with drama and negativity, wanting to get me to get out of line, but I did not. The entire event was giving Jeffrey vibes as he gaslighted me with lies and false narratives trying to defend his wrongdoings towards my son. I expressed to him that I had no intentions of wasting my day living in the past anymore. Despite his guilt for himself, I had forgiven him and moved on from all he did and didn't do a long time ago. Unfortunately, my son was not in the same headspace as me.

Nor did I expect him to be because a child does not have the cognitive capacity to think in such a manner. "Despite what you may think, I have never talked bad about you to our son or tried to make him hate you for what you did. I tell our son all the time that you are the reason I move the way I do." For it was you that taught me what hustling looked like." I made Omar aware that watching him hustle taught me a lot, and although my hustles were not illegal, he was the person I had learned how to be ambitious from. I told him that I didn't hate him for abandoning me the way he did because it helped me grow into a strong, independent woman who learned what she was truly capable of achieving. Had I stayed with him, I would have never gotten off my ass to do anything other than have my hand out and live with a basic mindset and lifestyle, and I had learned that God had other plans for me.

Omar was stunned by what I was saying, apologizing to me instantly. I could tell that he had allowed his own guilt and self-hate from how he had mishandled me and my son to be the premise for him to pick an argument. Never anticipating that the Nina I currently was would never give him that in response. Sure, he had done me and my child wrong in ways we did not deserve, and in the moment of the experience, it cut deep to my core and later to my son when he was old enough to observe and process the rejection he was receiving from his father. But what Omar didn't understand is that I had worked hard to instill feelings of love and understanding in my children. Because I had grown up lacking those emotions so much because of the things I endured. I never wanted any of my children to feel bitterness towards anyone teaching them that forgiveness was essential for their own well-being because I had learned from experience that carrying hatred for those that have harmed you only harms you further.

My son was willing to forgive and try to move forward, but he wanted to do so under his own terms, and although he was still a child, I felt it was not my or Omar's place to strip him of the authority to be able to do so for himself. Omar may have not agreed with me about how me and my son did things, but he left the conversation respecting our paradigm. My son and I did not hear from Omar anymore, although I felt guilty for setting up the meeting between the two of them. And pushing my son to give Omar a chance, I felt we gained some closure learning that Omar was still the same, and there was no happy conclusion because he was unwilling to do things differently. I was proud of myself for taking a stand for my son in the way he had requested and not backing down. Although there was no real resolve, I was happy that I could voice to Omar that I had forgiven him because that was something I had carried around for far too long. I was so proud of myself for keeping my composure even when he accused me of being a white woman, for that was something Jeff had done frequently.

I had come to terms with all of who I was, and no ignorant comment was going to lesson my Blackness or my womanhood. In reality, I knew that Omar knew that I was still with the shit, and no amount of change would ever take that away from who I was. I had just learned how to carry myself in a better way. Tucking in my street demeanor from my past and allowing my present to mold me into the best version of myself. If people interpreted my change as being white, then so the fuck what!

CHAPTER 12

Growing Pains

*G*rowth is a universal concept often analyzed based on physical, emotional, and sometimes material circumstances. There were many times in my life that I was able to measure my growth based on achievement and physical abundance. Seeing the visual components of elevation never stopping to measure the internal components of my growth. As a child, I often heard the phrase growing pains used on numerous occasions, never taking into account the significance of the term. However, it was something I had experienced many times. After going through the relationship trials with my ex-husband, losing friends that were never truly friends to begin with, and elevating my lifestyle, I started to see how my mental and spiritual process was beginning to shift. Things I used to be okay with were no longer permissible to my being.

And poor choices I used to make freely were no longer a part of who I was. It was as if my internal CPU had been shut down, restarted, and reprogramed with a level of higher standards that were more acceptable based on the woman I was becoming. It was as if my spirit was sending me new signals of how things should be done, leaving me no other options for programming other than the new upgraded program that was now being distributed on the inside at higher processing speeds. There were numerous times in my past when I had walked away from failed relationships feeling as though I had regained my power by adopting a no fucks attitude. Finding someone else and avoiding any actual level of intimacy by only allowing my new partner the opportunity of getting a taste of who I was in small portions. Stripping them of the ability to have the whole thing because in my mind giving the entire portion of myself to someone was a recipe for heartbreak and disaster.

This time I felt a change in me that could not be avoided. The change that had been cultivated from anxiety and fear from my experiences with Jeff and all that came with being with him. I started to feel as though I could not bring myself to move forward with anyone because the process to court me had now changed. It was no longer an easy-going process like it had been before. Because I now understood who I was, who I had been, and what it is I wanted and desired wholeheartedly as a woman. The thought of running into the wrong person again was hard to overlook as I turned down men left and right who wanted my attention. Often having them assume two things.

One, I was not interested because my husband still had a stronghold on my mind and heart. Or two that I was stuck up and thought I was too good. Seeing this bougie version of my spirit that was, in fact, a prejudgment and a poor judgment. Based on the fact that I had just recognized my worth five seconds ago. So, it was kind of hard for me to feel like I was too much for someone when I had just come to realize that I was enough. It's incredible how people will look at you and see a display of confidence that is not truly there based on your ability to hold your head high when walking through low situations. I had spent so much of my days being misunderstood that it would come as no surprise when that dynamic would escalate amongst the people within my community. Despite how awkward my environmental dynamics became; I was still internally shifting to a better place despite my anxiety.

My anxiety could be so heavy that I would not leave the house at all unless it were to go to work. I was trying to avoid the awkward stares I received from people who knew me and knew about specific components of my life. Running into men who would send me numerous inbox inquiries about dates and get no response. Later, they would run into me in public, giving me crazy looks due to their disagreement with my stance. After all, Jeff was out in the community having fun with multiple women. Allowing many men to feel like I was a fool not to be doing the same. I had realized the importance of taking my time with potential partners and vetting them adequately.

I also learned the importance of finding a partner who fits with the person I truly was and not the person I had pretended to be for so long. I had always managed to meet men who were not stable in the ways I was therefore creating a disconnect that made true intimacy impossible or short-lived. I had also managed to find men who were not as ambitious as me, so in turn, my ambition would often turn into arrogance in my partner's minds as they tried to understand why I had the desires I did. Oddly enough, during my period of growth, the majority of the exes from my past tried to pop back up in my life. And it was a cringey ass experience for me. The random inboxes, texts, and facetime alerts where men I had forgotten had ever existed tried to make themselves known to me. As I watched everyone pop up, trying to come back as if they thought that would be realistic.

Exes were messaging me telling me how they realized I was a great woman, and they had failed to see that. I would read the cliché messages thinking, boy, bye, as I tried to measure all of the audacity floating around in the atmosphere. To have exes send me inbox messages about their new cars, homes, and vacation spots, they wanted me to accompany them to. This made me assess how the devil stays busy because he will dangle a million poor prospects in your face before he moves over and allows a good man the room to walk down your path. All of a sudden, all of these old flames were popping up interested in me because they could now see the value they had disregarded. I turned down all offers, often hearing the same kind of responses that revolved around my ex being the catalyst for my decline in their interest. I thought about how numerous men had inquired why I had married my ex and gone through all that I did.

In comparison, standing now in the position of a single woman unwilling to give them a chance. Hearing my child's father convey how much love he had for me and how he was so in love with me after he had abandoned my child. The oldest story in the book is the story of the baby daddy who dogs you, abandons your child, and then watches you blossom, realizing he fumbled the bag and picked the wrong woman. Because now the side piece preference he had run with was no longer feeling like the right preference. As his fickle spirit becomes engulfed with watching you blossom into the woman you always were despite his inability to see. Based on his dire need to cater to the woman who was less of a woman and more of a freak. Realizing his sexual appetite had blocked his vision while blocking his blessing because now you wouldn't spit on his raggedy ass with someone else's spit!

Let's just say it was the irony for me! I thought about how men can be so predictable. Initially falling for you and your light, getting comfortable, and ready and willing to toss you aside when the next woman comes along with a wet mouth prepared to risk all of her morals for a little time, attention, and community penis. Realizing that no matter how they may break your heart or let you down, they always travel back around waiting for round two. Unfortunately for them, Nina was not interested in anything from the past unless it was a lost check I had somehow forgotten to cash! One day my ex-boyfriend Benz contacted me telling me that he had heard about all of the great things I had been doing, and he was proud to hear it. He had also been an ex who frequently contacted me trying to rekindle a no longer lit flame.

During our conversation, he remembered the days when I talked about wanting to create my own cosmetic line or write a book, never considering that I actually would. I thought back on my relationship with Benz, reflecting how he was one of the best partners I had ever been in a relationship with. Asking me to marry him numerous times and having me decline because during those days, I had an idea of what I wanted in a partner, and I didn't feel like he was ready. When in reality, it was me who was not prepared. Benz was great to both of my children, catering and caring. Always making it clear to me that he wanted a future with me that I was mentally unprepared for at that time. During the time I was in a relationship with him, I was working and going to school, and I felt like he was not doing much with his life.

He had gotten accepted into many great schools prior to us dating and had turned down the opportunities. Feeling content with life as it was while I felt differently. I felt as though he was not a good fit for me because he was not driven in the way I was. I would go to work, school, and then come home often feeling tired and annoyed that Benz was not doing much of anything with his day. I made excuses to pull back and walk away from the relationship because I didn't know how to convey my lack of interest in him. He was tall, dark, handsome, and extremely intelligent, and it frustrated me how he chose not to do more when he was capable of so many things. That day I remember talking to Benz and thinking about how my patience was so short with him, yet I could have so many moments of patients with Jeff, who was horrible to me.

I thought about the type of family Benz came from and the kind of man he had grown to be, realizing that I didn't give him the opportunity because, at that time, I was inpatient, too strong-minded, and not with the bullshit at all. A few weeks after I graduated college in 2012, I ended my relationship with Benz because I felt as though I was tired of waiting for him to step up to the plate and meet me at the level of life I was on. Realizing at that moment that had I been patient and a little less anal, I would have had a better life, marriage, and experience. I had let a good man get away because I was unwilling to work with him through minor flaws. Walking into a future with a man whose scars would prove to be dangerous, hinder some, and monumental.

So many times, I questioned if Jeff was my karma for breaking Benz's heart. During my relationship with Benz, I had been a different person. Often breaking up with him when he was not showing up in the ways I felt he needed to as my partner. Walking through life with no obligation to anyone other than myself and my kids. Frequently dating other guys looking for the better option. Consistently finding better alternatives, always coming to the realization that those better options always lacked certain inner qualities. I realized later that Benz had a quality about him that could not be duplicated. He had also been raised by a woman of God who taught him about respecting women and placing God at the center. Darleen was a great woman and always welcomed her home to my two children and me.

Shortly after I gave birth to my youngest daughter, she came to pay me a visit bringing my newborn gifts, sending Jeff over the edge because he had heard from one of his coworkers how fond Darleen was of me. After she had gone to a hair appointment where she had shared with the stylist, who happened to be Jeff's friend, that she always wished me and Benz would rekindle our relationship. I started realizing how I had always been so strong-minded about my visions about my life that I would often reject blessings due to them showing up in a different format than the ones I had envisioned. I would often share stories with my friends about the crazy behavior Benz would exhibit, but I did not understand that he had chosen those behaviors based on how I had been handling him. He wasn't a perfect man, but he was a good man, and I should have valued that more. Ironically enough, it took me going through the worst with a person who had been a bad person to me for me to see how good others had been in my past.

Over the years, Benz stayed in contact, and he had invited me out numerous times, but I would never take the opportunity. Telling myself I would not be that girl. You know, the type who only comes back because she's been dragged through the mud with a bad guy using the old guy as her redemption opportunity. I knew I could call on Benz at any time in my life, and he would show up honored, capable, and privileged to be my partner, a father to my children, and a husband, but I knew he deserved more than my epiphany. Sometimes second chances can be beautiful, but I knew our time had passed, and he was not my blessing, and I was not his.

That day I left our conversation realizing that I, too, had been a Jeff just to a different magnitude. After Omar, I hurt many people carrying my resentment for what he had done to me. Bringing it into new relationships with good men feeling as if I could not invest fully. Treating partners as if they were of no value to me due to my mental baggage that I was still gripping a firm hold of. Leaving relationships with men and giving them no explanation feeling like I didn't owe them anything because I had made my intent clear initially. I don't think it was mere luck that once I was truly ready to commit, it would be with someone who was not. I realized each time I discarded men in some of the same ways they often do women, I was adding to my karma tally. I was never truly prepared for the moment karma would walk into my life, ready to give me a taste of my own heartbreaking meds.

Heartbreak will humble your ass quick. It will also help you recognize all the times when you got it wrong and were unaware of that. Growth was allowing me to take accountabilities for all of my choices. Acknowledging that just because I had finally decided to be better and do better didn't mean things would be simplistic. I had been away in my past that in my young mind seemed permissible. Treating good partners poorly because, in my mind, all men were liars, cheaters, and untrustworthy. In reality, that was not the case, nor was it a good reason to discard other people's feelings and emotions. Society paints having a zero fucks mentality as being the way to go. Still, I had learned through experience that having no care regarding people and situations was the poorest choice of all.

I chose a cowards' path to avoid real intimacy due to fear and anxiety. Allowing myself to see that despite my experiences, all people deserved respect and an opportunity to show themselves. I had been looking at every man with the same poor judgments, anticipation, and negative outlook. Recognizing that I created my dynamic long before it ever manifested due to my thought process and my poor actions in reference to fear. Benz reached out to me numerous times during my divorce, and although it would have been easy to allow him in my space, I didn't. He was in a new relationship, and I didn't want to ruin his concentration with his new partner based on his old feelings for me. So, I kept my distance, kept conversation to a minimum, and did what I knew was right.

I could see how it was that a woman could become involved with men they knew were in a relationship. Telling themselves it's okay because he doesn't want her, he still loves me, and we make more sense. When in reality, whether those components are true or not, it still isn't right. The dynamic between Benz and me made me understand the dynamic between Jeff and Tonya a little better. At the end of the day, we are all humans living through a human experience. I came to understand that Tonya could see me and Jeff's dynamic clearly because no man who cared for a woman would have done half of what he did. So, she was simply taking her opportunity to get what she felt she wanted and deserved to have.

Should she have considered his marriage when he wasn't? She didn't owe me anything and was not responsible for respecting my situation when Jeff was my partner and did not. I realized that a side chick isn't always trying to hurt you when she seeks out your man. Most of the time she is just acting on her desperate desires to have what she sees everyone else has. Taking whatever opportunity comes her way because her poor self-image doesn't allow her to think in terms of karma or compassion. I could consider Benz's partner's feelings because I knew what it was like to be her. I also had never seen a woman act in that way and have successful results with a man.

Because nine times out of ten, the man you take becomes the man who will be taken! It's funny how God will grant us access to understanding our lives in depth by looking through a lens at someone else's life. One of the main components of who I was that was allowing me to have much better outcomes during my adverse trials was my ability to understand myself. I had allowed myself to become overwhelmed so many times when analyzing my life and choices during times when those experiences were not that big as I had initially felt they were. Later, I went through some of my hardest days and was able to walk away without bitterness in my heart due to the blessing of understanding. My oldest daughter had been in communication with her father, and although I was not sure where things would go with them, it was off to a good start. I started seeing how consistent he was being, and I decided that I would drop his child support agreement hoping it would be a nudge on the path to consistency.

He had been paying me eighty-three dollars a week since my daughter was about two years old, and although it was not much, he always paid it. I made the choice in good faith that it would show him how important it was for him to be consistent with his now fifteen-year-old child. Days turned into weeks, and weeks turned into months, and he had not dropped the ball as often as I had anticipated. Picking up our daughter every day after school. Taking her to lunch, Sunday family dinners, and learning who she was, and responding to that person in a way that showed true care. I started seeing the glow in my child emerge after finally having the dynamic with her father she had always wanted. Recognizing from the stories she shared with me how they were enjoying, loving, and helping one another.

For it was starting to seem as though her presence around him was helping him just as much as his was helping her. Finally, someone was seeing a successful conclusion in the realm of fatherhood, and it was happy to watch. But it was also hard to watch because I craved that dynamic for all of my children. Often reflecting on my poor choices as a young woman wishing I could rewrite history. So, all of my children could have the opportunity my oldest was now having. Eventually, I learned that thinking in that manner showed a sincere level of bitterness towards myself. I had finally managed to forgive the people who had harmed my children and me.

While realizing that I was failing to forgive myself. Recognizing that it was not my fault that things had gone the way they had. Sure, I had chosen these men initially, but I had no real way of knowing that they would be absent fathers. Understanding in the moment that I could only hold myself accountable for my choices. I had been through many unfortunate events concerning dealing with the hurt my children had developed due to not having two parents. But I had done the best I could to address their emotions. Speaking with them individually and as a group often trying to reflect on their feelings regarding this factor of their life.

I could never be the mother and the father no matter how hard I tried. And I could never encompass what a father embodies for them no matter how much I wanted to. But what I could do is make them aware that it was okay to feel regarding the matter. Teaching them that bitterness and hatred were not the right emotion and resolve regarding these broken selfish men. Who were also not at fault? For they too had been through their own issues with fatherhood concerning their parents. I expressed to my children that generational curses were often easier to recognize than break.

Encouraging them to recognize their pain, voice it, and try to heal so they would hold no bitterness in their hearts for men that were simply just that, men. We often stop to assess the wrong that has been done to us, and we never stop to think about where the behavior truly stems from. Thomas Hobbes once said that man's true nature is inherently evil and selfish (Hobbes 1651). Although we know this is not every man's true character, we have seen it be true many times.

What can truly be said or judged in reference to a man who is evil or selfish regarding his own pursuits? My oldest daughter's father was a mere baby himself when we had our first child. Could I really believe that it was a fair notion to expect him to take care of another life when he had not even grasped the ability to do so for himself at that time?

Still a child under his own mother's care. My son's father was a young man who had been incarcerated for years for drug trafficking. Who had not felt as though his own father had been present for him in the way he needed or wanted. Was it fair to expect a man who never knew the diligence of a father to be fully prepared to be a father? Then there is my ex-husband, who had lived through so many physical and mental trauma's love was not a notion he had felt he had ever truly witnessed. Growing into a young man who was hypersexual, scarred, uneducated, and lost within his own existence. Lacking the ability to provide for himself.

Often looking for his female partners to encompass the duties of that of a mother due to his keen desires to have the mother figure in his life that was absent from his childhood. Looking for his partners to love, protect, and provide for him in ways that were not appropriate to most. He was unable to for himself because of his dire feelings of bitterness that took over his ability to evolve. Should he be expected to take care of a child when lacking the ability to take care of himself? The answers were no, no, and no. But during those relationships, I was ignorant to the cultures each person had come from and how it had silently affected them. Enabling them to be the kind of parents for whom I had hoped.

I came to understand that they were also not completely at fault for their behavior. Because they had not come from environments where people expressed to them how wrong their wrongdoings were. Cradling spirits that roamed around them daily, telling them that it was me who was at fault. The new women in their lives screaming that I was a bitter baby mama until they conceived children, and it was now their turn to go through what me and my child had. Now reaching out to me with different renditions of the "good man" they had been celebrating when they were in their relationships. Now it was no longer he is a good man; she is the problem. It was now "Nina was right about him. As if they could not somehow see that before.

Now only able to corroborate my accounts when they were in the same position as me, which was disrespected and disregarded. Hobbs said that "The condition of man is a condition of war of everyone against everyone "(Hobbs,1651). Man is constantly picking and prying at one another, struggling to come to terms with who is in the lead. Who is in the right, and who is destined to win overall? Every man and woman for themselves. Most hold fraudulent spaces where they prefer to sit gloating at their ability to rise in situations where they often do not truly deserve to be the victor. As I have stated many times that men are creatures of habit.

That is why cliché sayings like how you get them is how you lose them. Or what he will do to one he will do to another has always had the ability to be proven undoubtedly true in most cases. Although we often explore these truths based on displayed behaviors, we never dive deeper trying to understand the core elements that allow these behaviorisms to take the lead in a person's conduct. We are all busy bees swarming around our own individual nests, trying to make a way, feeling that it is impossible to slow down and try to understand one another. Often, we feel as though it would be a disservice to ourselves because who really has that kind of time in reference to the assessment of others besides our paid therapists who often feel overwhelmed by the context of their mental explorations. The truth is we can, and we should take the time to understand.

Had I made the time early on in my life, I could have shielded myself from so many harsh experiences. I had finally reached a place where the knowledge I had encompassed had allowed me to look at all of my experiences with a new paradigm. Leading me down a path that could allow forgiveness regarding some very unforgiving actions. How can a woman look a man in the eye and say, I forgive you for harming my child psychologically? I forgive you for cheating on me. I forgive you for physically abusing me.

I forgive you for using me. I forgive you for harming me when I did not deserve to be harmed. The answer was simple she could do so with the spirit of God leading her. Holding her hand as she revisited times, places, and occurrences that stripped her of her physical and mental strength. She could do so with God and the knowledge that forgiving is an essential component of the healing process. After realizing that I needed to slow down, I started moving a lot slower in reference to my ambitions, understanding that things would get done when they got done.

I was still trying to unpack and get things where I needed them to be at home. Dedicating my next weekend off to finishing the remainder of the house. One morning I got started early, making a lot of progress within reason. Slowing down and stopping altogether when my body started conveying that I had done enough and was close to the realm of overdoing it again. I had always been a person who worked well under pressure because pressure had been a part of my dynamic most of my life. But I was also someone who worked well when they had been hurt. Often channeling my pain into progress.

I was coming to the understanding that I had been hurt a lot. And although I was healing from the hurt, the emotions were still very much a part of my being. So naturally, I poured my emotions into my work. Getting my grades back to honors status after taking a fall.

Finishing my second debut trilogy novel that I had been behind on and finally coming to a place where I could actually cultivate my story in a way that the words were finally hitting the pages. I had been working on my story for two years, never able to make progress. Therapy had been helping me to cultivate my story without crying during moments where my experiences were too emotionally taxing to recollect.

I sat down after being annoyed with all the things still taking place. Watching as the devil constantly tried to steal my joy and progress from under my feet. Standing tall and strong, reminding myself that God was allowing all of the adversity, pain, and trials for a bigger purpose. As I sat down in front of my laptop, that had now become my most prized possession. Thanking God at the end for allowing me to keep pulling rabbits out of a hat even during my most trying hours. I started losing weight after following my diet as the doctor had instructed. Experiencing less inflammation and dizziness during the week, and my sleep pattern started progressing slowly. I finally received a referral for weight loss surgery and started attending the required nutrition sessions before undergoing the procedure.

CHAPTER 13

Self-Care Is Not There

*A*fter getting things structured for myself quickly, I started feeling better, watching as my mental and physical health started experiencing resolve. One day I sat down to rest when my phone rang, and an odd number I did not recognize popped up on my screen. I answered the phone to find my youngest daughter's little cousin on the phone asking to speak to her. I put her on the phone, hitting the speakerphone icon, telling myself that the call was random, and I knew someone had put her up to calling. Sure, enough, I was correct, and I heard Jeff's mother on the phone trying to coach my daughter into asking me to come to her house. Telling her she wanted to see her. In my daughter's five years of living, she had never requested to see her or have her come by, and I felt like she was not acting genuine.

She had never treated my daughter like she treated her other grandchildren. This often-led Jeff and me to deduce from her words and behavior that she did not care for my daughter much. Assuming it was because she was an extension of me. She asked to speak to me, informing me she had lost her sister and brother-in-law in the same week. My father had told me that her sister had passed. Despite my hunch of the call being contrived, I offered her my condolences. She started asking me how me and my child were doing, although I knew she did not genuinely care.

Feeling certain she was happy we were no longer in the picture. I could hear the guilt that rested in her voice. I told her that I had moved and was trying to unpack, trying to rush off of the phone. I did not understand why she had been trying to make conversation with me when she had talked about me horribly and disrespected me more times than I could count. She asked how school was going for my daughter, and I told her things were going well. She tried to bring up more about her personal family life when I told her I had to go because I was in the middle of something. She told me that she wanted me and my daughter to see her when I was not busy.

Although I felt sorry for her due to her sister's passing, I knew she was not someone I could trust. For all I knew, she had been getting tired of Tonya and Jeff's relationship and was trying to use my daughter and me to place a hedge in between the two of them. And I was not going to put myself in a position to find out what she was trying to pull. This woman had lied on me, cursed me out repeatedly, talked about me, disrespected my child, and brought another woman to my home to be disrespectful. Leaving me to deduce that her reaching out was not sincere in good faith. So that day, I blocked her new number as well. Reminding myself that she had shown me how she felt about my child and me many times, and I did not need to go dancing with people I knew had been nothing but devils in my life.

The old me would have gone running over to her house in the past. Hoping that she would one day learn to accept and respect my baby girl and me. But the new me had not one desire for that dynamic. Maya Angelou highlighted the importance of us believing what people first show us and I had spent most of my life not believing people's actions after the first occurrence—holding on to good faith that people would change. Maybe if they could see who I was and understand my heart, they would love me. They would respect me, value me, and treat me with the same good that I treated them with. But I was not being realistic in my ways of wishing, and people would not do those things in reference to me because the people I wanted those dynamics with did not want to give it.

Days turned into weeks, weeks into months, and before you knew it, a year had gone by where I had been implementing these boundaries with my oppressors. Occasionally adding to the list of people, places, and terms that were no longer suitable for who I was at the current moment and who I wanted to become. Recognizing how people constantly tried breaking down my barriers. Hoping to invade my space and disregard my boundaries in the same ways they had in the past, feeling confused when they no longer could. Sending friend requests from new social media pages after recognizing they had been blocked. Calling me from new phone numbers consistently.

I guess it's true what they say. You never know what you have until it's gone. And they all now knew who Nina was and had the potential to be, but the gag is she would never again be that for them. And that was the current culture of the morning they were all so engulfed in. Thankfully, I no longer cared. Feeling the internal strength I now embodied every time I was able to ignore calls, friend requests, and messages sent to me through another, hoping to sway my newfound sense of awareness. I had forgiven all of the people who hurt me, but to their misfortune, I would not ever be foolish enough to allow them back in my space. A space they had never valued being in and never deserved.

I had spent a lifetime trying to rewrite narratives that God had shown me had been set in stone. Wanting to matter to someone somewhere and never have that fulfilled by anyone other than my children. I was learning from my mistakes and experiences, recognizing that God would one day send me a tribe of people who saw my light and didn't want to diffuse it. People who would see my heart and not want to use it. And people who would see the love I gave unconditionally and not want to take advantage of it. I realized that the love I thought I craved so much was due to my lack of self-love. I thought I was treating myself well when in reality, I had not been for an extended time. Because had I truly loved myself, then all of these negative people would not have been able to hold a space in time with me. Nor would I have allowed so many poor relationship dynamics into my life. I concluded that God had been trying to teach me something the entire time. I wanted people to recognize my worth, but I failed to do so for myself. As soon as I started genuinely loving and valuing myself, that outside validation I had been seeking from my people was no longer a desire or a necessity.

I noticed how God had always provided for me even when I could not truly see the magnitude of his favor and protection—seeing how he started showing up for me in ways I could have never imagined once I started showing up for myself. You see, this story doesn't end with me leaving an abusive marriage and finding my prince charming. Although I am sure, he exists somewhere waiting to cross my path. This story ends with me recognizing the trauma I had developed from my marriage. Piling it up and allowing it to merge with my unaddressed trauma from my childhood. Observing myself and understanding that I had developed anxiety regarding developing new relationships with strangers due to past disappointments from old relationships with backstabbing friends, hateful family members, and bad romantic relationships that left scars deeply embedded in my being. I was not in a position to find prince charming because the thought of a date, intimacy, or getting to know someone new was overwhelming for me. Based on these components, I continued with therapy and still am at the very moment.

I started to see the reoccurring dynamic of being the over-giver and how it affected my well-being. I had been pouring effortlessly into my children, family, friends, and job. Never stopping to recognize how much I had been neglecting myself. Although I had been pouring into my writing endeavors and education, the list regarding myself started and ended there. I had spent so much time observing how poorly others were treating me that I never stopped to recognize that majority of that treatment stemmed from my inability to treat myself properly. We all want to be loved and valued. But is it fair to expect others to value us in a way we have failed to value ourselves? I understood that I needed to make some changes concerning self-care. I focused on new eating and sleeping habits, recognizing that my weight gain had been possible due to my lack of healthy eating and exercise. Once I tackled this issue to the best of my ability. My sleep started to improve.

Leaving room for me to cater to self-care in a different, more enjoyable aspect. One morning I got up and decided to go to the nail salon to get a much-needed pedicure. Sitting in the chair and instantly feeling guilty for not bringing my daughters along. Reminding myself that they constantly had their time and care, and as foreign as it felt to me at the moment, it was essential that I break out of the guilty rut and enjoy the fruits of my labor. I was reminding myself that I deserved days, times, and experiences that were allotted to me and only me. And although this was true, it was hard to own all in one sitting. My ability to mother my children correctly was something I was always proud of and although I catered to their needs catering to my own often felt wrong even when it was not. I know someone read that line and felt my experience because it is their own. As women and mothers, we often deem ourselves as unimportant while trying to tackle the needs and desires of everyone else around us. Telling ourselves that the need of the many outweighs the needs of the few. Us being in the category of the few.

Overlooking our neglected bodies, desires, and need for life. Because our lives have become consumed with pleasing everyone while failing to please ourselves. I had become so consumed with wanting to show up for people properly that I could not show up for myself. Not fully understanding that self-care and self-indulgences were in the best interest of all of my people. A person who is responsible for numerous people and responsibilities can't show up properly if they are unhealthy, tired, and mentally drained. Recognizing that was giving me the fuel to try and make changes, although changing how I moved concerning self-care was extremely hard due to time constraints, career endeavors, and years of rewiring that needed to take place. So, I started taking baby steps.

I sat in the salon chair, glancing at my feet that were so damaged it looked as if I had been walking on stones for weeks. I was constantly scanning through the salon menu book to find the best pedicure that fit my neglected state. Selecting the most expensive option. Sitting down, trying not to focus on my cracked heels. As shame took over my entire state. Looking around the room at the other Albemarle County moms who sat in their chairs proudly. Noticing one woman who appeared to be ready for a nap long before her feet were ever touched. Watching her in envy as she closed her eyes, enjoyed her foot massage. Leaning back in her chair, appearing to be indulging in the glory of self-care in a way I could not.

I scrolled through social media, trying to fight the urge to call and check on my children, who were absolutely fine. As they clung to their decorated rooms filled with every toy, technologically advanced device, and snack a child could want. Enjoying their spoiled existences while their mother fought against letting herself enjoy a pedicure that she needed months ago. The irony is I did everything in my power daily to make my loved ones happy while never allowing myself a chance to be spoiled. Stupid! But it's like that for us mothers sometimes. Especially single mothers. We see our children's desires to fill the voids having an absent father brings, and we make it our duty to try our best to shield them from hurt; we know we can never truly allow them to escape. Part of being human is having human emotions, and I had spent fifteen years trying to shield children from hurt, Telling myself that giving them the best would keep them from that pain when in reality, it never would. So, I sat in my chair, spiraling off into thought about serious shit as usual. Drifting into more and more thoughts about life like someone had come along and shoved a stick of worries up my ass that could not be removed.

Clinging to these thoughts until I started feeling the best leg massage I had ever known take over. This was followed by a massage with hot stones that sent me into a blissful state of mind. Instantly telling myself, "Fuck them kids in my miss pat voice"! They are good! They are loved! They are well cared for! And most importantly, they are not here to take away from this moment! Nothing like a good massage to remind you that you too matter. Long story short, the nail tech worked on my feet for two hours! At that moment, I was reminded of an episode of Martin when Myra went to Sheneneh's salon and got her feet prepared. Let's just say that I was shocked she didn't have to pull the chainsaw out for me, too, given the poor state my feet were in. It was as if I had spent an entire six months walking on thorns and disappointment.

That day I tipped the salon twenty dollars as a show of my appreciation for how rejuvenated my feet were when I left. After the salon, I decided to go forward and complete my booking for a trip I had planned with my brother to celebrate my birthday. I had bought one plane ticket. I avoid buying the other due to my strong desire not to be away on a trip without my kids, consistently trying to think of ways to get out of going. Telling myself that it was not a good idea. While my brother chimed in on a FaceTime conversation with me and my mother, assuring me that my kids would be fine. I then decided I would only go for two days. So, you're going to pay a thousand dollars for a Plane ticket to go somewhere for two days; he asked as if he thought that was the craziest thing he had ever heard.

I get that you don't want to leave the kids, but you work hard, and you deserve to go more than anyone, he said. It was still not breaking through as I gambled with retracting from the whole week and cutting it down to two days. Finally, coming to terms with the fact that I was doing it again! Mishandling myself and making myself less of a priority. Because once again, I was making excuses to negate away from self-care and self-indulgences that I rightfully deserved. So, I took my brother's advice and booked the trip for the full week. Later booking a trip for summer for my family. Telling myself it would be an even exchange. I would go to Aruba and enjoy the coming of this newfound relationship with self-care. Leaving a few months later to explore Florida, universal studios, and a family vacation that had all the kids excited.

No one appeared to care that I was going to Aruba. Nor did anyone care that they were not coming with me. Leading me to realize that I was the problem. I had often made myself feel guilty for trying to do things for myself. And although at times, my kids could be spoiled and selfish, wanting me to include them, they had grown up and were now in the realm of teenager Ville. Not caring about my comings and goings in the way they used to. Leaving my youngest daughter to be the only one out of the bunch who minded my absence because she was five and still valued me in a way my oldest didn't at times. They weren't holding on to my way of doing things. It was me who was not letting go, so 'I took note of that and tried to move forward, designating outings, spa days, and alone time for myself. Placing self-care at the top of my neglected list of things I needed to change concerning myself.

Thanksgiving rolled around, and it had now been a year since the domestic incident with Jeff. After putting my foot down and setting up the proper boundaries along with the restraining order, he was finally fleeing from his normal attempts to bother me. Six months went by, and there was no more anxiety in regard to being contacted by entities I did not want to hear from. After getting no responses from her earlier request to see me, Roberta stopped reaching out to me. Later starting up again the week before thanksgiving. With Jeff following suit, trying to reach out to people in my circle as well. I watched as each call came through, deliberately ignoring all of her fraudulent attempts to reconnect with me. Thanksgiving day, she called and called, getting no answer again. Leaving me a voicemail, hoping to get a response in return for her efforts. The next day the calls would continue leading me to block her new number like I had done all the others. She had made it clear to me that she did not like, value, or care for my daughter or me. Yet here she was, blowing up my phone as if she had good reason. Although it made no sense to me why she would be reaching out, I knew her intentions were not favorable. She had wanted me gone for so long. Hating the sight of me, my daughter, and our dynamic with her son.

Always feeling as though us being present served as a roadblock for her and her intentions. Uplifting the idea of Jeff being with any other woman as opposed to being with his child or me. And doing whatever she could to make me feel like we were not welcomed into her family. Yet now that I had permanently removed myself from her reach, she was desiring to have a connection with the woman and child she never wanted around from the start. I had forgiven her for all of the harm she had caused my child and me. But what I was not going to do was give her the opportunity to do any of it again. I glanced at my phone, looking at her call back-to-back. It had now been two full weeks that she had been reaching out, looking for a response. I thought about all that had occurred. Thinking about all the times she used me.

Reaching out to me when things with Jeff and me were rocky hoping she could get me to pop back up. Desiring my return so she could drive a wedge through Jeff and Tonya's bond once she saw it getting serious with them. Only to turn around and do the same to me. Utilizing Tonya as a wedge and resource to ruin me and Jeff's dynamic once she felt like she saw it progressing. What she didn't know was that I had grown, and she would never be able to have access to me ever again. That day I blocked her new number. Vowing that I would keep my intentions pure and my focus right where it was. Shutting out all thoughts of the past.

I didn't know that while I had been implementing more boundaries concerning Roberta and Jeff, Roberta had been trying to reach out to my family despite my lack of response. My brothers contacted me via FaceTime, alerting me that Roberta had reached out to my mom after having no luck with reaching out to me. That day I instructed my mother to block Roberta. My mother informed me that

Roberta had inquired about how me and my daughter were doing. Relaying the message to me that she wanted to see us. At that moment, I reminded myself that she had proven who she was concerning my child and myself more than enough. This was now the third time I had given myself this reminder since the domestic incident, and I told myself it would be the last. I had forgiven a lot of my past. Finally, unwilling to open shut doors. Learning from my mistakes and keeping on my path to peace.

Roberta and Jeff's family had never welcomed my daughter into their lives like they did everyone else. At times it used to bother me tremendously. I often wondered why they would watch my social media stories religiously. Never forgetting to tune in. In contrast, they watched me post pictures of my daughter. Never liking one of them. I noticed how they never gave her a birthday or Christmas gift. Or a simple happy birthday via social media after viewing my post and stories during those special days. I often felt as though they did it deliberately. Silently trying to convey to me in a subliminal aspect that they did not welcome her like they did all the others. Watching as they showed love to Jeff's many female flings, their children, and people who weren't of any biological significance to them.

Being a young mom, I had gone through similar situations with all of my kid's family members. And at times, dynamics like this really cut deep. Often making me feel like people felt like me and my kids were not good enough. Coming to terms with things and recognizing our value once those components no longer mattered to me. As I watched how the same parties that excluded us for no reason now wanted to reshape those dynamics after realizing they were wrong. The only problem with that is that Nina White was now in a state of giving zero fucks. I was willing to forgive all of the harm and ostracization that had been done in reference to my kids and me. But what they all would not anticipate is I was no longer willing to reopen doors to those types of people. I would never be able to undo what had already been done. But I could reshape my heart to forgive while reshaping my mind to keep my boundaries in place with ugly entities. And that's what I did.

I didn't walk away, gaining everything I ever wanted. And at times, I felt like I had lost more during my enlightenment period than what I had achieved. Reminding myself that the things and people I had lost were no longer right for me. You see, I wish I could tell you that a better man came along, better friends, and my happily ever after was perfect, but it was not. I'm still healing, and I have found that healing is a lengthy process. My circle these days consists of my mother, my siblings, and my children. Although many seem to like the idea of me being in a new relationship, I have been able to recognize that I do not have that desire. Nor do I plan to welcome another until I have fully come to terms with my relationship experiences. Based on the things I have endured; I still have trust issues that I am still currently trying to work through.

Owning the fact that I am not ready for a relationship because the emotional and mental baggage from my previous relationships have not fled from me completely. I am now also able to recognize that my life is busy, and there is barely room for the already-present things. What would a relationship look like for a woman with my schedule? Working eighty-four hours a week, going to school full-time, and being a mom around the clock. I can only speculate that it would be very difficult for my potential partner and me. So, I keep those components in mind. At the same time, reminding myself that God will make room for a relationship when the time is right in my life. But for now, I am a long way away from having room for that kind of

SELF-CARE IS NOT THERE

addition. It's easy to make yourself feel like you desire things that you see other people desire for you.

And there were many times I acted in that manner. Listening to Barbra tell me that I needed a man and following through with that. Later recognizing that I was fine at that point in my life. And had I stayed true to my initial path, I would have never endured all that I did. Later learning to be true to myself. Walking into spaces proud of who I am. Owning my ambitious nature, discipline, gifts, and independence. I tell myself daily that there is nothing wrong with being a lone wolf. Because who I am is who I am. And at the end of the day, all I can do is be true to my essence. Society wires women to believe that they are not complete without the presence of a man. Leading many women in the Black community to endure things they should not. Based on the ideology that is planted in their minds. The ideology tells them it is better to be with the wrong man than not have a man at all. Leading women to feel like they are not walking towards a path of true happiness. Because what is happiness without a man? But that is not true. Nor do I ever want this to be true for my daughters or me. I now recognize that although having a partner has many perks being single does as well. I am learning to embrace this time of being to myself. Understanding all of who I am. While trying to work on my less favorable qualities. Striving to work through my issues so when the next man arrives, we can spend time embracing each other instead of trying to heal one another. I had spent so much of my life depending on

dynamics that were not truly desirable to me. Finally, I came to terms with what I truly did and did not want. Therapy helped me to start putting myself first and not feel guilty about it. I finally removed Jeff and all that was associated with him from my life and my children's life permanently. Keeping the two-year restraining order in place and eventually having him and all of his people leave me alone after they realized I was no longer accessible to them. Finally, having them respect my boundaries as they should have previously. You see, I have observed my role in all of the disrespect and figured out it only took place because I kept allowing it. And the answer to my problem was simple…. Stop allowing it. And that's what I did.

CHAPTER 14

Tis The Season To Move The Fuck On!

*T*o say that a lot had occurred in my life that was undesirable is most definitely an understatement. After all of the chaos with Jeff, I started viewing my life differently. Recognizing that I had made a habit of keeping people in my space who God could see did not fit—always sending me signals that my connections were not conducive to peace or happiness. These are the two components of life that I wanted so much. Not realizing that I was also acting as a catalyst of prevention concerning myself. I was stripping myself of the ability to have those two things due to my poor relationship dynamics.

During my first self-assessment regarding this issue, I initially presumed that my relationship with Jeffrey was what caused me to settle with life, but that was not entirely true. For it appeared to me upon my deep dive into the matter that this was something that was cultivated long before Jeffrey arrived. Looking back at all of the things I had allowed showed me who people were and how they felt about me. The faces that were always one way in my presence and another way during my absence. The friends who talked about me frequently behind my back. Sharing accounts of my life regarding my failed marriage with people they claimed they weren't fond of, laughing with my enemies about my shortcomings in relation to my ex-husband.

The fake friends that would often come to me repeating incidences where I had been discussed with women who had enjoyed giving their accounts of sex and lies with my ex-partner. Leaving out the parts of the stories where they laughed along with my enemies and shared inappropriate facts due to the status of our friendship dynamic. I pretended to be oblivious as to why my enemies thought they could talk about me to my friends. Later dissecting things further. I looked at the fact that people weren't discussing my friends with me because they knew they couldn't. This helped me to conclude that this was frequently happening with certain so-called friends because they too contributed to the conversation. You see, I often would listen to these stories and become so plagued with doubt, sadness, and insecurities trying to figure out why these things were taking place.

Hadn't I been a good wife, mother, and friend? Why were so many people trying to bring me down, including those in my circles? Why did the people I call friends and family enjoy this for me? The answer was simple they enjoyed it because there were not truly my people. They also kept these poor dynamics going because they knew I would allow it. I started to understand that due to things that had occurred in my childhood, I allowed people to mistreat me.

Welcoming the poor, dysfunctional energy into my space because it was all I had ever known. It's hard to stand up for yourself and say to people that you deserve better when no one has ever given you that kind of respect or treatment. My self-esteem had been beaten down so much that it was not triggering for me when I was mistreated. I was more uncomfortable with people who treated me kindly and spoke to my good qualities. I often tried to figure out the catch when someone spoke good and blessings over my being because that was something new for me. It would take time before I would come to realize how sad that dynamic truly was in regard to me and my future.

I often tried to make sense of the senseless, never understanding that these things were not for me to understand during those times. I should have understood that my enemies were only bringing this energy to certain people I called friends because they could see that they were not my friends. A hater will always be able to spot out another hater. Just as a thief can identify another thief without evidence that those components are present. The cold hard truth was most of the people around me thought more of me than what I thought of myself. Jumping to the occasion to throw negative dynamics in my face hoping to strip me of my being. The very being that made them love and hate me all at the same time. The being that made them look at me and see my potential, fearing the day I would wake up and see it for myself.

These frenemies acted on things they hoped would never come to be because they wanted to see me as nothing more than the teen mom and the young woman with relationship issues and struggles. I never realized that while they were getting a kick out of all of their ugliness and the ugliness of others, which was propelled in my direction. God was helping me to use those negative experiences to push myself forward both internally and externally. I thought about the friends who called trying to cover themselves in negative blanket statements such as "your little business," "your little books," or stating things like anyone can do school when they themselves had failed to do so numerous times. It led me to realize that people were infuriated at the idea of the possibilities of the things I was doing. It was not the initial action that scared them but the reaction that comes along with consistency. For example, two people can get into an ivy league college, start a business, and create a magazine brand. On the one hand, we have a person who does enough to get by, doesn't have a plan for the future, and retracts at the first sight of fear or adversity. On the other hand, we have an individual who strives to do their best, enters the room with a mapped-out plan, and has a resilient spirit.

Refusing to give up when faced with hurdles because this individual understands that hurdles are all a part of the process. Which one of these individuals do you think will succeed? The second individual will face the most trials, hatred, and disconnect amongst society because they have the makings to be great, and most importantly, they have the potential to succeed. It is easy to look at individual number two and see their potential and possibilities because we all know that consistency is a person's most significant resource. People were now looking at me and seeing my drive, intellect, consistency, and passion. Recognizing that those characteristics were some of the main ingredients to a cocktail of achievement. They were constantly checking in on me, trying to see if I had failed yet or given up. Plagued by the fact that neither of the two appeared to be taking place.

I remember speaking with an older family member one day that I had always looked up to and catching the undertones of shade. As I spoke with her and got a reply back as she went on to say, well, maybe you can after you get all your little degrees. It's incredible how people will attach the word little to significant achievements when trying to be passive-aggressive and ugly. The craziest part about it is that the people who usually speak in this manner have nothing "Big" to offer up. Shooting down all of your achievements and goals while having none of their own. What was it about my now that was so irritating to people? I saw how some of the same people who felt bothered by me and my "little achievements" showed love to people who bragged, boasted, flexed, and scammed their way into the spotlight. Bragging about their money, designer, homes, cars, etc.

Getting nothing but love and support from my people. In comparison, I stood in a space with nothing more than my humble offerings, goals, and aspirations getting nothing in response but negative behaviors. I often asked myself why the support was so different in regard to me. I Later realized people will always support something that is not genuine. The truth was I had given these dynamics way too much of my energy. So, I finally decided to part ways with all of it after seeing how trying to understand people who didn't matter was distracting. One of the main comments that was often thrown around is "she thinks she's doing something."

This one became one of my favorites! Which was often stated by some of the people I was the closest to. People I thought were happy for me who had managed to hide their true intent for as long as they could. Eventually, giving up and letting the ugly hang out, as they called me, spewing out microaggressions that had more to do with their own self-image than mine. The truth was I was doing a lot, and despite my ability to recognize my success, the people around me could see it loud and clear. Fearing the day, the seeds I was planting would grow into a beautiful garden of success. Often trying to act as weeds and plant killers sprinkling their gems of aggression, hatred, and negativity in my life trying to cloud my vision and abilities. I sat on the edge of my bed, glancing at my tapestry of The Diary of Janay Wilkerson.

I still felt amazed by the existence of the project itself. Despite some of the flaws and errors within the text itself, the book had been successful and had the potential to do more had I continued to market it in the way I originally had. I stopped making retail agreements for the book, keeping it in the stores I had initial relationships with while I tried to rework the original manuscript to get it to where it should be. As I stared at the tapestry, I became lost in my thoughts. Thinking about how God had showered me with favor even during some of my darkest days. During the process of me writing my first novel, I was drowning in misery, hurt, and confusion. Utilizing the formulation of the project as a way to offer myself a little light while being planted in the space of complete darkness. Telling myself that bringing the dream of authorship to life would plant me in a space I longed for more than anything.

Which was a space to create content of purpose. Content that could help another little girl, little boy, or grown-up in search of things the world does not offer freely at times. Day in and day out, listening as my partner tried to derail me mentally. Attacking my confidence, abilities, and spirit in general. At times I honestly think that the areas of my book that lack the proper structure were due to my lack of concentration. When I read the novel, I can still remember what was taking place in my life during the cultivation of each chapter. Recognizing where the trauma of Jeffreys abuse is present in my story. Taking over my ability to structure the novel as solid as I could have.

Despite the manuscript errors, the book still sold in all of the retail locations where it sat on the shelves in flawed form. I thought about all the feedback I had received where readers conveyed to me that they could see it being a movie. Was this God's way of speaking to me that the dream I have been dreaming since childhood is indeed one that I could have? The feedback where people expressed that despite the errors, they could see the story, loved the comedy I presented and felt I have a gift. All that kept coming to me during this moment was to think about what you could create with peace in your life! Think about how this could have turned out if Jeffrey weren't around to distort your confidence or concentration. Think about what you could create if you got rid of all of the fake friends who would rather compete than uplift you. The more I sat staring at the tapestry, the more thoughts were flooding in.

Allowing me to see that despite my many flaws, failures, and negative experiences, God was bringing things out of me that I always knew were there. It was as if I was in a car that was packed with packages that needed to be delivered for me to gain goodness. Inside the packages were gifts of self-love, confidence, aspirations, intelligence, selflessness, selfishness, dreams, and my life calling. All waiting to be hand-delivered to my cognitive doorstep while sitting in traffic. Waiting for the moment for the congestion to clear and the negative traffic to disperse so I could become who I was meant to be. That day I cried and cried after my stroll down memory lane. Thanking God silently for all that he had done in my life. Most people would have thanked God for the book that sold millions or was the most popular but not me.

That day I thanked God for the book that changed my life. The book that I was able to cultivate while being in a marriage filled with physical abuse, mental abuse, and infidelity. The book that helped me to realize that there is nothing that I can't do. The book that allowed me to understand that even if I don't execute something correctly the first time, I can pause, reflect, and return and try again until I get it right. The book that helped me to recognize that creative writing is truly my gift and calling. I wiped away my tears, ready to get on with my day when my phone rang repeatedly. I debated if I should answer after noticing that it was someone I had recently been retracting away from. Someone who had been my friend for sixteen years .

I had also looked up to her as a friend and role model and never had any negative ideas about her until after having grown in my own life. Shortly after realizing that, she too did not like seeing me have a positive increase because she was more comfortable with the imagery of the struggling, self-conscious teen mom she had initially become acquainted with those many years ago. I had learned so much from her in my past and had always felt like God put her In my life for a reason. Helping me to work through the hurt I felt when my oldest daughter's father went on to live his life without considering us. Leaving me to raise her on my own, instantly ripping away the love and basketball fantasy I had in my mind during those days. She had also helped me get a grip on what I could achieve as a teen mom. After all, she too knew the struggle because she had been a teen mom as well. What I would learn from her transition in regard to me is that everyone we start out with does not come into our lives to be a permanent entity. People are often seasonal, and her season was coming to a close.

The phone continued to ring while I sat, ignoring it. Watching as the call stopped, I prepared to go on with my day. I was making some hard choices regarding people I had known half my life, and no matter how steadfast I tried to be, it was difficult. My phone started to ring again, making this her third attempt in less than two minutes to try and reach out to me again. I picked up the phone despite my better judgment. About time you answered the phone, she said as if she had no recollection of why I stopped answering her calls. After having her be messy, more than enough. Calling me on three-way and making deceptive statements that I could read through instantly.

You see, I could always tell when she had me on three-way, and I was able to decern so because I had been a part of this dynamic with her and others. Hearing as she called me urging me to be silent while she called someone else on three-way wanting me to hear as she made passive-aggressive statements to them. Making the conversation about them after she hung up. Talking about people I didn't see, converse with, or care about. Funny how we sit in on these messy dynamics, never understanding that what they do to one they will do to another. Surely enough, it was now my time to endure this from her. "What you been up to, Nina"? She asked innocently. She was unaware that I could smell the stench of mess that dwelled in her loins from a mile away.

"Not much, just got home from work about to make my kids some breakfast and take a nap." I said, trying to convey, to her that her time on the other end of the phone was minimal. Due to me having no genuine desire to converse with her." I ran into Jeff;" she said as if she wanted a cookie for her encounter with him. "Oh, okay," I said, attempting to convey my lack of interest to her purposefully. "Yeah, girl, he was with his mom, and the Tonya girl," she said. "It looked like she had her daughter with them," she said as if she thought that detail somehow mattered. "Oh, okay," I said, still not giving her anything in response.

When she began unloading all of her messiness into the conversation. "Yeah, he was with his girlfriend," she said, placing extra emphasis on the word trying to trigger me. "They looked so happy together," and he looked good. "He was dressed up, and it looked like they were all going somewhere," she continued. I could hear the excitement in her voice as she went on giving details about what Jeff was wearing, doing, and saying to her during their conversation. When I stopped her in her tracks. "Well, that's nice, but I have to be honest and let you know that I don't care to hear about any of what he said to you. I know the truth, and so does he, and I am no longer in a place where I feel the need to discuss any of this."

"So, moving forward, if you see him or talk to him next time, keep the details to yourself. I've moved on with my life, and if he and Tonya are happy, I'm happy for them. Jeff was not right for me, and he and Tonya make more sense than he and I ever did," I concluded, leaving her mute on the other end. She tried to dissect the sincerity in my voice regarding her shady attempt to bother me emotionally. "So, Nina, what is your book about?" She asked, trying to change the subject. While still holding on to her desire to be petty in regard to me. "Which book, I replied," knowing which one she was inquiring about.

At the time, I had two books due for publication, and I knew her being the person she was, the only book she would be interested in is the one she could cultivate into her messy agenda. "The Baltimore Imprint? What's that about? "She asked as if she had no clue when we had initially discussed it two years ago when I first started drafting the book. It's about my life, I said in a light tone." So, let me ask you a question, is the stuff Jeff did to you going to be in there?" She asked, already knowing the answer to her shady question. "Yes, it is," I replied, keeping my responses short and sweet. "Well, how do you think that's going to make him feel?" She asked." Won't he be embarrassed that you're putting those details out about your relationship with him?"

"I don't know, and I honestly don't care," I replied. "I shared with Jeff that I was drafting the book and initially gave him the offer to help me create it. I started authoring the book when I was with him, offering him the chance to help me include the story of his background along with mine. Having him agree and retract from the verbal agreement after our relationship ended." I created the title, concept, and manuscript alone, deciding that I would continue with my goal for the project. I never considered his feelings because, truthfully, they were not valid to me due to me knowing my intent for the book." I feel like you sharing details about abuse and infidelity can ruin his reputation," she said as if that was not already the case before the book's development. "In the book, I'm not telling anyone's story but my own."

"If Jeff did not want me to be able to share about his behavior in regard to me, then he shouldn't have done those things," I said. "I'm not writing this story because I want to hurt him, humiliate him, or ruin his reputation. I'm writing this story because I want young women to know that they are the creators of their own destinies. I also want young men and women to understand the psychological effects abuse imposes on their partners." How many times had I thought less of myself, what I could do, or what I could have due to the trauma of the abuse from my relationships? "I didn't always feel worthy, nor did I always value myself because the abuse I had endured had wired me to view myself with the same low-value paradigm as my abuser. Think about how many women there are who are going through things like that now," I said. "With no one to turn to who has a proper understanding of their circumstance. Think about how many of them we know in our families, neighborhoods, and community in general. I want to share my accounts so women who have been through what I have can use it as encouragement."

" They can analyze my story and learn from my behaviors. I want women to realize that they do not have to subject themselves to poor treatment, abuse, or judgments because, in the end, God has a plan and a purpose for everyone. No matter how worthy or unworthy they may feel. My mother went through it and didn't have a resource, field guide, or support during her process. Instead, she had to learn on her own, later creating a road map to trauma that I followed unconsciously. So, I'm doing this for her, myself, my daughters, and women like me who don't feel worthy because their circumstances have trained them to believe otherwise." After I finished preaching and letting my passion fuel my energy while I conveyed the purpose of my publication to this devious person on the other end, I listened as she sat in silence. Even the devil himself could not argue with purpose and good intent.

That day I ended that conversation with her vowing to never converse with her again, and that's what I did. Suddenly, she had become a martyr of care for Jeffery, but it was not a genuine sentiment. Truth be told, she didn't like Jeff, respect him, or see any good in the person he was. She was only trying to speak up for him to try and irritate me. I often watched her become annoyed at the sight of growth concerning her siblings, friends, and family. Frequently talking negatively about people once they found love, financial abundance, elevated their relationship with God, became educated, or found some form of happiness due to personal growth. Placing those people in her dislike category because it was an easier task to subjectify people based on their ability to prosper than to own her feelings of unhappiness due to her dire need to grow regarding her own issues.

She could see my growth more than anyone because I had shared so many of my battles with her. Now that I was walking into my space, she felt I had changed. Now I thought I was someone! Now I had confidence! Now I was setting goals and executing them! Most importantly, now I was disengaging in the drama, toxicity, and ugliness that had initially been the catalyst for my stagnation and doubt! This led me to see how the majority of my circle I had accumulated during a time where stagnation and doubt ran rapidly through my being. Seeing how those dynamics left my being, so were these relationships as they should have because a lot had changed for the better.

Although those people knew I had always desired to be better and have better, they never thought I would. So naturally, when they started seeing growth, they would retreat away because that growth was uncomfortable for them to sit in on. Mainly because it made them analyze their own beings. Taking in that if I could make specific changes with a lot more baggage, they could do the same. I started to see that these changes made more sense than what I wanted to admit. So, I decided it was time to get the fuck over it, keep moving forward, and keep moving towards the path God was laying out for me. Out with the old and in with the new. For the new came wrapped in positivity that the past did not.

I started to realize that many of the things that felt so personal were not as personal as I thought. Sometimes we think people are hating us for our growth because it's us. When in reality, they are hating us because our growth offers positive and negative reflections that they are not willing to accept. These people saw my growth and could recognize that it was also possible for them while also acknowledging that they had not made many changes regarding their lives. Sixteen years later, life still looked the same, whereas my life constantly evolved even during the darkness. I was showcasing a level of favor that can be frustrating when you look down and realize you, on the other hand, are still sitting in the same pile of mud and misery as you were the day you met this person that is now growing in ways you are afraid to. When you start to grow and elevate to better spaces, people have a few choices in regard to you and your progress. They can learn from you and take in what you did and apply it for their own betterment.

They can also congratulate you and wish you the blessings and abundance you deserve from the footwork you are willing to do that is never a cakewalk due to the obstacles that come along with holding yourself accountable. Or they can ignore your growth, throw shade, spew out hate, trying to knock you off your course. While secretly wishing for your downfall and depreciation. Sad as it might be, many often choose the last option because it is the most pleasurable route and it's also the easiest. Once I took in that cup of truth, I started to understand that the task ahead of me would most likely always be met with great adversity.

Nonetheless, it was still a road worth traveling, so due to that, I decided to put all the negativity behind me and move on. I couldn't change how anyone was acting in regard to me, but I could change how I dealt with people. I could do so by tucking in my ego, holding onto positive intent in regard to my endeavors, and cutting any and all parties out of my life who showed these poor behaviors in relation to me.

A few days later, I was riding in my car on my way to take my daughters out to lunch for my oldest daughter's sixteenth birthday when I got a notification on my phone screen. Informing me that Jeff had sent me one hundred and fifty dollars via cash app. Christmas was approaching in a few days, so I figured Jeff attempted to give a Christmas gift for my youngest daughter while also trying to bait me in with communication. Knowing my way and assuming that I would have to contact him at least to say thank you. Under normal circumstances, I would have. I thought about how it had been an entire year, and he had never sent anything for our child or inquired if she needed anything. You don't get respect for doing what you should be doing, especially when you choose never to do anything. That day I decided it was in my best interest not to respond. He could have done this a long time ago and chose not to. When school started, and he realized she was going off to kindergarten and would need school supplies, clothes, and food to prepare her lunches. Instead, he gave nothing. Or previous holidays, but rather, he did nothing. Not realizing that he was still currently sticking to this deadbeat pathology of only providing once in a blue Christmas. He had purchased himself a new vehicle and was back living the flex lifestyle, so I had been told. For him to think that sending 150 dollars was sufficient enough for him to get anything in response would have to mean that he was delusional. I used to look at things like that and feel grateful, saying out loud, at least he finally gave her something. Unfortunately for him, I was no longer the woman willing to settle or take the less that was being offered to my children.

Voiding the gesture altogether, reminding myself that Jeff was not an adequate provider because he didn't want to be. Taking my daughter to target to let her spend the money and move on with our day, never giving the gesture a second thought because my daughter was worth more than 150 dollars, petty attempts to show insincerity, and all the lax energy that her father was willing to give concerning her care. It was now the second Christmas since my departure from the relationship, and it was the happiest I had been for a long time. Christmas morning, I arrived home ready to wake all of the children to open gifts when Melvin Jr called asking me to wait for his arrival. I showered, slipping into my new Christmas nightgown and fuzzy socks, ready to relax. Laying on the sofa looking at loads of gifts, reflecting on how just five years ago, I was in a different space. Thinking about all the times my mom had shown up for me and purchased all of my kid's things in the past because I couldn't afford to.

I reflected on how for the past five years, I was able to provide in ways I never thought I would be able to after struggling for so long. I lay glancing at my home, thinking about the many lifestyle upgrades I had been blessed with within a short time through my hard work and favor. I thought about how the previous Christmas had been depressing for me due to the incident with Jeff, him giving my child nothing and his dynamic with Tonya. It's funny how we go through things that knock us down emotionally, craving a space of peace. Feeling like the sting of the pain will never go away. Feeling the imprint of confusion once we assess that the hurt, we thought would never leave us has left our side. I took in this epiphany on that Christmas morning. Evaluating how the pain was so far gone, I could no longer remember its sting.

Let me just say that to become over it is a blessing because you never know how beautiful a peaceful life is until your resting in it. That day I enjoyed my holiday as me and my brother Melvin Jr watched the kids open their gifts. While my brother Gavin joined along via facetime. Enjoying the bliss of the many blessings that had befallen my children, my siblings, my mother, and myself. I silently thanked God for the avail as I enjoyed the peace and love that comes with a holiday surrounded by goodness and loved ones. I recognized that it was truly the season to move on, be happy, and welcome all of the new possibilities that lay ahead waiting to be grabbed and imprinted into my future. I kept my distance from people who had mistreated me. I accepted my state of loneliness as a time to cultivate a better me.

Healing from the trauma of my past so when the right people showed up, I'd be free of anxiety looking at them with a new paradigm instead of placing them in categories due to fear that they'd be like people from my past. I started taking anxiety medication to help me with my frequent feelings of anxious outpour. Finding that the medication was not right for me. Trying natural methods like breathing exercises and meditation and having some resolve. Depreciating my nervous events to one or two times a week as opposed to the multiple times a week I had been experiencing them before. I got registered for my last few classes at Liberty University. I prepared myself to graduate with my bachelor's and move into my master's program.

Getting myself one step closer to becoming Dr. Nina White and utilizing my experiences to help people recover from their trauma. I kept writing, completing novels on my laptop, and focusing on how to start the process to create the millions of scripts that roamed around in my head waiting to be cultivated. I stopped planning for the recultivation of my earth grain brand. Placing the goal of relaunching on the backburner until I could come back to it and be in a space where giving it my all was probable. It stings when you have to say no to something you enjoy, but I had been shown the progress that comes with sacrifice so many times in my life. This helped me to lay my Earth Grain business goals to rest peacefully. Although I didn't want to do that, I started to see how my caregiving business goals, authorship, and Psychology were correlational.

So, I walked away from my cosmetics line temporarily, holding onto the things that were doable for my current living environment. Capricorns are often ambitious in a way that can seem outer-worldly to most. Due to their keen ability to wake up each day willing to go get it on their own no matter what hurdles stand in their way. Although that is usually how I had been functioning, I realized it was ok to take my time and let God lead me to my aspirations. Driving the bus had made me tired, anxious, and annoyed by my own stupidity. Sure, God had instilled certain qualities in me, but he had not done so with the hopes that I would lean more on those qualities than I would him. I assessed my moves, motives, and mission and decided to lay down my hands and allow God to lead me in the right direction. I told myself that as long as I stayed consistent eventually, I would obtain the results I work towards daily.

Happy endings are often depicted in stories and television as the end all be all of adversity. And although we know firsthand that adversity never completely disappears, we like to hope that our happy ending will rid us of the ugly disappointments that the world has to offer. My story doesn't end with me riding off with my knight in shining armor into the sunset or becoming the next Steven King or R.L. Stine in female form, but my story does end with me learning my limits, abilities, and beauty. Finally, I came to terms with who I am and who I was. Recognizing that although many have tried and most likely will continue to try. No one can strip me of the light and purpose God has granted me. Somewhere there is a young girl or woman going through the things I have telling herself she does not deserve better. Telling herself that due to the environment she came from, better is not an option. But I am living, breathing proof that thoughts and beliefs like those are blasphemy. I've been through some harsh experiences in my life. Committing myself to three different relationships with three men who never reciprocated loyalty to me or their children. Leaving me to provide for our children alone. I've been disrespected, used, abused, and completely disregarded by my ex-husband, his family members, my own family members, and friends. I could have walked away from each experience broken, weak, hopeless, and tired. Although I felt most if not all of those emotions at times, I walked away with a better understanding of myself, my environment, and the possibilities the future holds in regard to me. I could have given up and kept a negative outlook in regard to life and people; instead, I ended up gaining the strength to walk away, grow, and prosper in the same ways people had always assured me I never could or would. Resting in the solace that God's favor and purpose for my life were far more unwavering than any of the devilish attempts to break my spirit ever were.

Life is never as open and shut as we would like, but we have to remain strong in the belief that there is always better waiting around the corner for us. We just have to be willing to be strong enough to seek it out. God walks with us daily. Monitoring our lives observing as we make poor choices. Offering us a moment to wake up daily with the opportunity to make changes. I had not been watered in the way I wished I would have, and at times that was hard for me to accept. Often questioning what it was about me that was so unlovable. Walking through my childhood feeling inadequate when I should have felt nothing but love and hope. Carrying those same feelings of inadequacy with me into young womanhood. Allowing people to mistreat me, never questioning the dynamic because it was one, I had known for far too long. I say that to say this: Rise up, little Black girl, for there is a power that dwells so naturally within your spirit. Rise up in the morning, greeting the sun as it blesses your melanin with strength and energy to get through another day of uncertainties. You are light, you are strength, you are knowledge, you are care, you are love, and you are loved. Face your oppressors daily with a smile and a thought that this too shall pass. Pray for them when they wish you ill. And rise to the occasion of being the underdog for the bible reminds us that those that are last shall one day be first. Laugh at the devil as he tries to dance on your spirit. Hoping to strip you of your ingredients that can never truly be watered down. Allow your mind's eye to be alert as your intuition tells you all of the things you would like to believe you don't already know. Respect your body, for it is your temple.

A supple place and space that no man or woman should be allowed to grace without the proper approach. Respect the energy field that roams around you daily. Propelling negative forces that wish to diminish the field of energy waves that are customed made. Designed to fit you and only you. Embrace your uniqueness, flaws, and all. As you look at your reflection and notice the beauty that is yours and yours alone. Hold it, cherish it, water it, and tuck it away safely when you feel that tucking it away is better at the moment.

Feed your mind good thoughts and your heart positive self-talks as you roam through a universe that was never truly created with you in mind. Own all of who you are while accepting all that you are not. Never let others place limitations and doubt on what God has for you. You are light, you are strength, you are knowledge, you are care, you are love, and you are loved. Though you may not always recognize it, you are a phenomenal entity with phenomenal purpose. Who God is waiting on to acknowledge, observe, and understand what that purpose consists of. Rise up, Black girl and let the sun hit your face; let God be your strength while you roam this unknown space. Be strong in your character and abundant in quality and take your light with you and give no apology. You are light, you are strength, you are knowledge, you are care, you are love, and you are loved.

There is never any real way to deny ourselves access to the hurt and pain that the world dishes out amongst the selected. But there is always room for hope, progress, and healing. I went through all these things, and sadly enough, there is a lot more I could have included that would have made people question how one person could have the agility to endure so many unthinkable things. But I selected the things I did for a reason. Since the beginning of time, abuse, trauma, failed relationships, and doubt have plagued all women from all different backgrounds. Although no race or group of women are exempt from knowing these hard truths, women in the Black community have been made to feel by many that we deserve some of those very adverse traumatizing actions to be inflicted upon us. Teaching ourselves that we are sitting in these unfortunate spaces because we have to when the truth is better is something that is available to everyone.

We just have to be willing to do the footwork. When I was doing the footwork, I admit it felt just as harsh as my hurt, trauma, and toxic lifestyle. I told myself that I wanted to give up and wait on God to do it for me. When God was showing me that we were a team and in order to get out of the black hole I was in, I would have to work in accordance with him to gain relief. I don't know your reasoning for picking up this book and making your way through its pages. Maybe you know someone who is a trauma victim, or you are a victim of trauma yourself. Whatever your reasoning is, encourage someone or yourself to find healing.

Addressing issues that have left us scarred is not easy, and I still have moments where I am overwhelmed by the scars of my past. I often remind myself that healing is a lifelong journey. Write down your thoughts, journal your experiences, seek counseling, and try and eat healthy meals. For we are everything we put in our bodies, and healing is as much an internal process as an external one. Sleeping as best as you can and doing things like drinking water, going for walks, and meditating can offer you a substantial amount of relief. Make a list of all the bad things you have endured, followed by a list of all the good things you would like to see happen in your life. Recognize that all that you have experienced, both good and bad are contributions of knowledge and wealth because they have all allowed you to learn more no matter how good or bad the experience was for you.

Peace and blessings are a manifestation that reaches your cognitive space once you have learned from your mistakes, created change, and discovered your proper life path. Rely on the lessons you've learned to lead you to your blessings. Manifest better and stay strong during the process. Don't allow yourself to sit in spaces where God and your body are communicating are not for you. Whenever I tried to stick it out with a fake friend, a hater, a cheater, and an oppressor in general, my body always communicated something to me to let me know I was making a poor choice. I began to observe how the stress of my environment and relationship choices always manifested in my body. As my body sent me an indication that I was on the wrong track. You can feel when people and places are not suitable for you. It may not come to you all at once, but being in the wrong environment, you will eventually catch on and identify.

Trust what you feel and see and act in your own best interest. Cultivate your change by addressing your scars and removing those who are still trying to inflict new scars upon your being. Talk to yourself positively daily, listen to positive affirmations on YouTube, and do whatever you can to cultivate peace within your day. Most importantly, talk to God and ask for the things you truly want, no matter how close together or far apart those things may be, for she that is willing to ask can be made ready to receive. I hope that my story can create some change for others going through it, and I hope my timeline of events offers realistic observation allowing people to see that all fairy tales take time, patience, and consistency. My story is not over, and I hope my next chapter is filled with imprints of peace, recovery, progress, and happiness as I continue on my journey to becoming the person God wants me to be. And I hope you will join me next time for another telling Imprint of the life and experiences of Nina White. Until next time pray, live in peace, and ask God for all it is that you deserve and desire.

"Do not judge, or you too will be judged. For in the same way you judge others, you will be judged, and with the measure you use, it will be measured to you.

"Why do you look at the speck of sawdust in your brother's eye and pay no attention to the plank in your own eye? How can you say to your brother, 'Let me take the speck out of your eye,' when all the time there is a plank in your own eye? You hypocrite, first take the plank out of your own eye, and then you will see clearly to remove the speck from your brother's eye.

"Do not give dogs what is sacred; do not throw your pearls to pigs. If you do, they may trample them under their feet and turn and tear you to pieces.

"Ask, and it will be given to you; seek and you will find; knock, and the door will be opened to you. For everyone who asks receives; the one who seeks finds; and to the one who knocks, the door will be opened.

"Which of you, if your son asks for bread, will give him a stone? Or if he asks for a fish, will give him a snake? If you, then, though you are evil, know how to give good gifts to your children, how much more will your Father in heaven give good gifts to those who ask him! So, in everything, do to others what you would have them do to you, for this sums up the Law and the Prophets. (Mathew 7 7-12 NIV)

References

Hobbes, T. (1969). Leviathan, 1651. Menston: Scolar P.

Mathew 7 7-12 NIV

www.ingramcontent.com/pod-product-compliance
Lightning Source LLC
Chambersburg PA
CBHW060857120626
46553CB00001B/115